A Key to the
OLD TESTAMENT

David L. Edwards is the author of many books which have been well received. 'Here once again', wrote a reviewer, 'is that marvellous fluency and lucidity, that ability to present complex and conflicting facts and situations completely fairly, those magisterial judgements which combine penetrating insight and down-to-earth common sense, and with it all a sheer readability' (*Church Times*). His most recent books are three volumes of a history of *Christian England* (revised as one volume in 1989), *The Futures of Christianity* and *Essentials: A Liberal-Evangelical Dialogue* with John Stott. Now Provost of Southwark Cathedral in London, he was formerly a Fellow of All Souls College, Oxford, and Dean of King's College, Cambridge.

This introduction to the study of the Old Testament, first published in 1976 and reprinted, has been brought up to date for this edition. It was written in Westminster Abbey while the author was Sub-Dean and the Speaker's Chaplain in the House of Commons. It draws on enthusiasm and experience as a preacher and as Editor of the SCM Press, 1958–66, when he began the publication of the series of standard scholarly books, the Old Testament Library.

A Key to the
OLD TESTAMENT

David L. Edwards

with a new chapter (1989) on
The Old Testament Today

Collins
FOUNT PAPERBACKS

Originally published by William Collins Sons
and Co. Ltd, Glasgow, 1976
First published in Fount Paperbacks 1978
This revised edition published
by Fount Paperbacks, London, in 1989

Printed and bound in Great Britain by
William Collins Sons & Co. Ltd, Glasgow

The biblical quotations are from the New
English Bible, second edition © 1970 by permission
of Oxford and Cambridge University Presses

Contents

Preface

The reason why this book was written may be gathered in the first chapter, but on these more personal pages I want to confess that what I say there about the things that can put modern people off the Old Testament is based on my own experience. When I was a schoolboy I had only a vague knowledge of the Old Testament apart from a few bits which were familiar, even over-familiar. When I started to study religion systematically in my training as a Christian priest, I reckoned the Old Testament the least important part of the course.

Gradually I became interested. I found that the New Testament, if taken by itself, could result for me and (it seemed) for others in a piety which was sentimental and escapist. But when in common with many others of my generation I turned to the religions of the East for light, I found that they also were often remote from the world of my newspaper and my daily experience. My own need drove me to open the Old Testament more humbly; and there I found the realism I was seeking. I found, too, that when I used for myself the key provided by the biblical scholars I entered a world full of interest and liveliness.

Although such experiences left me with an enthusiasm for the Old Testament, they did not leave me competent to translate the Hebrew language. But here also I have had some luck. In 1970 the Old Testament and the Apocrypha were published in the New English Bible. That translation put into twentieth-century English the results of the studies of Britain's leading authorities in the field, directed for the Old Testament by the late Sir Godfrey Driver and for the Apocrypha by Professor W. D. McHardy. In recent years a number of other fresh translations have appeared, all with many merits. I think in particular of the Revised Standard Version (1952) and the Jerusalem Bible (1966); and now, in 1976, I look forward to the completion of Today's English Version. But as I have used the New English Bible, I have become more and more grateful for its guidance.

Now I offer the non-specialist student and reader this presentation of the Old Testament. It enjoys a singular privilege. The Oxford and Cambridge University Presses have allowed me to quote extensively from the New English Bible. They have even given me special permission to substitute for the phrase 'the LORD', which has become customary in almost all English Bibles, the word 'Yahweh', which was the name of God in Ancient Israel.

I am indebted to Margaret Conn for the care she has lavished on the typescript; to Canon Joseph Robinson for reading the proofs; and to Westminster Abbey for the leisure in which to write this book, in a house between the Abbey and Parliament.

Preface (1989)

It is a great encouragement to me that there is a demand for an updated edition more than a dozen years after I offered this book to my fellow students and fellow amateurs. I have corrected four small errors which had lingered in the text, but most of the results of further study and reflection are in a new chapter (12), together with suggestions about recent books. I could have rewritten the whole book without any explicit reference to recent discussions, but that would have been expensive and perhaps less interesting than an attempt to come to terms with new work by historians and theologians. However, there seemed no need to include the new chapter in the Index. I am glad to retain the dedication to a dear friend who died in 1987.

D.L.E.

CHAPTER I

Discovering the Old Testament

WHY READ IT?

What is wrong with our religion or lack of it? Many answers can be given to that question. Here is one, for people interested in Christianity. It is based on the assumption that we should all know what was wrong with our cookery, or our science, if three-quarters of what has been discovered were ignored. Part of what is wrong here is that we are trying to have Christianity – or we are trying to get to know what it is about, or we are trying to get at the truth in it – while refusing to take seriously three-quarters of the Christian Bible.

For one reason or another, all too many of us nowadays have never been given the key needed to open the Old Testament. Our education never included a coherent account of it. In the past many congregations used to hear substantial lessons from the Old Testament, explained by careful sermons. Now fewer people go to church; and when they do go, they hear less about the Old Testament. Facing these facts need not mean a dismal pessimism about our own time. Many current trends are creative. But the danger exists that the Old Testament may be forgotten apart from a few snippets. This means that for practical purposes we may be losing the sense of being the heirs of Ancient Israel. For many generations Christians, as well as Jews and Muslims, regarded the Old Testament as their heritage. They went out into the unknown with Abraham; they crossed the wilderness with Moses; they blew the trumpets with Joshua; they heard the Lord speak with the child Samuel; they wept with Ruth; they fought and conquered with David; they dreamed dreams of glory with prophets and psalmists. Handel's *Messiah* or Haydn's *Creation* meant all the more to them because of the words. For many today that whole world has become a foreign country.

However, it is easy to see why the Old Testament is now often neglected. Many people feel passionately that its effect has been, on the whole, disastrous, for it has been made to serve the arrogance, bitterness, and ruthlessness of groups which have identified themselves with God's Chosen People. It is easy to find in the Old Testament a God who is bad-tempered, quick to take offence, slow to forgive, proud of the righteousness of his wrath, utterly merciless in punishing his enemies. And it is easy to see how that angry Jehovah was the projection of the anger in very human hearts. Such use of the Old Testament has not merely provided fuel for men's private quarrels; it has also fed tragic and ruinous hatreds between religions, denominations, classes, races, and nations. Accordingly many who long for more good humour in human affairs long for the death of that Old Testament God to be complete. Goodbye Jehovah!

Many people also believe that it is very difficult, if not impossible, to find an intellectually honest attitude to the Old Testament. The events described in it took place more than two thousand – in many cases, more than three thousand – years ago. Yet the Old Testament's accounts of these events, going back to the creation of the world, have been traditionally viewed as free from error. As a natural reaction to that treatment of the Old Testament as infallible, many modern people have gone to the opposite extreme of thinking that it is all a lot of fairy tales. Between these extremes, how is an honest modern reader to know where to stand?

The duty to be honest includes honesty in religious argument. But much of the use made of the Old Testament in the Christian Church in the past now seems highly artificial and unfairly polemical. The Bible has been combed for predictions of the future, specially for prophecies of Christ's birth and second coming at the end of the world.

These passages have been torn out of their original contexts and used shamelessly in the propaganda of Christian denominations or sects. Inevitably Jews object to such a treatment of their own scriptures, but plenty of non-Jews object too.

After an education which did not include the Old Testament, and in an atmosphere full of a suspicion about it, the modern reader encounters many obstacles if he is inquisitive enough to explore it for himself. The Old Testament is a long book. Indeed, it is not a book but a library of books; and even a normal reader who knows very little of their origins quickly sees that these books were written at different dates for very different purposes. How is the reader of the Old Testament, which normally is printed without any notes, to sort it all out? Bewilderment is increased by the fact that (apart from an edition of the Jerusalem Bible in 1975) the Old Testament is not printed in the order in which it was written. The first chapter of *Genesis* is one of the later pieces, while the last book, *Malachi*, is in fact a prologue to others now printed before it.

Clearly the Old Testament is a jungle, but if one sets out to hack one's way through it without a guide one is liable to be lost and depressed. Does one get to the end of *Genesis*, which seems to be a mixture of name-lists and legends? Does one persevere through *Exodus*, where some tall stories are followed by some short laws, and through the priests' manual called *Leviticus*? If so, one is still liable to perish in the wilderness of *Numbers* before one can – if one so wishes – enlist under Joshua for the conquest of Canaan. The historical books which follow are relatively easy to understand, except that without a guide one is always asking oneself what connection they have with true history. Then comes another problem: *Chronicles* goes over much of the same ground, but with conspicuous differences. *Job* and the psalms are obviously great poetry, but how can one have the patience to read *Proverbs*? What is the cynicism of *Ecclesiastes* doing in the Old Testament? Apart from

Lamentations and that strange book *Daniel*, the rest of the Old Testament consists of prophets. But without some knowledge of the historical background, it is very often impossible to tell what these prophets are talking about.

Again, what is one to make of the books called 'the Apocrypha' (or 'Deuterocanonical books')? These are now included in Bibles accepted by Catholic, Protestant, and Orthodox Churches alike; for example, they appear in the 1973 ecumenical edition of the Revised Standard Version, 'the Common Bible'. But traditionally the Churches have disagreed about their status. Since the days of Luther and Calvin Protestants have refused to give these books equal authority with the Old Testament. One of their reasons has been that when the rabbis gathered at Jamnia to settle the 'canon' (official contents) of the Jewish scriptures in the first century AD, they excluded these books. But these books (with the exception of *2 Esdras*) were in the earlier Greek translation of the scriptures (the Septuagint), and were accepted by almost all Christians up to the Reformation. At the Council of Trent they were definitely included in Holy Scripture for the Roman Catholics (with the exceptions of *1 and 2 Esdras* and the *Prayer of Manasseh*); at the Synod of Jerusalem in 1672, for the Eastern Orthodox.

A modern reader exploring the Apocrypha independently is likely to be puzzled. Why should the novel called *Tobit* in the Apocrypha be regarded as less edifying than the one called *Esther*, which is in the Old Testament? And why should the beauties of the books called *Ecclesiasticus* and the *Wisdom of Solomon* in the Apocrypha – the nearest that Ancient Israel came to doing philosophy – be regarded as non-scriptural, while the prophet Obadiah's patriotic denunciation of the neighbouring state of Edom forms one whole book of the Old Testament? Incidentally, the question why Obadiah deserves a place grows when we discover that almost half his little book is virtually identical with Jeremiah 49:7–22. The *Letter of Jeremiah* in the Apocrypha is not by him; but the book of Jeremiah in the Old Testament is not entirely by him, either.

These questions are enough to indicate that the problem of the contents of the Old Testament cannot nowadays be regarded as settled. And this problem is bound up with a wider and more important question. What is the authority of the Old Testament for modern man, whether or not it includes the Apocrypha? That is a question more often asked than answered.

The difficulties involved in any reader's pilgrimage through the Old Testament are so formidable that it is easy to see why many readers decide never to make the attempt. The effort does not seem worth while. Many ask: why read *Genesis*, when one can get books out of the library giving the latest knowledge about astronomy, evolution, and the long progress of primitive man? Why try to reconstruct Joshua's conquest of Canaan when today's newspaper is full of today's crisis in the Middle East? Why study the prophets' commentary on the history of a few centuries in the life of tribesmen probably always numbering less than a million, when the spiritual wisdom of the world is available to us? And why value the life of King David, when we have the life of Jesus Christ?

If modern people are persuaded that some background is needed by the Christian Gospel – some large society which sets the scene by asking the questions to which the Gospel is said to give the answers – they often need to be convinced that the Old Testament still provides a necessary background. We all know that a new world has arisen on the foundations of science and technology; that in this new world a new culture has grown with new prophets, new singers, new landmarks, new questions; and that it is actually more than one world. There is the Western world, free but in a mess. There is the Communist world, which pays a heavy price for its discipline. There is the international 'youth' world. There is the African world; there is Latin America; there is India. Many modern people ask why it is necessary to bother about the Old Testament when the urgent task is to relate Christianity to these contemporary worlds. In the second century a shipowner and amateur theologian who had considerable influence in Rome and elsewhere, a man named Marcion, publicly urged that Christians should abandon the Old Testament. He said plainly that the God described in it was not the God and Father of Jesus Christ and was not relevant to the new age. Today, when Christians as well as others are fascinated by the novelty of the age, Marcion often seems to have won.

When we reckon with such obstacles to the study of the Old Testament in our time, we cannot be surprised that it is fast becoming the unknown three-quarters of the Christian Bible.

THE SCRIPTURES OF JEWS AND CHRISTIANS

But it is there! And it remains one of the great possessions of the human race. For example, some of its heroes feature in the Koran and are therefore sacred to Muslims. Innumerable other examples exist to show the influence of these scriptures of the Jewish people – who remain a puzzle in world history.

The sheer endurance of the Jews is breathtaking. Their homeland was conquered by many armies sent by many empires, yet in 1948 the state of Israel was born again. During the Middle Ages the Jews seemed to have no place in the Christian civilization of Europe or in the Islamic civilization of the Middle East. Yet they survived – and more. In our own century the rulers of Europe attempted the final solution of the 'problem' by exterminating them; and Arabs, more pardonably angered by their return to Palestine, pledged themselves to drive them into the sea. Yet our century, like many previous ages, is spiritually in debt to the Jews. It owes much to them as pioneering businessmen, scientists, writers, musicians, artists, and entertainers; it owes much to their human warmth and their family life; and intellectually ours is the age of Marx, Einstein, and Freud. As Israel Besht, the founder of the Hasidic movement in eighteenth-century Russia, wrote: 'Like the soil, everyone treads on the Jews. But God has put into the very soil the power to bring forth all kinds of plants and fruits.'

Far beyond the state of Israel the Jewish community exists in the *Diaspora* or Dispersion. Some Jews are strictly 'orthodox'; others, more assimilated into the general life of society, are merely 'conservative', 'reformed', or 'liberal'. But all Jews who are not completely secularized live by these scriptures to a greater or lesser extent, and probably it would be true to say that all Jews are somehow conscious of themselves as inheritors of this unique spiritual wealth. Are they a religion? Are they a race? Are they a nation? They cannot agree among themselves. But they can agree on the sheer fact that these scriptures are their heritage. A greater understanding of such writings is surely a way to a greater understanding of modern Jewry.

Exploring the Old Testament is also a way to understand Christianity – a job that needs to be done before we can begin to think about making Christianity relevant to scientists, to Communists, to young people, or to anyone else. The English word 'Christ' is a reminder that the Greek *Christos* was the Hebrew *Messiah*, whose coming was foretold in the Old Testament. When we pick up the Old Testament, we hold in our hands the library of the school and synagogue which educated Jesus of Nazareth, called the Christ; we are weighing the mental food of the adult Jesus; and we are touching what touched the imaginations and the basic convictions of the first Christians.

Mark reflects this when he tells us that immediately after the baptism of Jesus, 'a voice spoke from heaven: "Thou art my Son, my Beloved; on thee my favour rests" ' (1:11). It is a kind of shorthand which cannot be understood without some knowledge of the Old Testament. *Baptism* 'in token of repentance, for the forgiveness of sins' (1:4) was what the Jews did to their converts (the 'proselytes'), remembering passages in the Old Testament such as 'wash yourselves and be clean' (Isaiah 1:16). *Thou art my Son, my Beloved* is a quotation from one of the psalms used to honour a king in Jerusalem (2:7). *On thee my favour rests* is a quotation from a prophet's description of God's suffering servant (Isaiah 42:1). By joining the mass baptism in the river Jordan, Jesus identified himself with his fellow-Jews in their need to be cleansed. He was 'King of the Jews', as the charge which Pilate fixed over his head was to state; but the kingdom he claimed was to be reached through service and suffering.

The story of the testing of Jesus in the wilderness (Matthew 4:1–11; Luke 4:1–13) is not only an echo of the testing of the people of Israel under Moses in the wilderness. It also shows Jesus comparing one Old Testament text with another, and arranging them in an order of life-controlling importance. 'Tell these stones to become bread' – as Moses had obtained *manna*, the food believed to be miraculous, in the wilderness. But the reply comes: 'Scripture says, "Man cannot live on bread alone; he lives on every word that God utters"' (Deuteronomy 8:3). Satan now quotes Psalm 91:10–13:

No disaster shall befall you,
no calamity shall come upon your home.
For he has charged his angels
  to guard you wherever you go,
  to lift you on their hands
for fear you should strike your foot against a stone.

But the reply comes in another *Deuteronomy* passage (6:16): 'You must not challenge Yahweh your God . . .' And when the devil shows Jesus the kingdoms of the world in their glory, Jesus clings again to *Deuteronomy* (6:13): 'You shall fear Yahweh your God, serve him alone and take your oaths in his name.'

That story of his solitary ordeal after his baptism hints

that during many silent hours, days, and years Jesus pondered the significance of the scriptures of his people. Another story shows that he drew strength for his last ordeal from his sense of communion with the great figures of the Old Testament. In a strange mystical or psychical experience, 'they saw Elijah appear, and Moses with him, and there they were, conversing with Jesus . . . and now suddenly, when they looked around, there was nobody to be seen but Jesus alone with themselves' (Mark 9:4,8) – a Jesus who was now prepared 'to endure great sufferings and to be treated with contempt' (9:12).

Were the life and teaching of Jesus of Nazareth in accordance with the great tradition of the Old Testament? Were they the best fulfilment of its promises? Were the Jewish scriptures to any extent now replaced by a more authoritative declaration of the will of God? Had a new agreement or covenant or testament been concluded between God and man, so that Paul was right to announce the replacement of the 'old covenant' (2 Corinthians 3:14, the passage from which came the Christian phrase 'the Old Testament')? Were the Christians, the new people of God, dispensed from the Jewish religious law? These were the questions on which the earliest Christian preaching fastened.

The letters of Paul are saturated in the Old Testament, and the earliest of the gospels, Mark's, plunges straight into it. 'In the prophet Isaiah it stands written: "Here is my herald whom I send on ahead of you, and he will prepare your way. A voice crying aloud in the wilderness, *Prepare a way for the Lord; clear a straight path for him*." ' The fact that the first of these sentences is actually a quotation from the prophet called Malachi, not from Isaiah, is an indication that the first Christian preachers including Mark used collections of proof-texts or 'testimonies' from the Old Testament; and that in the collection which Mark possessed, this quotation was attributed to the wrong prophet.

Luke's gospel claims that such preaching began on the afternoon of the first Easter Day. ' "How dull you are!"

Jesus answered. "How slow to believe all that the prophets said! Was the Messiah not bound to suffer thus before entering upon his glory?" Then he began with Moses and all the prophets, and explained to them the passages which referred to himself in every part of the scriptures' (24: 25–27). One way of understanding Luke's moving story of the walk to Emmaus is to see it as evidence of the importance of the 'Law of Moses and the prophets and psalms' (24:44) in the first Christian generation's preaching. Thousands of Jews, persuaded by this revolutionary interpretation of their own scriptures, were at that time saying: 'Did we not feel our hearts on fire as he talked with us on the road and explained the scriptures to us?' (24:32).

Many non-Jews who were already impressed by the Jewish religious tradition were converted to Christianity by the argument that 'the Gospel' or 'the Way' was the supreme fulfilment of these scriptures. A typical scene occurs in *The Acts of the Apostles* (8:26–40). Philip finds 'a high official of the Kandake, or Queen, of Ethiopia, in charge of all her treasure' returning home from Jerusalem, 'sitting in his carriage and reading aloud the prophet Isaiah'. 'Do you understand what you are reading?' asks Philip. The Ethiopian civil servant who has bought this book as a souvenir of his trip answers: 'How can I understand unless someone will give me the clue?' And without hesitation Philip gives the clue, as a Christian evangelist.

Such quotations illustrate the detailed use of the Jewish scriptures by Jesus and his first followers. But the role played by Judaism in the birth of Christianity was not mainly bookish. The central claim of early Christianity was that Jesus had been vindicated despite his crucifixion; this vindication demonstrated the truth of his message. And the message of Jesus came amidst the Jewish life of Palestine.

Not only did Jesus teach the public through parables based on the details of that life; the message which his parables conveyed also presupposed a Jewish audience. For

the message was that the 'kingdom of God' was very near.
That phrase was Jewish. More: the idea of the reign of God
on earth was the outcome of many attempts by the Jews to
achieve a human government which would act in accordance with what they understood to be the divine will. More
still: the Jews would not have longed for God to reign had
they not believed so deeply in God. Their hope of this
kingdom was a hope that God would act to clear his name.
Such a hope does not arise out of leisurely philosophical
speculation; it comes out of agony. It does not arise in
circles where the question of God's nature and will is treated
as unimportant, or where the reality of God seems remote,
or where the existence of God seems improbable. The
question which Jesus claimed to answer – namely the
question: when will God rule on earth as in heaven? – was
a question asked by a highly God-conscious society.

It would seem that any person of any generation who
would understand the New Testament must also understand
at least the outlines of the Old. But there remains the question:
can twentieth-century hearts be set on fire by any interpretation of this ancient literature? If that question is to be
answered convincingly, it must be discussed in an intellectually honest way, using modern knowledge of Ancient
Israel and its books. That involves understanding something about how the books came to be written, and what
were their principal purposes. But it involves more. A heart
is not set on fire by cold historical information. We need to
feel for ourselves the significance of those long-dead
Israelites. Only then shall we be convinced that these
books, inherited by all Jews and all Christians as Scripture,
are alive for us today.

THE THRILL OF DISCOVERY

In the nineteenth and twentieth centuries AD there has been
excitement from time to time over the discoveries of
archaeology in the lands of the Bible. The empires which

rise and fall in the Old Testament have been illuminated as never before. In Palestine new standards were set by the skill of the University of Chicago's excavation of Megiddo which began in 1925, and since the Second World War the excavations of Jericho by the British under Kathleen Kenyon, of Shechem by the Americans under G. Ernest Wright, and of Hazor by the Israelis under Yigael Yadin, have rightly attracted worldwide attention. But the largest sensation to date has been caused by the 'Dead Sea scrolls' at Qumran.

The discovery began when a Bedouin goatherd idly threw a stone into a cave in 1947 and heard a pot smash. About a quarter of the scrolls are important as confirmation of the text of the Old Testament. Before they came to light, it was thought that the oldest text of a substantial part of the Old Testament (Genesis 39:20 – Deuteronomy 1:33) was that of Aaron ben Asher, written about AD 850 and now in the British Museum. The oldest complete text, the Aleppo Codex, was written about a century later and is now at the Hebrew University in Jerusalem. Smaller portions found in the storeroom of the old synagogue in Cairo, found in AD 1890, date from the sixth and seventh centuries AD. But included among the Dead Sea scrolls are texts a thousand years or so older than Aaron ben Asher's, representing every book in the Old Testament except *Esther*. In detail they show the variation that was possible before the scribes of the Pharisees fixed the 'Masoretic' or 'traditional' text as part of their reconstruction of Judaism after the fall of Jerusalem to the Romans in AD 70. But the main fact about these Dead Sea scrolls – most notably, a well-preserved scroll giving the whole book of Isaiah – is that they show the faithfulness with which the text of the Old Testament was transmitted from a time long before the birth of Christ. The text was protected because it was so deeply respected.

Can the twentieth century share much, or any, of that respect? Thanks to archaeology, at point after point our understanding of the Old Testament has been enriched in

recent years. Attempts have been made to cash in on this
public interest by claiming that 'archaeology proves that
the Bible is true.' Actually, archaeology cannot do that –
not in the most important sense of the word 'true'. For
while archaeology provides an amazing and thrilling confirmation of some details in the Old Testament, the men
and women who made these stories cannot be dug up.
Even if we were allowed to apply modern, scientific
techniques to the cave which Jews and Muslims alike
venerate as the burial-place of Abraham, Isaac, and Jacob,
once purchased from the Hittites (Genesis 23:1–20), we
should probably feel not much nearer to the age of the
patriarchs. Even if we could discover the authentic grave of
that titanic figure, Moses – about whom it is written: 'he
was buried in a valley in Moab opposite Beth-peor, but to
this day no one knows his burial-place' (Deuteronomy
34:6) – we might find no more than a little dust. Above all,
we could never reach the 'truth' of what these Israelites
claimed about their God. Such claims are not to be
measured by an archaeologist's tape, for this God does not
lie in visible fragments like an ancient pot. Even if we
received permission to dig for the foundations of Solomon's
temple – in earth sacred to Jews since David built here an
altar on the threshing-floor of Araunah the Jebusite (2 Samuel
24), sacred also to Muslims because here by tradition
Abraham was prepared to sacrifice his son Isaac (Genesis 22),
the site of Herod's Temple where Jesus worshipped, since
AD 691 the site of the Muslim Dome of the Rock – our
spades could never clink against the treasure of faith.

Far more amazing and thrilling than any dig in archaeology is the fact that the Old Testament itself exists, await-
ing discovery by any reader who will take a guided tour.
Over the last hundred years many excellent guides have
appeared. Many new translators and many scholars at
work on the Hebrew have devoted endless care and great
skills to these ancient books. Great progress has been made
with the questions which a modern reader needs to have

answered: how the Old Testament was written, what was the purpose of each author, what relation his writing had to the real history of Ancient Israel, and how the different books, as interpretations of this history, built up Israel's faith. No previous generation had the privileges which ours can now enjoy if we are prepared to use modern translations and the results of this investigation by the scholars. The exploration of the Old Testament under that expert guidance is far more interesting than anything which the spade can unearth.

It helps us to see what riches remain for our enjoyment if we appreciate how near we came to having no Old Testament at all. Originally every book was written on a single scroll. For a considerable period there were probably only a few copies. Not only was this some two thousand years before the invention of printing (outside China); it was also long before these books were regarded as belonging together to 'the scriptures'. This process was only completed by the rabbis in the first century AD, although a more informal agreement about 'the scriptures' had been established before that to cover almost all the books.

Such records could easily get lost – particularly when the two capitals, Samaria and Jerusalem, were pillaged and destroyed by foreign armies. And some *were* lost. In the 'Books of Kings' surviving in the Old Testament there are references to fuller accounts of the different reigns then available. There was a separate history of the reign of Solomon (1 Kings 11:41). When the kingdom was divided after Solomon's death, official scribes seem to have kept the annals of their kings at the northern and southern courts (1 Kings 14:19,29, etc.). The 'Book of the Wars of Yahweh' is also quoted (Numbers 21:14). In the book of Joshua (10:13) there is a reference to 'the Book of the Upright' – the source of David's lament over Saul and Jonathan (2 Samuel 1:18). There were collections of other laments, including Jeremiah's for King Josiah (2 Chronicles 35:25). All these books have now disappeared. If the books which we know as the Old Testament had also been lost, and had recently been discovered in some cave, the sensation and the delight would have been worldwide.

In 1908 a small, soft limestone plaque was dug up at Gezer, twenty miles north-west of Jerusalem. From the roughness of the letters, and from the variety of their forms, the inscription on this tablet seems to have been written by a schoolboy or adult as an exercise in writing, rather than as an official record. Traces of earlier writing on the plaque can just be discerned. The text is simple. It is a list of the main activities in the agricultural year, month by month – the olive harvest, sowing grain, other planting, pulling flax, the barley harvest, the rest of the harvest, vine-tending, the summer fruit. It was probably written in the tenth century BC, and is the earliest example of Hebrew writing that has survived. That is exciting. But it is more exciting to have in the Old Testament from the same century a long, vivid, frank, and intimate account of the emotional conflicts at the court of King David, written with great maturity and sophistication.

The ancient city of Beth-shan, the chief market town of the plain of Jezreel, has been partially excavated (mainly in 1921). Two temples have been found, with fragments of the city wall. This helps us to visualize the day, about 1000 BC, when the Philistines found Saul and his three sons lying dead after the battle on the nearby Mount Gilboa. They cut off his head before they 'deposited his armour in the temple of Ashtoreth and nailed his body to the wall of Beth-shan'. But in the Old Testament (2 Samuel 1:17–27) we have David's lament when he heard the news:

Hills of Gilboa, let no dew or rain fall on you,
   no showers on the uplands!
For there the shields of the warriors lie tarnished,
   and the shield of Saul, no longer bright with oil.
The bow of Jonathan never held back
from the breast of the foeman, from the blood of the slain;

the sword of Saul never returned
  empty to the scabbard.

Delightful and dearly loved were Saul and Jonathan;
  in life, in death, they were not parted.
They were swifter than eagles,
  stronger than lions.

Weep for Saul, O daughters of Israel!
  who clothed you in scarlet and rich embroideries,
  who spangled your dress with jewels of gold.

How are the men of war fallen, fallen on the field!
  O Jonathan, laid low in death!
I grieve for you, Jonathan my brother;
  dear and delightful you were to me;
your love for me was wonderful,
  surpassing the love of women.

Fallen, fallen are the men of war;
  and their armour left on the field.

In 1908–10 sixty-five inscriptions were found in the ruins
of the royal palace of Samaria, written on pottery by skilled
scribes using reed pens and black ink. They are invoices or
labels sent with oil and wine from twenty-seven places,
probably in the royal estates; and they date from the ninth
century BC. That is interesting. But it is more interesting to
have in the Old Testament lifelike pictures of the luxury
in Samaria from the major poet-prophets, Amos and
Hosea. In these pictures we can watch the wine being
drunk.

In 1846 a young Englishman, Henry Layard, found in
the main square of the ruined Assyrian city of Nimrud a
black limestone obelisk, now in the British Museum,
London. On it the great conqueror, Shalmaneser III,
boasted of his campaign of 841–0 BC. Jehu, King of Israel,
or his ambassador, is portrayed kneeling before the emperor
and offering tribute as a token of his submission. This
tribute is carried by thirteen porters, like him wearing

fringed tunics and cloaks, tasselled caps and pointed shoes, and like him bearded and Hebrew-looking. Seemingly it is the only contemporary attempt at a portrait of an Israelite king to have survived – although presumably it was not carved after any detailed study of Jehu's face, and perhaps Jehu did not appear in person for this humiliating ceremony.

This act of homage is not recorded in the Old Testament, but in the second book of Kings (9:30–36) we have a graphic account of Jehu in a very different and more lively posture, a year or two before. He has just seized the throne and has come to Jezreel to dispose of his arch-enemy, Queen Jezebel.

> Now Jezebel had heard what had happened; she had painted her eyes and dressed her hair, and she stood looking down from a window. As Jehu entered the gate, she said, 'Is it peace, you Zimri, you murderer of your master?' He looked up at the window and said, 'Who is on my side, who?' Two or three eunuchs looked out, and he said, 'Throw her down.' They threw her down, and some of her blood splashed on to the wall and the horses, which trampled her underfoot. Then he went in and ate and drank. 'See to this accursed woman,' he said, 'and bury her; for she is a king's daughter.' But when they went to bury her they found nothing of her but the skull, the feet, and the palms of the hands; and they went back and told him.

One hot day in Jerusalem in 1880 an Arab boy who had been bathing in the Pool of Shelah (Siloam) explored a tunnel in the rock, and discovered an inscription carved in Hebrew not long before the Assyrian siege in 701 BC. It tells how the workmen digging the tunnel from the Pool of Siloam here joined another gang digging from the Virgin's Spring. 'There was heard the voice of a man calling to his fellow, for there was a crevice . . . And on the day of the piercing through, the stone-cutters struck through the rock each to meet his fellow, axe against axe. Then ran the

water from the Spring to the Pool . . .' That inscription
enables us to recapture the panic when the inhabitants of
Jerusalem attempted to secure their water supply against
the dreaded Assyrian army; and it helps us to appreciate
the engineering feat. But it is even more impressive to read
in the Old Testament a detailed account of what an Assyrian
siege felt like, including the taunts of the Assyrian commander. 'Where are the gods of Hamath and Arpad?
Where are the gods of Sepharvaim, Hena, and Ivvah?
Where are the gods of Samaria? . . . Among all the gods of
the nations is there one who saved his land from me?'
(2 Kings 18:13-19:3). And in the Old Testament we have
a commentary on the crisis by no less a man than Isaiah.

When Henry Layard unearthed the emperor Sennacherib's throne-room in Nineveh in 1849 he found a large
relief on the wall showing that Assyrian army's siege of
Lachish, thirty miles south-west of Jerusalem; this is now
in the British Museum. In 1935-8 a guard-room in Lachish
itself was excavated, and twenty-one fragments of pottery
were discovered. On them are written letters of Yaosh, the
military governor, during the Babylonian invasion, in
589-8 BC. 'We are watching for the signals of Lachish,' one
letter says, 'according to all your lordship's orders, for we
cannot see Azekah.' Presumably these were fire signals to
give military directions, and the reason why none could be
seen from Azekah may have been that the Babylonians had
already captured that fortress. Another letter complains
about 'the words of the princes which only weaken our
hands and slacken the hands of those who are told about
them'. Evidently there were defeatists in the Israelite
upper class. Such letters are fascinating. But it is even more
valuable to have in the Old Testament the autobiography
of one of the great men of history, the prophet Jeremiah.
He was the leader of the defeatists in that crisis, and as his
own book records he was accused of 'weakening the hands
of the soldiers' (38:4).

In 1882 an excavation ended in the ruins of ancient

Babylon. One of its discoveries was a clay cylinder, now in the Metropolitan Museum of Art, New York. In the long inscription, Cyrus the Persian recorded that Marduk the god of Babylon had welcomed his triumphant entry (in 549 BC) to put an end to the misrule of Nabonidus, the last of the Babylonian emperors. He also recorded that he had returned many images of the gods of other cities to their sanctuaries which had been in ruins for some time. 'I also gathered all these cities' former inhabitants and returned them to their homes.' That inscription is evidence of the propaganda value of the liberal policy of the Persians in their conquest of the Babylonian empire. But more important evidence about these dramatic changes is to be found in the Old Testament – the decree in which Cyrus allowed the rebuilding of the Jerusalem temple, and the ecstatic poetry with which a Jewish prophet, a genius whose name we do not know, greeted the end of the exile.

In 1962 forty business documents, or fragments of them, were discovered in a cave nine miles north of Jericho. They date from 375–335 BC, and so far as we know are the oldest manuscripts on papyrus (the ancient form of paper, imported from Egypt) to have survived in Palestine. But in the Old Testament we have fragments of the memoirs of the great reformers Nehemiah and Ezra, and moving echoes of the attempts of prophets to restore their people's morale, and the psalms of the restored temple. These psalms have been found worthy to express the sorrows, sins, and delights of multitudes in many centuries, around the globe. Sabbath by Sabbath, Sunday by Sunday, day by day, these psalms are still used and loved.

THE STRANGE FAITH OF THESE PEOPLE

They were one of the most eloquent peoples in the history of mankind. Even in disaster they took comfort from talking and writing about it, pushing language to its frontiers and even playing with their broken hearts. An example of their unabashed delight in words comes in the collection of *Lamentations* attached to the book of Jeremiah. As we read it in English, we experience the power of this grief over the fate of Jerusalem. But in the Hebrew it consists of five poems; four of these are acrostics, where each of the twenty-two stanzas begins with a different letter of the Hebrew alphabet. These were people who thought it natural and right to make their laments shapely; people who enjoyed the hymns at a funeral.

Supremely they were eloquent in an area where most people have always been tongue-tied. They talked with gusto about God: not abstractly about his nature, but concretely about his relationship with them. Even Moses was refused permission to gaze into the face of God, but he was allowed to glimpse God moving on. 'You shall see my back, but my face shall not be seen' (Exodus 33:23). The rear view fascinated them. The Jews never produced a work of systematic theology until Saadya ben Joseph's *Jewish Faith and Knowledge* in AD 933; what they produced was an infection in their enthusiasm for God.

They knew slavery in Egypt and exile in later empires, and many disasters in between, but they never finally forgot their conviction that their God was present and active in their lives. Indeed, they dared to believe that this God so loved them that he had made an agreement or covenant to be their God. They frequently accused themselves of many appalling breaches of this bargain with their God, but they did not commit the final sin: they did not give up. In their story of how their ancestor Jacob had wrestled with God, they said that he had cried: 'I will not let you go unless you bless me' (Genesis 32:26). That was true of them, generation by generation.

Much of their faith was patriotic and tribal. Their God would bless them, they hoped, with victories, harvests, many children, long peace. But their faith was allowed to criticize their pride, and they honoured the prophets who denounced them in the name of their God. The messengers of the time began: 'This is the word of my master.' An early example comes in Genesis 32:4, where Jacob tells his messengers to say to his brother: 'My lord, your servant Jacob says . . .' But these prophets began with the claim that this was the word of their God. And then they had an astonishing, shattering courage and freedom to say what seemed to them right.

Their God was unique. He had a name like an ordinary god; in the Hebrew consonants his name was equivalent of YHWH in English (they did not write vowels). The name is nowadays usually given as 'Yahweh' as an approximation to the original pronunciation. But the name became so sacred that it was not spoken or written in normal circumstances. When vowels were added to the Hebrew Old Testament, they added here the vowels of *Adonai*, meaning 'Lord'; and when the Old Testament was translated into Greek, they substituted the Greek *ho kurios* for YHWH. The English translation is 'the LORD' and that is how Yahweh is referred to in most English Bibles. 'Jehovah' is simply a word used in the Middle Ages before scholars found out that 'Yahweh' was more accurate.

There was a strict prohibition against any image of Yahweh. When in 63 BC the Roman general Pompey entered the innermost sanctuary of the Jerusalem temple, the Holy of Holies, he was astounded to find it empty. While the artists of the ancient world employed their skills in carving and painting images of their gods, orthodox Jews delighted to make insulting remarks about all such 'idols':

> Their idols are silver and gold,
>   made by the hands of men.
> They have mouths that cannot speak,
>   and eyes that cannot see;
> they have ears that cannot hear,
>   nostrils, and cannot smell;
> with their hands they cannot feel,

with their feet they cannot walk,
and no sound comes from their throats.
Their makers grow to be like them,
and so do all who trust in them (Psalm 115:4–8).

The people of the Old Testament, being frail, could not
always maintain this lofty attitude. There is an old story
which suggests that at one time a devout worshipper could
have his own image of Yahweh in his home, and his own
son as a priest to perform in front of it (Judges 17). Centuries later in the Jerusalem temple itself there were still
various objects which were, no doubt, images of Yahweh
to some. But orthodox Jews came to condemn and abhor all
images of their God – and all images of all other gods, and
of anything which might be mistaken for a god.

For long they regarded other gods as possessing some
reality, at least in other lands. They could not help doing so.
Their Yahweh was not the only divinity in their experience.
He had to stand comparison with the gods of the massive
temples in Egypt, Assyria, and Babylonia – gods who
seemed to bless invincible empires. He had his own little
land, but the very names of that land told a tale. In this
'Canaan' the gods of the Canaanites were often far more
seductive, and in this 'Palestine' the gods of the Philistines
often looked far more impressive. Finally Yahweh had to be
compared with the sun, moon, and stars, which many
worshipped in the ancient world. At one time, under
Assyrian influence, there were in and around Yahweh's own
temple in Jerusalem altars where sacrifices were burnt 'to
the sun and moon and planets and all the host of heaven'
(2 Kings 23:4–5). Even the stern preaching of *Deuteronomy*
admitted some reality in foreign worship. 'Nor must you
raise your eyes to the heavens and look up to the sun, the
moon, and the stars, all the host of heaven, and be led on to
bow down to them and worship them; Yahweh your God
assigned these for the worship of the various peoples under
heaven' (4:19).

But they came to know that such worship was not for them, for 'the gods whom earth holds sacred are all worthless' (Psalm 16:3). To be on the safe side, they even banned 'the degrading practice of making figures carved in relief, in the form of a man or a woman, or of any animal on earth or bird that flies in the air, or of any reptile on the ground or fish in the waters under the earth' (Deuteronomy 4: 16–18). It was the ruin of their art, but the making of their religion. No possibility of misunderstanding must arise about their allegiance. 'You are the people whom Yahweh brought out of Egypt, from the smelting-furnace, and took for his own possession, as you are to this day . . . Do not make yourselves a carved figure of anything which Yahweh your God has forbidden. For Yahweh your God is a devouring fire, a jealous god' (4:20,23,24). So we do not know exactly what they looked like, but unmistakably we know what they believed.

Theirs was a faith which in its most vital days was always subject to correction. Not only were visual images of God condemned. Even favourite images of him in words were often questioned. The prophets who felt called to speak the mind of Yahweh came to know that the cost was the sacrifice of all their stability: they must be prepared to leave families and jobs, to denounce their own nation and religion. In the early period the role of a prophet included domestic tasks such as finding lost property, so that the first book of Samuel explains that 'what is nowadays called a prophet used to be called a seer' (9:9). But Jeremiah felt called 'to pull down and to uproot, to destroy and to demolish' whole nations including his own (1:10), so that the rarest form of courage was needed:

This day I make you a fortified city,
  a pillar of iron, a wall of bronze,
    to stand fast against the whole land (1:18).

They told a story of another of their great prophets, Elijah. When he felt isolated and defeated he went back

through the wilderness to 'the mountain of God' where
Moses had seen the glory and received the Law (1 Kings
19). They might easily have told this story so as to show
how Elijah was consoled by the old religion of Yahweh as
the mountain-god, the volcano-god, the storm-god. These
were images of God very familiar to the Israelites in their
scriptures, particularly in their psalms. Instead, they said
this. 'Yahweh was passing by: a great and strong wind
came rending mountains and shattering rocks before him,
but Yahweh was not in the wind; and after the wind there
was an earthquake, but Yahweh was not in the earthquake;
and after the earthquake fire, but Yahweh was not in the
fire . . .' And after that? A low sound? A small voice? An
inner voice? Or the silence?

The true prophets of Yahweh never thought that their
words had pinned Yahweh down. But they were so sure of
the devouring fire and the speaking silence that they felt
driven to say something. What they said always came out
of their experience, which included ecstasies and trances.
We meet in the first book of Samuel 'a company of prophets
coming down from the hill-shrine, led by lute, harp, fife, and
drum and filled with prophetic rapture'; and we read how
'God gave Saul a new heart' and 'the spirit of God suddenly
took possession of him, so that he too was filled with
prophetic rapture' (10:5-10). On a later occasion Saul
'stripped off his clothes and like the rest fell into a rapture
before Samuel and lay down naked all that day and all that
night' (19:24). And when Elisha's prophetic powers were
flagging, a minstrel's music could revive them (2 Kings
3:15). But religious experience was for the Israelites not
entirely like a drug.

Joy came out of it, but so did the regulation of business
and politics. Dancing went into it, but so did sober thought
and the prick of the conscience. Its centre was ecstatic, the
spirit naked before God, the heart making music in worship;
but always it was tested by its ability to guide day-to-day
life morally. It was never an escape. To choose it was to

'choose life' (Deuteronomy 30:20).

The Israelites derived their religion through their experience of the real world, and they let it speak to the real world. Their prophet Micah (6:6–8) summed up the priorities which in the end they acknowledged:

> What shall I bring when I approach Yahweh?
> How shall I stoop before God on high?
> Am I to approach him with whole-offerings or yearling
>   calves?
> Will Yahweh accept thousands of rams
>   or ten thousand rivers of oil?
> Shall I offer my eldest son for my own wrongdoing,
>   my children for my own sin?
>
> God has told you what is good;
>   and what is it that Yahweh asks of you?
> Only to act justly, to love loyalty,
>   to walk wisely before your God.

In one of the hymns used in the Jerusalem temple (Psalm 40:6–8), this sense of priorities is expressed even more boldly:

> If thou hadst desired sacrifice and offering
>   thou wouldst have given me ears to hear.
> If thou hadst asked for whole-offering and sin-offering
>   I would have said, 'Here I am.'
> My desire is to do thy will, O God,
>   and thy law is in my heart.

Psalm 15 is a portrait of the worshipper who is welcomed by Yahweh:

> O Yahweh, who may lodge in thy tabernacle?
> Who may dwell on thy holy mountain?
> The man of blameless life, who does what is right
> and speaks the truth from his heart;
>   who has no malice on his tongue,
> who never wrongs a friend

and tells no tales against his neighbour;
the man who shows his scorn for the worthless
and honours all who fear Yahweh;
who swears to his own hurt and does not retract;
who does not put his money out to usury
and takes no bribe against an innocent man.
He who does these things shall never be brought low.

That sounds complacent. But the religion of Israel was, at its best, far from being self-righteous. Its self-criticism, its humble penitence, is voiced in another psalm (51:16,17):

Thou hast no delight in sacrifice;
if I brought thee an offering, thou wouldst not accept it.
My sacrifice, O God, is a broken spirit;
a wounded heart, O God, thou wilt not despise.

The relationship between Yahweh and Israel was a love which was totally unsentimental. This is seen in the use which the prophet Amos makes of the sound of a lion. Twice in the same short poem (3:1–8) he draws religious lessons from this frightening sound. The first reference is to the lion's private growl over his prey. The growl is inevitable. No less inevitable is the fact that Yahweh controls and causes everything that happens to his people, even disaster.

Does a young lion growl in his den
    if he has caught nothing? . . .
If disaster falls on a city,
    has not Yahweh been at work?

The second reference is to the lion's public roar against his enemies. The roar inevitably spreads terror. No less inevitable is the fact that when Yahweh speaks his servants repeat his words; when he sends disaster, his prophets do not flinch.

The lion has roared; who is not terrified?
Yahweh has spoken; who will not prophesy?

To 'prophesy' meant not peering into the distant future in order to satisfy mere curiosity, but having such an insight into the trends of the present that some future consequences were seen. And Amos now repeated as the word of Yahweh the claim that the disasters beginning to afflict Israel were punishment sent by Yahweh to his rebellious people:

For you alone have I cared
among all the nations of the world;
therefore will I punish you
    for all your iniquities.

Typical of the luminous integrity of Israelite religion at its best is the reply which Amos makes when Amaziah, the smoothly snobbish priest in charge of the royal chapel at Bethel, attempts to silence him. Amaziah expresses the general attitude that religious enthusiasts are contemptible and, when they can make themselves heard, troublesome. 'Be off, you seer!' he shouts. 'Off with you to Judah! You can earn your living and do your prophesying there. But never prophesy again at Bethel, for this is the king's sanctuary, a royal palace.' To which Amos replies in words of unfading splendour: 'I am no prophet, nor am I a prophet's son; I am a herdsman and a dresser of sycamore-figs. But Yahweh took me as I followed the flock and said to me, "Go and prophesy to my people Israel"' (Amos 7:10–15).

Also typical of the best tradition is a picture we are given of a less famous prophet, Micaiah, addressing great men courageously. In front of him are the two kings of Israel and Judah, 'seated on their thrones, in shining armour'. Around him are four hundred so-called 'prophets' who have been urging these kings to wage war on their national enemy. Their cry has been 'Attack!' But Micaiah says, simply and quietly, that attack would mean defeat: 'I saw all Israel scattered on the mountains, like sheep without a shepherd' (1 Kings 22:1–28).

Israelite prophecy, based on a vision of Yahweh lifted high above the littleness of his worshippers, often proclaimed the defeat and scattering of Israel. But the Israelites' faith in the divine shepherd did not depend on their nation's success. They loved to sing 'Yahweh is a warrior' (Exodus 15:3), and they loved to speak of their God as 'Yahweh of Hosts'. Probably the 'hosts' were the army of Israel, but that is not certain and the phrase may refer to the hosts of heaven – to subordinate gods, or perhaps to the stars. Yahweh was not a God who guaranteed victory to the army. To find out what he was, we have to read the Old Testament with sympathy. For when we meet the people who lived and wrote these books, we, too, begin to catch a rear view of their extraordinary, invisible, sovereign, and triumphantly independent God.

Twice in the Old Testament kings wait breathlessly while watchmen shout reports. 'The watchman went up to the roof of the gatehouse by the wall and, looking out, saw a man running alone . . . The man came nearer and nearer. Then the watchman saw another man running . . . The watchman said, "I see by the way he runs that the first runner is Ahimaaz son of Zadok"' (2 Samuel 18:24–27). So they brought the news to King David of the defeat of the rebellion led by his son, Absolam. 'The watchman standing on the watch-tower in Jezreel saw Jehu and his troop approaching and called out, "I see a troop of men . . . The driving is like the driving of Jehu son of Nimshi; for he drives furiously." "Harness my chariot," said Jehoram' (2 Kings 9:17–21). So Jehu came to kill King Jehoram.

The modern archaeologists and scholars have acted like those watchmen. They have told us that people are coming to meet us. These men and women are walking, running, driving furiously into our time out of the history of Ancient Israel. Now we must get up to meet them.

CHAPTER 2

Meet the People

MEN AND WOMEN

The Old Testament corrects any idea that the people in it were either more or less than human.

In the disapproving words of Isaiah (3:18–23) we are given a list of some of the fashions which adorned the women of Ancient Israel: 'anklets, discs, crescents, pendants, bangles, coronets, head-bands, armlets, necklaces, lockets, charms, signets, nose-rings, fine dresses, mantles, cloaks, flounced skirts, scarves of gauze, kerchiefs of linen, turbans, and flowing veils.' Some of the Hebrew words used in that list are so rare that modern translators have difficulty in deciding exactly what Isaiah meant, and we can have fun comparing the translators' efforts. For example, the Revised Standard Version gives us head-bands instead of discs, scarfs instead of coronets, sashes instead of necklaces, and handbags instead of flounced skirts. But the general picture is clear, and it is not inhuman.

The Israelites took a human pride in their children:

Happy are we whose sons in their early prime
    stand like tall towers,
    our daughters like sculptured pillars
    at the corners of a palace (Psalm 144:12).

The girls grew up. In the *Song of Songs*, one of them is tenderly undressed by her bridegroom:

How beautiful you are, my dearest, how beautiful!
Your eyes behind your veil are like doves,
your hair like a flock of goats streaming down Mount
    Gilead.

Your teeth are like a flock of ewes just shorn
    which have come up fresh from the dipping;
each ewe has twins and none has cast a lamb.
    Your lips are like a scarlet thread,
        and your words are delightful;
    your parted lips behind your veil
        are like a pomegranate cut open.
Your neck is like David's tower,
    which is built with winding courses;
a thousand bucklers hang upon it,
    and all are warriors' shields.
Your two breasts are like two fawns,
    twin fawns of a gazelle . . . (4:1-5)

We can look at the bridegroom through her proud eyes:

My beloved is fair and ruddy,
    a paragon among ten thousand.
His head is gold, finest gold;
    his locks are like palm-fronds.
His eyes are like doves beside brooks of water,
    splashed by the milky water
        as they sit where it is drawn.
His cheeks are like beds of spices or chests full of perfumes;
his lips are lilies, and drop liquid myrrh;
his hands are golden rods set in topaz;
his belly a plaque of ivory overlaid with lapis lazuli.
His legs are pillars of marble in sockets of finest gold;
his aspect is like Lebanon, noble as cedars.
His whispers are sweetness itself, wholly desirable.
Such is my beloved, such is my darling,
    daughters of Jerusalem (Song of Songs 5:10-16).

We can see that girl become a tireless housewife:

She chooses wool and flax
and toils at her work.
Like a ship laden with merchandise,
she brings home food from far off.

She rises while it is still night
and sets meat before her household.
After careful thought she buys a field
and plants a vineyard out of her earnings.
She sets about her duties with vigour
and braces herself for the work.
She sees that her business goes well,
and never puts out her lamp at night.
She holds the distaff in her hand,
and her fingers grasp the spindle.
She is open-handed to the wretched
and generous to the poor.
She has no fear for her household when it snows,
for they are wrapped in two cloaks.
She makes her own coverings,
and clothing of fine linen and purple.
Her husband is well known in the city gate
when he takes his seat with the elders of the land.
She weaves linen and sells it,
and supplies merchants with their sashes.
She is clothed in dignity and power
and can afford to laugh at tomorrow.
When she opens her mouth, it is to speak wisely,
and loyalty is the theme of her teaching.
She keeps her eye on the doings of her household
and does not eat the bread of idleness.
Her sons with one accord call her happy;
her husband too, and he sings her praises:
'Many a woman shows how capable she is;
but you excel them all' (Proverbs 31).

Or perhaps in his absence she is far less loyal to her husband:

I glanced out of the window of my house,
I looked down through the lattice,
and I saw among simple youths,
there amongst the boys I noticed

a lad, a foolish lad,
passing along the street, at the corner,
stepping out in the direction of her house
at twilight, as the day faded,
at dusk as the night grew dark;
suddenly a woman came to meet him,
dressed like a prostitute, full of wiles,
flighty and inconstant,
a woman never content to stay at home,
lying in wait at every corner,
now in the street, now in the public squares.
She caught hold of him and kissed him;
brazenly she accosted him and said, . . .
'I have spread coverings on my bed
of coloured linen from Egypt.
I have sprinkled my bed with myrrh,
my clothes with aloes and cassia.
Come! Let us drown ourselves in pleasure,
let us spend a whole night of love;
for the man of the house is away,
he has gone on a long journey,
he has taken a bag of silver with him;
until the moon is full he will not be home' (Proverbs 7).

Or perhaps she depresses her husband as they share a
one-room cottage through the boredom of a winter's day:

Endless dripping on a rainy day –
that is what a nagging wife is like (Proverbs 27:15).

We can see the bridegroom, now a careful farmer:

Will the ploughman continually plough for the sowing,
    breaking his ground and harrowing it?
  Does he not, once he has levelled it,
broadcast the dill and scatter the cummin?
  Does he not plant the wheat in rows
  with barley and spelt along the edge? . . .
Dill is not threshed with a sledge,

and the cartwheel is not rolled over cummin;
   dill is beaten with a rod,
      and cummin with a flail.
Corn is crushed, but not to the uttermost,
      not with a final crushing;
his cartwheels rumble over it and break it up,
      but they do not grind it fine (Isaiah 28:24–28).

Or perhaps he has become a craftsman:

So it is with every craftsman or designer
who works by night as well as by day,
such as those who make engravings on signets,
and patiently vary the design;
they concentrate on making an exact representation,
and sit up late to finish their task.
So it is with the smith, sitting by his anvil,
intent on his iron-work.
The smoke of the fire shrivels his flesh,
as he wrestles in the heat of the furnace.
The hammer rings again and again in his ears,
and his eyes are on the pattern he is copying.
He concentrates on completing the task,
and stays up late to give it a perfect finish.
So it is with the potter, sitting at his work,
turning the wheel with his feet,
always engrossed in the task
of making up his tally;
he moulds the clay with his arm,
crouching forward to apply his strength.
He concentrates on finishing the glazing,
and stays awake to clean out the furnace
                    (Ecclesiasticus 38:27–30).

Or perhaps he has become a very important and very
pompous person:

If I went through the gate out of the town
to take my seat in the public square,

young men saw me and kept out of sight;
old men rose to their feet,
men in authority broke off their talk
and put their hands to their lips;
the voices of the nobles died away,
and every man held his tongue.
They listened to me expectantly
and waited in silence for my opinion.
When I had spoken, no one spoke again;
my words fell gently on them;
they waited for them as for rain
and drank them in like showers in spring.
When I smiled on them, they took heart;
when my face lit up, they lost their gloomy looks.
I presided over them, planning their course,
like a king encamped with his troops (Job 29:7–25).

THE STRONG BEAUTY OF NATURE

Such were some of the people of Israel. And we can look at their land in the *Song of Songs*:

For now the winter is past,
the rains are over and gone;
the flowers appear in the country-side;
the time is coming when the birds will sing,
and the turtle-dove's cooing will be heard in our land;
when the green figs will ripen on the fig-trees
and the vines give forth their fragrance (2:11–13).

That is spring. Here is summer, described by Isaiah:

when the heat shimmers in the summer sun,
when the dew is heavy at harvest time.
Before the vintage, when the budding is over
and the flower ripens into a berry . . . (18:4–5)

And the crown of the year is pictured by a psalmist:

Thou dost crown the year with thy good gifts
and the palm-trees drip with sweet juice;
   the pastures in the wild are rich with blessing
and the hills wreathed in happiness,
the meadows are clothed with sheep
and the valleys mantled in corn,
   so that they shout, they break into song (65:11–13).

We can return to the *Song of Songs* for another glimpse of
the sensuous delight of the harvest, appropriately linked
with the joy of sex:

Your belly is a heap of wheat
fenced in by lilies . . .
You are stately as a palm-tree,
and your breasts are the clusters of dates . . .
May I find your breasts like clusters of grapes on the vine,
the scent of your breath like apricots
and your whispers like spiced wine . . . (7:3–9)

Such richness of life was to be enjoyed, not analysed.
Among the proverbs of Israel we read:

Three things there are which are too wonderful for me,
   four which I do not understand:
   the way of a vulture in the sky,
   the way of a serpent on the rock,
   the way of a ship out at sea,
   and the way of a man with a girl (30:18–19).

Even the smallest things in nature aroused wonder and
pleasure. As another proverb puts it:

Four things there are which are smallest on earth
   yet wise beyond the wisest:
   ants, a people with no strength,
   yet they prepare their store of food in the summer;
   rock-badgers, a feeble folk,
   yet they make their home among the rocks;
   locusts, which have no king,

yet they all sally forth in detachments;
the lizard, which can be grasped in the hand,
yet is found in the palaces of kings (30:24-28).

These simple proverbs could, however, be expanded into
a panoramic view of the majesty and wealth of nature, and
of its intricate and inexhaustible loveliness. In one of the
psalms we hear this people's thanksgiving to their God for
their land:

Thou dost make springs break out in the gullies,
   so that their water runs between the hills.
The wild beasts all drink from them,
the wild asses quench their thirst;
the birds of the air nest on their banks
and sing among the leaves.
From thy high pavilion thou dost water the hills;
the earth is enriched by thy provision.
Thou makest grass grow for the cattle
   and green things for those who toil for man,
bringing bread out of the earth
and wine to gladden men's hearts,
oil to make their faces shine
and bread to sustain their strength.
   The trees of Yahweh are green and leafy,
   the cedars of Lebanon which he planted;
the birds build their nests in them,
the stork makes her home in their tops.
High hills are the haunt of the mountain-goat,
and boulders a refuge for the rock-badger.

Thou hast made the moon to measure the year
and taught the sun where to set.
When thou makest darkness and it is night,
all the beasts of the forest come forth;
   the young lions roar for prey,
seeking their food from God.
When thou makest the sun rise, they slink away
   and go to rest in their lairs;

but man comes out to his work
   and to his labours until evening.
Countless are the things thou hast made, O Yahweh.
Thou hast made all by thy wisdom;
 and the earth is full of thy creatures,
   beasts great and small (104:10–25).

In *Job* we come across a poem about the riches beneath the earth, discovered by the miner:

While corn is springing from the earth above,
what lies beneath is raked over like a fire,
and out of its rocks comes lapis lazuli,
dusted with flecks of gold.
No bird of prey knows the way there,
and the falcon's keen eye cannot descry it;
proud beasts do not set foot on it,
and no serpent comes that way.
Man sets his hand to the granite rock
and lays bare the roots of the mountains;
he cuts galleries in the rocks,
and gems of every kind meet his eye;
he dams up the sources of the streams
and brings the hidden riches of the earth to light
                      (28:5–11).

At the climax of *Job* are reminders of the earth's stupendous creation:

Who set its corner-stone in place,
when the morning stars sang together
and all the sons of God shouted aloud?
Who watched over the birth of the sea,
when it burst in flood from the womb? –
when I wrapped it in a blanket of cloud
and cradled it in fog,
when I established its bounds
fixing its doors and bars in place,

and said, 'Thus far shall you come and no farther,
and here your surging waves shall halt'? (38:6–11)

Rain in the desert is an example of nature's inexplicable
bounty:

Have you visited the storehouse of the snow
or seen the arsenal where hail is stored,
which I have kept ready for the day of calamity,
for war and for the hour of battle?
By what paths is the heat spread abroad
or the east wind carried far and wide over the earth?
Who has cut channels for the downpour
and cleared a passage for the thunderstorm,
for rain to fall on land where no man lives
and on the deserted wilderness,
clothing lands waste and derelict with green
and making grass grow on thirsty ground? (38:22–27)

Towards the end of *Job* we find word-pictures of animals –
the mountain-goat, the wild ass and ox, the ostrich, the
horse, the hawk, the vulture, the whale, the crocodile. The
picture most often exhibited is that of the horse:

Did you give the horse his strength?
Did you clothe his neck with a mane?
Do you make him quiver like a locust's wings,
when his shrill neighing strikes terror?
He shows his mettle as he paws and prances;
he charges the armoured line with all his might.
He scorns alarms and knows no dismay;
he does not flinch before the sword.
The quiver rattles at his side,
the spear and sabre flash.
Trembling with eagerness, he devours the ground
and cannot be held in when he hears the horn;
at the blast of the horn he cries 'Aha!'
and from afar he scents the battle,

the thunder of the captains and the shouting

(39:19–26).

But the horse has often been celebrated as the friend of man. It says more about the Israelites' love of life that the author of *Job* could produce an equally accurate and admiring portrait of the fearsome crocodile (40:15–41:34). The prophet Joel, describing a plague of locusts, halts in his panic for long enough to celebrate the strength and efficiency of this horror:

> Before them the land is a garden of Eden,
> behind them a wasted wilderness;
> nothing survives their march.
> On they come, like squadrons of horse,
> like war-horses they charge;
> bounding over the peaks they advance with the rattle
> of chariots,
> like flames of fire burning up the stubble,
> like a countless host in battle array.
> Before them nations tremble,
> every face turns pale.
> Like warriors they charge,
> they mount the walls like men at arms,
> each marching in line,
> no confusion in the ranks,
> none jostling his neighbour,
> none breaking line.
> They plunge through streams without halting their
> advance;
> they burst into the city, leap on to the wall,
> climb into the houses,
> entering like thieves through the windows (2:3–9).

THE TRAGEDY OF LIFE

One of the most attractive features of the Old Testament is its collection of these (and many other) pictures of people and nature – poems which are 'like apples of gold set in silver filigree' (Proverbs 25:11). But such celebrations of life are by no means unique in the world's literature. Far rarer was the ability of the Israelites to uncover the pain as well as the beauty in the riddle of human existence. Through many centuries they have been able to speak to hearts full of sadness, or at least empty of illusions, because their vision of life so definitely included autumn. The prophet Micah laments:

> Alas! I am now like the last gatherings of summer fruit,
>   the last gleanings of the vintage,
>   when there are no grapes left to eat,
> none of those early figs that I love.
> Loyal men have vanished from the earth,
> there is not one upright man.
> All lie in wait to do murder,
> each man drives his own kinsman like a hunter into the
>   net (7:1–2).

A similar but stronger passage is Isaiah's 'Song of the Vineyard' (5:1–7). It begins like the pleasant kind of song at a country wedding that is found in the *Song of Songs*. It turns into a lament over the useless vineyard – a reminder of nature's hostile side, which the farmers of Ancient Israel met to the full as they cultivated the often not very fertile soil. But instead of complaining of difficulties unfairly inflicted on man, the song ends by condemning man. Ultimately it is a song about the grief and fury of God, betrayed by his own people.

> I will sing for my beloved
>   my love-song about his vineyard:
> My beloved had a vineyard
>   high up on a fertile hill-side.
>   He trenched it and cleared it of stones
>   and planted it with red vines;
> he built a watch-tower in the middle

and then hewed out a winepress in it.
He looked for it to yield grapes,
   but it yielded wild grapes.

Now, you who live in Jerusalem,
   and you men of Judah,
judge between me and my vineyard.
What more could have been done for my vineyard
that I did not do in it?
Why, when I looked for it to yield grapes,
   did it yield wild grapes?
Now listen while I tell you
what I will do to my vineyard:
I will take away its fences and let it be burnt,
I will break down its walls and let it be trampled under-
     foot,
   and so I will leave it derelict;
it shall be neither pruned nor hoed,
but shall grow thorns and briars.
   Then I will command the clouds
   to send no more rain upon it.

The vineyard of Yahweh of Hosts is Israel,
   and the men of Judah are the plant he cherished.
He looked for justice and found it denied,
   for righteousness but heard cries of distress.

Such reflection on the tragedy of life was one of the most
powerful forces in creating the art of history-writing, for
the oldest historical book known to us is included in the
Old Testament (2 Samuel 9–20 with 1 Kings 1:1–2:12).
This book is a narrative fuller than any carved or written
historical record surviving from the many-splendoured
civilizations of Mesopotamia, Egypt, India, or China. It is
almost three thousand years old, and almost five hundred
years older than the work of Herodotus, often called the
father of Greek history. It is known to scholars as 'the
succession narrative' because it tells of the succession to

King David; and almost certainly it was written under his successor, Solomon.

The work is anonymous. Naturally it has been examined to find the identity of its author, who must have had first-hand knowledge of some of these events (although he was not afraid to recount conversations between members of the royal family in their bedrooms – the biblical equivalent of keyhole journalism). The most likely candidate seems to be Abiathar, a son of one of the priests whom Saul massacred at Nob as a punishment for sheltering David. Attaching himself to David (1 Samuel 22:20) he became one of the king's closest associates, but was exiled by Solomon to his estate at Anathoth with the words: 'You deserve to die, but . . . you carried the Ark of Yahweh before my father David, and you shared in all the hardships that he endured' (1 Kings 2:26–27). Perhaps the prophet Jeremiah, who came from this same village of Anathoth five miles north-east of Jerusalem, was one of his descendants.

Since David and Solomon founded the House of David so much praised by prophets and psalmists, and since they exalted Ancient Israel to a pinnacle of power not known at any other time, we might expect this book to brag of their exploits. Certainly the museums of the West are littered with boasts about the feats accomplished by the rulers of Mesopotamia and Egypt. But no such bombast is found here.

As the minimum, we might expect the emphasis to be on David's virtues. Certainly other writing about David brings out the characteristics which made men glad to work, fight, and die for him – the consummate political skill with which he, who had spent his boyhood with his father's sheep, secured the throne of a united kingdom; the generalship which won freedom from the Philistines and acquired an empire, it seemed miraculously; his courage, dignity and patience under many tests; his respect for other men's courage (as when he refused to drink the water brought from the well at Bethlehem by soldiers who risked

their lives to show their affection); his musical powers (as
when his harp-playing soothed King Saul); his charm,
which knit to him the heart of Saul's son Jonathan; his
generosity in sparing Saul's life when Saul had turned
against him and was hunting him down as an outlaw; his
tenderness in mourning for Saul as well as for Jonathan,
and in restoring Saul's estates to Jonathan's crippled son;
his high spirits as he danced 'without restraint' before the
Ark of Yahweh being carried in triumph to rest in his new
capital, Jerusalem.

But this narrative of David's decline is so realistic that in
it David ceases to be the hero. The story is prefaced by the
solemn warning of the prophet Nathan that the king is not
a fit person to build a temple to Yahweh in Jerusalem: 'Are
you the man to build me a house to dwell in?' (2 Samuel
7:5). And then tales are told which vividly reveal the
true character of the man in maturity and age.

The flaw in the hero shows when he arranges the killing
of Uriah so that he may be free to marry Uriah's wife,
Bathsheba. The indiscipline of his sex life has tragically
suitable consequences when David, who can govern an
empire and win the devotion of soldiers, fails to control his
sons. He fails with Amnon, who rapes his half-sister and
whose love for her then turns to bitter hatred. He fails with
the more coldly-calculating Absalom, who waits and
schemes before murdering Amnon and then claiming the
kingdom for himself. He fails with Adonijah: 'never in his
life had his father corrected him or asked why he behaved
as he did.'

David's lament when he hears of Absalom's death
deserves its fame for its elemental simplicity. 'O my son!
Absalom my son, my son Absalom! If only I had died
instead of you! O Absalom, my son, my son!' That grief for
Absalom echoes David's earlier agony of mind as Bathsheba's baby dies. 'David,' we are told, 'prayed to God for
the child; he fasted and went in and spent the night fasting,
lying on the ground. The older men of his household tried

to get him to rise from the ground, but he refused and would eat no food with them. On the seventh day the boy died, and David's servants were afraid to tell him. "While the boy was alive," they said, "we spoke to him, and he did not listen to us; how can we tell him that the boy is dead? He may do something desperate." ' But his grief for these two sons is ultimately a lament for David himself, the hero conquered by his own weakness, the man of blood condemned to reap his own harvest. And the only consolation we are offered is that after all such is the universal human condition. As David says when Bathsheba's baby has died: 'Now that he is dead, why should I fast? Can I bring him back again? I shall go to him; he will not come back to me.'

The transfer of power from David to Solomon is recounted not as the glorious fulfilment of the divine promise to inaugurate an age of splendour but as the sordid affair it was – David now so old that he could not keep warm and could take no more than a fatherly interest in the pretty girl who warmed him up; Adonijah enlisting the support of the commander-in-chief and of Abiathar the priest, and boasting that he is to be king; Bathsheba (herself no chicken) plotting with the commander of the palace guard and arranging the rushed coronation of Solomon by Zadok the priest and Nathan the prophet; the dying David instructing Solomon to secure the deaths of Joab and Shimei.

To Ancient Israel, that was what it meant to be human: to be trapped in a web of lust, violence, greed, despair, death. The horror struck them all the more because the physical charm was so great – David who when young was 'handsome, with ruddy cheeks and bright eyes', and who when mature was the fabulous warrior; Bathsheba bathing on the roof of her house, 'and she was very beautiful'; the 'beautiful' Tamar for whom the boy Amnon fell 'sick with love'; Absalom with his appealing vigour and glamour, and his great head of hair; Adonijah who was 'very handsome'. They saw the skull beneath the skin. They saw that

in very truth men are a puff of wind,
    all men are faithless;
put them in the balance and they can only rise,
    all of them lighter than wind (Psalm 62:9).

But they saw amid the tragedy the true dignity of man. In this story David rises to authentic heroism when humble, most notably when he has to flee from Jerusalem during Absalom's rebellion. At that time he forgives Shimei who showers curses and stones on him. 'You are worth ten thousand of us,' say his men; and for the time being it is true. And some of the men he meets then are truly noble men. Ittai the Gittite, a Philistine mercenary, stays loyal with the sublime words: 'Wherever you may be, in life or in death, I, your servant, will be there.' The eighty-year-old Barzillai brings David provisions, but after David's victory he refuses the reward of a place at court. He is too old for all that; he prefers his own home, and sends his son instead. And the potential glory in being human – the potential glory in being the son of David – comes out when the dying David tells Solomon: 'I am going the way of all the earth. Be strong and show yourself a man.'

THE WISDOM OF DISILLUSIONMENT

The riddle of man, so beautiful, so clever, and so weak, a copy of God made of dirt, fascinated the thoughtful in Ancient Israel. They knew that the rich man and the poor man were made alike in the womb (Job 31:15), and they asked: *made for what?* So they advanced to their own stage of wisdom.

A considerable body of literature about 'wisdom' has survived from the ancient world. It attempted to make sense of nature and history: more practically, it taught useful knowledge ranging from etiquette to elementary science. Some of the men who wrote and supported this literature seem to have done so as a hobby, but others earned

their livings by educating the well-born young as leaders of
the community. Some of this literature was in short sayings
or proverbs, some in stories, some in songs or poetic medi-
tations; and examples of all three varieties are found in the
Old Testament. In Israel's folklore if not in real life, King
Solomon was the greatest and most typical teacher of such
varied wisdom. We are told: 'He was wiser than any
man . . . He uttered three thousand proverbs, and his songs
numbered a thousand and five. He discoursed of trees,
from the cedar of Lebanon down to the marjoram that
grows out of the wall, of beasts and birds, of reptiles and
fishes. Men of all races came to listen to the wisdom of
Solomon, and from all the kings of the earth who had heard
of his wisdom he received gifts' (1 Kings 4:31–34).

Such wisdom was to a large extent international. For
example, in the Old Testament a collection of proverbs
(22:17–23:11) is based on the Egyptian Book of Amenmope,
written about 1300 BC and discovered in AD 1922. But there
is no parallel in Egyptian or other ancient literature with
the way in which the Old Testament explores the *limits* of
human shrewdness and human strength. In Ancient Israel
as nowhere else, the sum of civilized wisdom was seen in the
confession that man knew nothing, and could do nothing,
in comparison with the mystery that encompassed him.

It is astonishing that *Ecclesiastes* and *Job* were included
among the scriptures of Israel, for these examples of
'wisdom' contain many attacks on pious complacency and
many confessions of agnosticism and despair. Both their
language and their thought suggest a late date, perhaps
some 250 years before Christ. The word which they usually
use for God is not Israel's own word 'Yahweh'. It is *El*, or
rather the plural *Elohim*. This international Semitic name
for God is still familiar to us through *Allah* of the Muslims.
Job, written in a Hebrew which has been greatly influenced
by Arabic, is located beyond the frontiers of Israel, in the
land of Uz (or Edom). It contains not a single reference to
any event in the history of Israel. And *Ecclesiastes* might

almost be a commentary on this 'saying of Agur son of Jakeh from Massa' which is one of an originally Edomite collection now found among the Old Testament's proverbs (30:1-14):

> I am weary, O God,
> I am weary and worn out;
> I am a dumb brute, scarcely a man,
> without a man's powers of understanding;
> I have not learnt wisdom
> nor have I received knowledge from the Holy One.
> Who has ever gone up to heaven and come down again?
> Who has cupped the wind in the hollow of his hands?
> Who has bound up the waters in the fold of his garment?
> Who has fixed the boundaries of the earth?
> What is his name or his son's name, if you know it?

An unknown 'teacher' or 'speaker' (in the Hebrew, *qoheleth*) wrote the book which usually retains its Greek title *Ecclesiastes*. He presents himself as a rich king 'greater than all my predecessors in Jerusalem'. He had refused his body no pleasure it craved; and whatever his eyes coveted, he had obtained. But his repeated verdict is that everything is empty. 'The end of all man's toil is but to fill his belly, yet his appetite is never satisfied' (6:7). The work involved in getting, so he teaches, is itself the only reward — for the same fate overtakes the man who labours hard and the idler, the wise man and the fool. 'It is a sorry business that God has given men to busy themselves with' (1:13).

What makes him describe all human achievement as 'chasing the wind' is, supremely, the empire of death, which makes life meaningless. 'For man is a creature of chance and the beasts are creatures of chance, and one mischance awaits them all: death . . . All go to the same place; all came from the dust, and to the dust all return. Who knows whether the spirit of man goes upward or whether the spirit of man goes downward to the earth?' (3:19-21). Death is the subject most worth thinking about, for only

death is lasting. 'The day of death is better than the day of
birth . . . Grief is better than laughter . . . Wise men's
thoughts are at home in the house of mourning' (7:1–4).

Some remnants of the old wisdom survive, for this teacher
continues to teach shrewdness, prudence, discretion,
caution, and moderation. He is practical about the prizes
of a well-ordered life. 'Divide your merchandise among
seven ventures, eight maybe, since you do not know what
disasters may occur on earth' (11:2). 'Eat your food and
enjoy it, and drink your wine with a cheerful heart . . .
Always be dressed in white and never fail to anoint your
head. Enjoy life with a woman you love all the days of your
allotted span here under the sun, empty as they are . . .
Whatever task lies to your hand, do it with all your might'
(9:7–10). But soon the joys of youth are followed by old age
with its lack of purpose and pleasure; this is the theme of
chapter 12, Lear-like in its senile gloom.

Almost all the colour of life has been blotted out by the
cloud of fate, and that cloud can never be pierced by man.
'There is nothing good for a man to do here under the sun
but to eat and drink and enjoy himself; this is all that will
remain with him to reward his toil . . . I applied my mind
to acquire wisdom and to observe the business which goes
on upon earth, when man never closes an eye in sleep day
or night; and always I perceived that God has so ordered it
that man should not be able to discover what is happening
here under the sun. However hard a man may try, he will
not find out; the wise man may think that he knows, but he
will be unable to find the truth of it' (8:15–17).

THE EXPERIENCE OF EVIL

Apart from a few conventional references to religion (some
of which may well have been added by a later editor),
Ecclesiastes says little about God. That is deliberate. 'Go
carefully when you visit the house of God. Better draw near
in obedience than offer the sacrifice of fools, who sin without

a thought. Do not rush into speech, let there be no hasty
utterance in God's presence. God is in heaven, you are on
earth; so let your words be few' (5:1-2). But *Job* has words
about God which are not few. They were all prompted by a
phenomenon which the author of *Ecclesiastes* observed with
his usual defeatism: 'I saw the tears of the oppressed, and I
saw that there was no one to comfort them' (4:1).

Job sums up human existence as no better than slavery:

Has not man hard service on earth,
and are not his days like those of a hired labourer,
like those of a slave longing for the shade
or a servant kept waiting for his wages? (7:1-2)

The author bitterly recalls a psalm (8:4-5) about the
glory of man:

What is man that thou shouldst remember him,
mortal man that thou shouldst care for him?
Yet thou hast made him little less than a god,
crowning him with glory and honour.

And he parodies that to take account of the realities of
his experience:

What is man that thou makest much of him
and turnest thy thoughts towards him,
only to punish him morning by morning
or to test him every hour of the day? (7:17-18)

His pessimism about life makes him long for death – the
death which was still an enemy in *Ecclesiastes*.

For then I should be lying in the quiet grave,
asleep in death, at rest,
with kings and their ministers
who built themselves palaces,
with princes rich in gold
who filled their houses with silver.
There the wicked man chafes no more,
there the tired labourer rests;

the captive too finds peace there
and hears no taskmaster's voice;
high and low are there,
even the slave, free from his master (3:13–19).

But this longing for death is not accompanied by any
clear faith that death will bring rewards to the deserving.
No, death seems to be the end of all but the most shadowy
kind of life. Man is worse off than a tree:

If a tree is cut down,
there is hope that it will sprout again
and fresh shoots will not fail.
Though its roots grow old in the earth,
and its stump is dying in the ground,
if it scents water it may break into bud
and make new growth like a young plant.
But a man dies, and he disappears;
man comes to his end, and where is he?
As the waters of a lake dwindle,
or as a river shrinks and runs dry,
so mortal man lies down, never to rise
until the very sky splits open.
If a man dies, can he live again?
He shall never be roused from his sleep (14:7–12).

So God has to reward the deserving before death; and
Job begins with a folk-tale which cheerfully asserts that
God does. 'There lived in the land of Uz a man of blameless and upright life named Job, who feared God and set his
face against wrongdoing. He had seven sons and three
daughters; and he owned seven thousand sheep and three
thousand camels, five hundred yoke of oxen and five
hundred asses, with a large number of slaves. Thus Job
was the greatest man in all the East.' A reference by the
prophet Ezekiel (14:14) shows that this was a common
folk-tale: 'Even if those three men were living there, Noah,

Daniel and Job, they would save none but themselves by their righteousness.'

The folk-tale was now continued to the effect that God permitted 'the Adversary' (*Satan*) to test Job's piety by a series of disasters – with the result that Job remained blamelessly devout, saying meekly:

> Naked I came from the womb,
> naked I shall return whence I came.
> Yahweh gives and Yahweh takes away;
> blessed be the name of Yahweh (1:21).

And the end was happy: 'fourteen thousand head of small cattle and six thousand camels, a thousand yoke of oxen and as many she-asses . . . There were no women in the world so beautiful as Job's daughters . . . He saw his sons and his grandsons to four generations, and died at a very great age' (42:12–17).

But before that traditional end to the tale is told, *Job* plumbs the depths of misery and ascends the heights of eloquence in order to expose the shallowness of the conventional belief in God. The conclusion is that those who have claimed that God always adjusts his rewards and punishments before death according to the individual's merits 'have not spoken as you ought about me'(42:7). This radical book is a courageous attack on all naïve or calculating piety – and on all the neat explanations of why the pious are made to suffer life's misery and slavery.

It looks as if the courage of such an attack was too much for some early readers of *Job*. The long speech of Elihu in chapters 32–37, a speech notably inferior to the rest, seems to have been added to the first edition of the book as one more attempt to argue that if a man suffers he must be a sinner. The three friends of Job have already trotted out all the orthodox wisdom with this theme – and Job has rejected it because it fails to tally with his experience.

Job mocks these teachers of wisdom:

No doubt you are perfect men
and absolute wisdom is yours!
But I have sense as well as you . . . (12:2–3)

The book laughs at these teachers' pompous assurance:

We have inquired into all this, and so it is;
this we have heard, and you may know it for the truth
(5:27).

And even more boldly this book mocks their claim to a
supernatural inspiration by producing a parody of it:

A word stole into my ears,
and they caught the whisper of it;
in the anxious visions of the night,
when a man sinks into deepest sleep,
terror seized me and shuddering;
the trembling of my body frightened me.
A wind brushed my face
and made the hairs bristle on my flesh;
and a figure stood there whose shape I could not discern,
an apparition loomed before me,
and I heard the sound of a low voice:
'Can mortal man be more righteous than God,
or the creature purer than his Maker?' (4:12–17)

Moving beyond such sarcasm, Job is ready to defend his
own righteousness seriously before man and before God, to
the bitterest end:

If he would slay me, I should not hesitate;
I should still argue my cause to his face (13:15).

I will maintain the rightness of my cause, I will never give
up;
so long as I live, I will not change (27:6).

And it is an immense tribute to the religious tradition of
Israel that when Job makes the final survey of his case
(chapters 29–31), the emphasis is not on the purity of his

worship but on the morality of his daily life. He affirms
that he has obeyed the laws which mean most – the laws of
chastity, of compassion, of honesty. Yet Job is allowed to
suffer terribly! That is what tempts him to the ultimate
despair, as it tempted a psalmist to say that 'the Most
High neither knows nor cares' (73:11).

Job supplies no clear answer to the agony which it articu-
lates, but it does indicate the direction in which the most
thoughtful in Ancient Israel believed that an answer
might be found. When put briefly, such pointers to the
ultimate truth may seem like the smug and bogus answers
of Job's friends; it is only their setting in the agony of real
life that gives them their integrity and their power to con-
vince. So we listen with the reverence which human
suffering and sincerity always command:

> O earth, cover not my blood
> and let my cry for justice find no rest!
> For look! my witness is in heaven;
> there is one on high ready to answer for me.
> My appeal will come before God,
> while my eyes turn again and again to him (16:18–20).

> But in my heart I know that my vindicator lives
> and that he will rise last to speak in court;
> and I shall discern my witness standing at my side
> and see my defending counsel, even God himself,
> whom I shall see with my own eyes,
> I myself and no other (19:25–27).

The radically honest author of *Job* knows no easy proof
that God is near, or that God is interested:

> If only I knew how to find him,
> how to enter his court,
> I would state my case before him
> and set out my arguments in full;
> then I should learn what answer he would give
> and find out what he had to say . . .

If I go forward, he is not there;
if backward, I cannot find him;
when I turn left, I do not descry him;
I face right, but I see him not (23:3-9).

This book presents the evidence in nature that there is a Creator of unfathomable power, but it knows the objection:

These are but the fringe of his power;
and how faint the whisper that we hear of him! (26:14)

Indeed, the book offers no philosophical answer at all to 'the problem of evil'. It simply affirms that God lives when the orthodox descriptions of him lie dead. It simply repeats that man has been gripped by the sheer fact of God:

I knew of thee then only by report,
but now I see thee with my own eyes
Therefore I melt away;
I repent in dust and ashes (42:5-6).

And it says that even when his vision fails, man can know God in the darkness:

Therefore I am fearful of meeting him;
when I think about him, I am afraid;
it is God who makes me faint-hearted
and the Almighty who fills me with fear,
yet I am not reduced to silence by the darkness
nor by the mystery which hides him (23:15-17).

And when they say that man can know God, and lose him, and know him again, these books are not being exclusively masculine. Abraham's wife is *both* Sarai or 'Mockery' *and* Sarah or 'Princess'. She laughs once in cynical bitterness (Genesis 18:10-15). She laughs again because 'God has given me good reason to laugh' (21:6). Her daughter-in-law Rebecca is at first 'very beautiful' and a model of kindness (24:15-27). She becomes possessed by 'bitter grief' (26:35) and thinks nothing of tricking the blind old man she is supposed to be nursing (27:5-17). Finally she is buried with him in great honour (49:31). Eve is part of Adam when Adam is made from the dust (2:7). Separated from him, she remains 'bone from my bones, flesh from my flesh' (2:23). Men and women sin and suffer and go on together.

These, in their joys and griefs, in their doubt and faith, are some of the men and women who come towards us out of these books. It is impossible to read these people's books and still to contrast the Old Testament with 'life'. They knew life in its intoxicating and terrifying fullness. As a poem in *Ecclesiastes* indicates, they knew

> a time to be born and a time to die;
> a time to plant and a time to uproot;
> a time to kill and a time to heal;
> a time to pull down and a time to build up;
> a time to weep and a time to laugh;
> a time for mourning and a time for dancing;
> a time to scatter stones and a time to gather them;
> a time to embrace and a time to refrain from embracing;
> a time to seek and a time to lose;
> a time to keep and a time to throw away;
> a time to tear and a time to mend;
> a time for silence and a time for speech;
> a time to love and a time to hate;
> a time for war and a time for peace (3:2–8).

The Birth of a People

THE STORIES OF THE SHRINES

Because man is gregarious, an ape in a pack, every individual is partly made by his or her community. But this was specially true of the Israelites. They regarded themselves as significant chiefly because they were members of a group which possessed, so to speak, a corporate personality.

According to a grim old story preserved in the book of Joshua (chapter 7), the invading Israelites have been repulsed from a Canaanite city named Ai – and have concluded that their God is angry with them. It is discovered a man called Achan has kept some loot after a previous victory; he has offended against the will of Yahweh that 'every single thing' should be destroyed. So he is stoned to death, and with him are destroyed his sons and daughters, his oxen, asses and sheep, his tent and all his property. Every single thing that was his was infected by his guilt. Israel's prophets and law-givers later insisted that the guilty individual alone should be punished, but that ancient story stands as a reminder that any growth of individualism in the history of this people arose in soil where the sense of a corporate identity flourished more naturally. The element of individualism is strong in *Ecclesiastes* and *Job*, but almost everywhere else in the Old Testament we find that the Israelite achieved his self-understanding through his sense of belonging to a people.

An illustration of this intense group-mindedness and patriotism comes when the farmer is told to put the first-fruits of the harvest into a basket, and take it to the priest. Then he is to recite a creed about the birth of his people:

My father was a homeless Aramaean who went down to
Egypt with a small company and lived there until they
became a great, powerful, and numerous nation [the
farmer is to say]. But the Egyptians ill-treated us,
humiliated us and imposed cruel slavery upon us. Then
we cried to Yahweh the God of our fathers for help, and
he listened to us and saw our humiliation, our hardship
and distress; and so Yahweh brought us out of Egypt
with a strong hand and outstretched arm, with terrifying
deeds, and with signs and portents. He brought us to this
place and gave us this land, a land flowing with milk and
honey. And now I have brought the firstfruits of the soil
which thou, O Yahweh, hast given me.

That creed is set out in *Deuteronomy* (26:5–10), a book
which was published in 622–21 BC, and it refers to an escape
from Egypt some six hundred years before. Although it
should not be used as evidence about the details of that
escape, it is usually thought to be in part much older than
622–21, and certainly it demonstrates the continuing significance of the history of Israel in the daily life of the people.

It is, in fact, one of many pieces of evidence in the Old
Testament showing that the twelve tribes of Israel repeatedly strengthened their corporate spirit by telling
stories about their origins. This cannot surprise us. Modern
nations place great emphasis on the history of the discovery,
or the revolution, or the expedition when the nation was
born. The saga of the founders is drummed into the
memories of schoolchildren and celebrated by public
holidays. Even tough-minded adults are expected to know
all about 1066, Joan of Arc, the defeat of the Moors,
Columbus and Captain Cook, the Declaration of Independence, the Storming of the Bastille, the Great Trek, the
Long March under Mao, civil disobedience under Gandhi,
or Castro's guerrilla operations.

Some scholars believe that the farmer's creed in *Deuteronomy* was recited at the open-air shrine at Gilgal, between

Jerusalem and the river Jordan. According to tradition, it was at Gilgal that all the Israelites were circumcised, to show by that uniform of their flesh that they were a whole and separate nation; and there they had their first harvest festival. It was then and there that Joshua, we are told, had his vision of the 'captain' of the army of Yahweh, who declared that 'the place where you are standing is holy' (Joshua 5:2–15).

There is, however, also evidence of an assembly of the tribes at another shrine – at Shechem, between the two hills, Gerizim and Ebal, at the crossroads of the main north-south and east-west roads in Canaan. *Deuteronomy* (chapter 27) describes the altar there. It is made of undressed stone (for this religion is older than the Iron Age), but it is carefully inscribed with 'all the words' of the tribes' laws. The twelve tribes of Israel are then to recite blessings on the law-keepers and curses on the law-breakers. Six of the tribes are to stand on the slope of Mount Gerizim in order to say the blessings, and six on the slope of Mount Ebal in order to say the curses. Tradition said that this ceremony, too, was started by Joshua, who at Shechem 'recited the whole of the blessing and the cursing word by word, as they are written in the book of the law' (Joshua 8:34).

It is possible that the ceremony at Shechem spread the idea that the law of Israel had been given by Yahweh to Moses on Mount Sinai – for the evidence about the gathering at Shechem does link the tribal law with Sinai, while the farmer's creed with which we began makes no mention of Sinai.

Shrines such as Gilgal and Shechem were holy places for many centuries before the Israelites arrived in Canaan. The archaeologists have uncovered Canaanite buildings at Shechem; the destruction of the Canaanite temple there is recounted in the book of Judges (chapter 9). But the Old Testament shows that it was thought necessary to associate these sanctuaries with the founders of Israel, so that many legends of the holy places arose. In much the same way the Koran attributes the foundation of the once pagan shrine at Mecca, the Kaba, to Abraham, the father of the faithful, assisted by his son Ishmael. *Genesis* (12:7–8) tells of Yahweh's appearance to Abraham at Shechem, at a time when 'the Canaanites lived in this land.' Yahweh's message to Abraham was: 'I give this land to your descendants' – and in response Abraham built an altar. Abraham's grandson Jacob built another altar at Shechem. This was dedicated to El-Elohey-Israel (Genesis 33:18–20). Near it were buried all the heathen idols of Jacob's household (35:1–4), and there the tomb of Jacob's son Joseph was honoured (Joshua 24:32–33).

The takeover of other Canaanite sanctuaries by the Israelites as local tribal shrines is reflected in other *Genesis* stories. One of the most famous shrines was at Bethel, probably named after the god Beth-El. This place ten miles north of Jerusalem was, we are told, visited by Abraham (Genesis 13:3) – and by Jacob, who

came to a certain place and stopped there for the night, because the sun had set; and, taking one of the stones there, he made it a pillow for his head and lay down to sleep. He dreamt that he saw a ladder, which rested on the ground with its top reaching to heaven, and angels of God were going up and down upon it.

Yahweh was standing beside him and said, 'I am Yahweh, the God of your father Abraham and the God of Isaac. This land on which you are lying I will give to you and your descendants. They shall be countless as the dust upon the earth, and you shall spread far and wide, to north and south, to east and west. All the families of the earth shall pray to be blessed as you and your descendants are blessed. I will be with you, and I will protect you wherever you go and will bring you back to this land; for I will not leave you until I have done all that I have promised.'

Jacob woke from his sleep and said, 'Truly Yahweh is in this place, and I did not know it.' Then he was afraid and said, 'How fearsome is this place! This is no other than the house of God, this is the gate of heaven.' Jacob rose early in the morning, took the stone on which he had laid his head, set it up as a sacred pillar and poured oil on the top of it. He named that place Beth-El; but the earlier name of the city was Luz (Genesis 28: 10–19).

It is related that at nearby Penuel, where there was a ford across the river Jabbok, Jacob wrestled with 'a man' and was told that he had been striving with God – the origin, we are told, of the name 'Israel' or 'God strove' (Genesis 32:22–32). This story may be an echo of a local legend about a river god. It is not surprising that when Jeroboam was setting up his kingdom in the 920s, after a rebellion against the royal and religious authority of Jerusalem, he restored Shechem and Penuel, and rebuilt Bethel as a national shrine (1 Kings 12:25–13:34). Some of the earliest notions of sacredness which the Israelites had were strong in these places – although Genesis 14:18–20 shows how Jerusalem, which was to become so much the centre of their religion, could be linked with Abraham through the story of his meeting with Melchizedek 'king of Salem . . . priest of God Most High' (El-Elyon).

Other sanctuaries were taken over by Israelite tribes. Some were in the territory of Judah. One in the hill country near Bethlehem was Hebron, later to be the capital of King David before he took Jerusalem. It was (and is) the highest town in the land. By tradition Abraham talked among the nearby oaks of Mamre with three angels (Genesis 18:1–15), and was buried in the nearby cave of Machpelah with his wife Sarah, to be joined by Isaac and Jacob with their wives (49:28–33). Another shrine was at Beersheba, where three roads crossed. There Abraham invoked 'the everlasting God' (which seems to be a reference to a local deity called El-Olam), as did Isaac and Jacob (21:33–34; 26:23–33; 46:1–4). Another shrine, at Mizpah, was associated with Jacob and a company of angels (31:25–32:2).

Curiously enough Shiloh, which replaced Gilgal and Shechem as the central shrine until it was destroyed by the Philistines, is not associated with the patriarchs by any legends which the Old Testament has preserved. Indeed, this temple in the hills between Shechem and Jerusalem became in Israel's folk-memory the place where Yahweh's just wrath had been executed (1 Samuel 4). 'God forsook his home at Shiloh' (Psalm 78:60). 'What I did to Shiloh I will do to this house' was the warning which Jeremiah heard in Jerusalem (7:14); 'I will make this house like Shiloh and this city an object of ridicule to all nations on earth' (26:6). But earlier references in the Old Testament show us the tribes' central shrine in action.

'The whole community of the Israelites met together at Shiloh and established the Tent of the Presence there,' we read (Joshua 18:1). During a clash between the tribes four hundred virgins were allowed refuge around this shrine (Judges 21:13) – only to be taken as wives by some Benjamites when the girls 'came out to dance' at the time of the 'pilgrimage in honour of Yahweh, made every year to Shiloh' (21:15–22). Elkanah the father of the great prophet Samuel 'used to go up from his own town every year to worship and to offer sacrifice to Yahweh of Hosts in Shiloh' (1 Samuel 1:3). It was a holiday when the priests of Shiloh expected pilgrims to get drunk (1:13–16). It was a time of celebration, an appropriate background to the song of Samuel's mother Hannah:

My heart rejoices in Yahweh,
in Yahweh I now hold my head high;
my mouth is full of derision of my foes,
exultant because thou hast saved me.
    There is none except thee,

none so holy as Yahweh,
   no rock like our God.
Cease your proud boasting,
   let no word of arrogance pass your lips;
for Yahweh is a god of all knowledge:
   he governs all that men do (2:1-3).

By regular pilgrimages to its own shrine and to the league's central shrine, a tribe would gradually build up its morale and its unity with fellow-members of the league. (Are we not familiar with the need of united states to salute their flag?) Twelve was a usual number in a league; it may have become customary because each tribe could then do a month a year at the central shrine. Such leagues of twelve existed among Israel's neighbours the Aramaeans, the Ishmaelites, and the Edomites, and reference is made to them in *Genesis* (22:20-24; 25:12-15; 36:10-14). An alternative number was six. The technical name of such a league is 'amphictyony', meaning 'those who live round about' the central shrine. And some evidence of the need to build and rebuild the corporate spirit of the twelve tribes of Israel is contained in the fact that the Old Testament includes four different lists of who the twelve were. The list in Genesis 49 (the Blessing of Jacob) differs from that in Deuteronomy 33 (the Blessing of Moses); and Numbers 26 differs from them both and from Judges 5. A league whose membership varied in this way certainly needed exercises which memorably celebrated its common ancestry and rejoiced in its common God.

THE PATRIARCHS IN LEGEND AND IN FACT

But who were Abraham, Isaac, and Jacob? We cannot know much, for we cannot get at the historical truth behind the stories told in these shrines – or around the cooking-pots as the tribesmen gathered of an evening in the camp or the village.

There is no ancient mention of these men outside the Bible, and no biblical evidence can be proved to date from their time, between 2000 and 1300 BC. It must make a modern reader suspicious of the accuracy of the *Genesis* stories when he notices (for example) that the anecdote of the patriarch's wife who was passed off among enemies as his sister is such a good story that it is told no fewer than three times: about Abraham in Egypt (12:10–20), about Abraham in Gerar (chapter 20), and about Isaac also in Gerar (26:1–11). The tale of Hagar, Abraham's concubine, and her son Ishmael is told twice, with variations (chapter 16 and 21:1–21). A close inspection reveals many little contradictions between one story and another, or within the one story. Such faults in the narrative have stimulated scholars to analyse the different sources from which these stories come. And a close inspection shows that some details in these stories are out-of-date. For example, 'the country of the Philistines' is mentioned as early as Genesis 21:32, whereas the truth is that the Philistines arrived in Palestine about 1200 BC.

This does not, however, mean that the stories about Abraham in Mesopotamia – 'the land between the rivers' Tigris and Euphrates – have no historical foundation at all. The first stories about Abraham put him in or near places where civilization came early in the Middle East. Mention is made of Ur the capital of the Sumerian empire (and then a port on the banks of the Euphrates), and of Haran some six hundred miles to the north-west. Abraham's move from Ur to Haran may dimly reflect the fact that the Sumerian empire around Ur was overthrown some two thousand years BC by an invasion of Westerners or Amorites, whose chief cities included Haran and Mari.

Despite the excitement of the excavation of Ur under Sir Leonard Woolley in 1922–34, it is no use digging around in the hope of finding Abraham's house, for he is never said to have been a pillar of urban society. On the contrary, he is always described as belonging to the well-known class of

Amorite breeders of sheep and cattle, who moved on to fresh pastures when need and opportunity arose. We can well imagine Abraham having to move – for Mesopotamia has never been a fertile land apart from the rich plain in the north between the Tigris river and the Zagros mountains (to be the heartland of the Assyrian empire around Nineveh) and apart from the irrigated delta of the south where the Tigris and the Euphrates flow through swamps to the Persian Gulf. In 'Mesopotamia' proper, between the two great rivers, agriculture is confined to the river banks. Here, in what has become Iraq, agriculture began; but it is astonishing that cities were built so soon after the beginning of the systematic cultivation of the land, for the country offers no stone, wood, or metal.

Modern archaeological discoveries have unearthed some parallels between the Bible and the records of Mesopotamia. Nahor, the name of Abraham's grandfather and of his brother (Genesis 11), is the name of a city near Haran. Serug and Terah are also place-names. Some customs reflected in the *Genesis* stories are found also in tablets written at Nuzi in the fifteenth or fourteenth century BC – customs of a concubine's son being adopted as the heir of a man whose wife had not borne a son; of a wife being treated as a sister when legally this was to her advantage; and of household gods serving as property deeds (which was why Rachel 'stole her father's household gods' in Genesis 31:19).

The impression given by *Genesis* that Abraham, Isaac, and Jacob led their flocks freely over the Middle East and enjoyed generally peaceful relations with the local rulers fits in with conditions possible at various points in the seven hundred years from 2000 to 1300 BC.

Egyptian records have survived which show how even that great empire could not dominate Canaan thoroughly. An extraordinarily graphic narrative tells how Sinuhe, a court official in disgrace, escaped across the guarded frontier and took refuge in Canaan in 1962 BC. Many

place-names including *Urushalimmu*, the earliest surviving
mention of Jerusalem, occur in the 'execration texts', small
earthenware statues and pots inscribed with curses against
rebels – and then smashed as a magic means of restoring
Pharaoh's empire in the nineteenth century BC. Around
1480 BC Egyptian authority was reasserted in a campaign
celebrated on obelisks which survive at Karnak, but about
a century and a half later the Hittites took over. They were
an Indo-European people probably coming from the
Balkans into what is now Turkey about 2000 BC, and they
conquered quite an extensive empire. (They are mentioned at Genesis 23:3, 26:34, 36:2). About 1220 BC
their empire collapsed under the pressure of new peoples
wanting their land, and they more or less vanished from
history until modern archaeologists got to work on their
ruins.

Archaeologists have also uncovered something of the early
history of Canaan. They give us a picture of a fairly prosperous network of fortified cities from about 3000 BC. There
was, however, no central authority. The cities sometimes
fought each other, were often the victims of raiding nomads,
and could not resist an Egyptian or Hittite army. The area
cultivated was simply what was needed to feed the cities and
villages where the farmers sheltered by night. Using this
evidence, we do not meet Abraham, Isaac, or Jacob. But
we do meet a situation in which it would have been
possible for a breeder of sheep and cattle, driven from
Mesopotamia by necessity, to find pasture for his herds in
Canaan without too much trouble from Egyptians, Hittites,
or Canaanites.

Whether or not the patriarchs spent much time in
Canaan, Jacob's son could be called a 'homeless Aramaean'
(Deuteronomy 26:5). The word 'Aramaean' was used to
cover a widespread movement of nomads from the steppes
into the more prosperous parts of the Middle East such as
Canaan and Syria between 1800 and 1200 BC. Another clue
is that Abraham is called 'the Hebrew' (Genesis 14:13).

Hapiru, or a similar term such as the Egyptian *'prw*, was a word used all over the Middle East to refer to people on the fringes of society – usually, when they were making a nuisance of themselves. It is mentioned in the tablets excavated at Nuzi, for example, but its use can be traced in many places and at many times over five hundred years before we meet 'the Hebrew midwives' at Exodus 1:15. Scholars debate about whether the word refers to a class or to a people but agree that it would have been an apt word for semi-nomads such as Abraham, who could grow prosperous but who never settled as a farmer in an empire or as a member of a Canaanite city state.

Many tribes and nations are being born off-stage as the drama of the Amorites or Aramaeans or Hebrews unfolds in *Genesis*. Some of the stories make the point that Israel's neighbours, who were often Israel's bitter enemies, could still be related to Israel in a half-forgotten way. They were all (to use the modern term) 'Semites'. The nomadic Ishmaelites, for example, whom the Arabs regard as their ancestors, are said to be among the descendants of Abraham. The name Ishmael means 'God hears', and an unexpectedly sympathetic poem is repeated about them (Genesis 16: 11–12). The Edomites are said to be descended from Isaac's son Esau about whom there is a similar poem (27:39–40). But the Moabites and Ammonites are said to have had their origin when Abraham's nephew, Lot, indulged in a bout of drunken incest (19:30–38). In chapter 30 of *Genesis* when we are being told stories about the birth of Jacob's twelve sons (with the rival mothers Rachel and Leah), we feel that we are being given jokes such as the tribes of Israel would tell against each other – although we cannot now recover the point of every joke. And a long poem about the sons of Jacob (Genesis 49) gives us some clues to the lost history of these twelve tribes. Other parts of the Old Testament tell us of 'the captivity in Egypt' and 'the captivity in Babylon'; this chapter tells us a little about the captivity in Canaan, when the tribes which were to constitute Israel formed themselves within the land they were to claim.

Although Reuben comes first, the poem warns: 'you shall not excel.' Although later Levi became the priestly tribe excluded from normal landowning, here it is a secular tribe wielding 'weapons of violence'. And although later the tribe of Simeon was absorbed into Judah, here it is presented as the 'brother' of Levi. The explanation seems to be that Reuben, Levi, and Simeon were tribes which never secured a substantial holding of land. By contrast, praises are lavished on the successful Judah.

Although the tribe of Zebulun settled in the Galilean hill country, this poem declares: 'Zebulun dwells by the seashore.' This may mean that these Hebrews hired themselves as labourers to the Canaanites of the coastal plain. Issachar is also said to have 'submitted to perpetual forced labour'. Then Dan is called 'insignificant' but 'a viper', and Gad is 'raided by raiders, but he raids them.' These seem to be references to the positions of these tribes on the borders of Israel to the north and east, perpetually involved in frontier wars. Asher and Naphtali are described as prosperous, for they occupied the fertile land of Galilee. Joseph, too, is a 'fruitful tree' in its area (later called Samaria); but in history it was to be broken up into two tribes, Manasseh and Ephraim (Joseph's sons in *Genesis*). The little tribe of Benjamin is called a 'ravening wolf' – a reference to its struggle to make a living in the country between Jerusalem and Jericho.

So the poem is full of fascinating clues to a history now forgotten. But clearly it was not a speech delivered by any historical Jacob.

The scholars who have studied these traditions most deeply, comparing them with the traditions of the surrounding peoples, conclude that each nation or tribe claimed its own father or founder. Stories were told about him which were thought to dignify customs practised by that nation or tribe, or to illustrate its characteristics, it might be humorously. Believing in a common ancestor was a way of concluding a treaty, for the story shared in common established a blood-brotherhood even if history had not already done so. It is quite possible that the tribes which eventually constituted Israel had very scattered origins. It is also possible that originally the founders called Abraham, Isaac, and Jacob did not belong to the same family. But the form which the stories have taken in the Bible does show what the people of Israel then wanted to believe about their origins and those of their neighbours.

Whoever they may have been, these founders were not regarded as examples of morality. The stories told about them emphasize many human weaknesses. Hosea (12:3–4) refers to Jacob:

> Even in the womb Jacob overreached his brother,
> and in manhood he strove with God.
> The divine angel stood firm and held his own;
> Jacob wept and begged favour for himself.

The greatness of these men, as they appeared in Israel's traditions, was that in their wanderings they met the true God. But they did not worship Yahweh, the God of Israel, by name. Legend had it that Abraham invoked Yahweh (Genesis 12:8), and even that Adam's grandson did (4:26), but the evidence is much stronger that the Israelites began to worship Yahweh many centuries later, when they were escaping from Egypt. Hints are preserved in *Genesis* that originally 'the God of Abraham' may have been separate from 'the Fear of Isaac' (31:42–53); and 'the Strong One of Jacob' different both from 'the Shepherd of Israel' and from 'God Almighty' or El-Shaddai (49:24–25).

However, if Abraham, Isaac, and Jacob each had his own god, that marks an advance on the pagan practice of worshipping many gods associated with natural objects (for example, Sin the Sumerian moon goddess). And it indicates some progress from the idea of the local god worshipped at a shrine, or by the river Jabbok. For 'the

God of Abraham' was not tied to any sanctuary. Because he was the god not of a place but of a person he could appear in Mesopotamia and say: 'Leave your own country . . . and go to a country that I will show you' (12:1). Such a god could one day be viewed as the Creator of the whole earth. And 'the Strong One of Jacob' could be strong over a man's life. He could make demands even when dealing with the crook and twister that Jacob was. Such a god was – or was capable of becoming – the Lord of history and the really Strong One, the King who was 'holy, holy, holy'. The fact that each patriarch and his household were dedicated to his god could lead to the stage when all the tribes which claimed Abraham, Isaac, or Jacob as 'father' felt themselves a holy because dedicated people. Jacob's name, Yaqob-El, means 'May God protect'.

Such trust in the tribal god could lead to Israel's faith in Yahweh. Thus there was some continuity between the gods of these Founders of Israel and the Yahweh whose glory Moses proclaimed. Some – but not much!

ISRAEL IN EGYPT

'My father' – let us recall again the Israelite farmer's creed – 'was a homeless Aramaean who went down to Egypt.' We cannot, however, be sure how many of the tribes of Israel ever were in Egypt. Scholars who have examined the evidence have often concluded that among the tribes *not* in Egypt were Judah, Simeon, and Benjamin. 'Judah' seems to have been originally a place-name in Canaan. The reference to the settlement of 'Simeon' in the area already claimed by Judah (Joshua 19:1–9) shows that these tribesmen were late arrivals. 'Benjamin' is a word meaning 'people of the south'; its use seems to reflect the tribe's formation in the south of Canaan.

There is nothing improbable in the tradition that some nomadic tribesmen or *Hapiru* people sought better pasture for their flocks and herds – or, if the worst came to the worst, employment as labourers – within the kingdom of Egypt. The surviving Egyptian records show that this was a regular practice. These Hebrews would have been so insignificant that it is not surprising that in these records no trace has survived of Israel in Egypt. It is therefore impossible to recover any firmly historical foundations for the *Genesis* story of the rise of Joseph from Hebrew slave to Prime Minister. However, it is possible that this story reflects conditions when Egypt was ruled by invaders from the Middle Eastern steppes, the Hyksos, between 1720 and 1550 BC. The Hyksos were far more formidable than any Hebrews. They conquered Egypt and Canaan with their chariots, and ruled efficiently. It is possible that they were prepared to use Hebrews such as Joseph.

The end of the Hyksos dynasty in Egypt may well be reflected in the biblical statement that 'a new king ascended the throne of Egypt, one who knew nothing of Joseph' (Exodus 1:8), but if so that statement scarcely does justice to the Pharaohs who succeeded the Hyksos. One of them, Amenhotep IV, was a frail youth who fanatically tried to enforce the worship of the sun god Aten and changed his name to 'Splendour of Aten' (Akenaten). About 1370 BC he established a new capital unpolluted by the traditional Egyptian worship. In the remains of this place (the modern Tell el-Amarna) a peasant woman in AD 1887 accidentally unearthed some of the imperial archives of Akenaten, including letters from frontier guards recording the admission of nomads into Egypt – and one from the ruler of Jerusalem warning Pharaoh that unless he sent archers the land would fall into the hands of the *Hapiru* people. On a tomb at Tell el-Amarna is carved a hymn to Aten. This seems to have had an indirect influence on Psalm 104 among the hymns of the much later temple in Jerusalem.

The immediate effect of Akenaten's zeal in the worship of the sun was to divide and weaken the Egypt he left to his son-in-law, the Pharaoh Tutankhamun (or Tutankaten) now famous for the magnificence of the contents of his tomb discovered in AD 1922. But the imperial power was restored by Rameses II, whose reign covered the first forty years or so of the thirteenth century BC. He built a vast new palace which has been partially excavated. There is a reference to it in *Exodus*: 'They were made to work in gangs with officers set over them, to break their spirit with heavy labour. This is how Pharaoh's store-cities, Pithom and Rameses, were built' (1:11). It is quite likely that nomadic Hebrews who had been allowed into Egypt were used in this way, and it is highly improbable that the Israelites would have invented such a humiliating story about their ancestors.

There is no good reason to deny that some of these Hebrews escaped from Egypt; and the probable date of this 'Exodus' is around 1250 BC. It would not have been an event inscribed by the Egyptians in one of their temples. The first Egyptian mention of Israel known to us dates from the reign of Merneptah, the successor of the great Pharaoh Rameses. Set up about 1220, this black granite pillar boasts of a victorious campaign to pacify Palestine. 'Canaan is plundered . . .' it reads; 'Ashkelon is taken; Gezer is captured; Jenoam is blotted out; the men of Israel lie desolate; their children are no more . . .' This campaign is not mentioned in the Old Testament.

The biblical stories of the escape have grown out of many traditions. Above all they have been shaped in the stories recited at the Passover feast (the *seder* loved by Jews to this day) in answer to a boy's question: 'What is the meaning of this rite?' (Exodus 12:26). The first fourteen chapters of *Exodus* can easily be read as 'lessons for Passover'. But above them all, and above many subsequent chapters of the Old Testament, towers one personality – who in his turn is dominated by his God.

Although remembered as 'the most humble man on earth' (Numbers 12:3), Moses was one of the architects of many nations' history. A poem about him is preserved, with Yahweh speaking:

If he were your prophet and nothing more,
I would make myself known to him in a vision,
   I would speak with him in a dream.
But my servant Moses is not such a prophet;
he alone is faithful of all my household.
   With him I speak face to face,
   openly and not in riddles.
   He shall see the very form of Yahweh.
How do you dare speak against my servant Moses?

                             (12:6–8)

The name 'Moses' comes from the Egyptian for 'Son'. It seems to be only half the man's original name; perhaps he was the son of a father whose name sounded too Egyptian to please the Israelites. The nephew of Moses had another curious and Egyptian name: Phinehas, meaning 'Negro' (Exodus 6:25). Moses may have been completely Egyptian in descent, but if so it is hard to account for the interest he took in the Hebrews. The story of how he was found as a baby in a rush basket and adopted by Pharaoh's daughter sounds very like the folk-tale which is told about the birth of Sargon, founder of the Akkadian empire about 2360 BC. Moses is said to have left Egypt for a time and to have married a wife, Zipporah (which means 'Bird') during his exile. She was a Midianite and her father, Jethro, owned sheep (Exodus 2:16–22). The Midianites were a nomadic people. Their centre was the inhospitable region between Palestine and Arabia, near the gulf of Aqaba, but Moses need not have gone that far to meet them.

Jethro was remembered in the traditions of Israel as a priest – and it is probable that the name of the god he worshipped was none other than Yahweh. The name is certainly very old. Three thousand years before Christ some Babylonian names included 'Yau' which seems to have been the name, or part of the name, of a god. What the name originally meant cannot now be known for certain. The most probable explanation is that it was a cry of greeting to God: 'Oh He!' The cry of 'Ya-hoo' comes very readily to the human voice in excitement; it is still preserved in the Muslim world, for it is used by Sufi dervishes when crying to Allah.

Whatever may have been the remote origins of the name, what matters more is the content with which it was filled when Moses began using it. *Exodus* gives the traditions that Moses first encountered Yahweh when acting as a shepherd for his father-in-law, and that he and his father-in-law later sacrificed to Yahweh together (3:1–2; 18:5–12). Some support may be lent from an Egyptian source. Inscriptions at Soleb in Egypt dating from about 1370 BC include references to 'the land of the *shasu yhw*'. *Shasu* was an Egyptian term for nomads, and the reference seems to be to the settlement of some ex-nomads whose god was Yahweh; this may mean the Midianites.

Another clue may be found in the subsequent history of the Kenites, a group (it seems originally Midianite) which joined the tribesmen of Israel. The name means 'Smith', suggesting that they were blacksmiths by origin, in the small copper or iron mines which we know were already worked in the time of Moses. In the book of Judges (1:16) we read that 'the descendants of Moses' father-in-law, the Kenite, went up with the men of Judah from the Vale of Palm Trees to the wilderness of Judah . . .' In later passages of the Old Testament the Kenites appear as Yahweh-worshippers.

Although we cannot be sure how the name of Yahweh arose, the atmosphere of its use in Israel's worship does suggest the desert of Arabia or Sinai rather than the shrines of Palestine or the cities of Egypt. It is an atmosphere of freedom from earthly rulers, combined with a feeling of awe before the divine mystery, producing a rare courage and a rare comradeship with one's companions in danger. These are features in the religion of the desert, and they can still be seen in some Arabs.

Some six centuries after the time of Moses, the purity of

religion and morality in the time of wandering through the wilderness was still valued so highly that a group of Israelites called the Rechabites obeyed these commandments: 'You shall never drink wine, neither you nor your children. You shall not build houses or sow seeds or plant vineyards; you shall have none of these things. Instead, you shall remain tent-dwellers all your lives . . .' (Jeremiah 35:6–7).

This puritan group was named after Rechab the father of Jehonadab who was Jehu's assistant in the massacre of the Canaanite priests (2 Kings 10:15–29). That is a reminder that the religion of the desert should not be treated sentimentally. The desert is a harsh place; it breeds harsh men with harsh ideas. Exodus 4:24–26 preserves a frightening little fragment of primitive religion among the Midianites. 'While they were encamped for the night, Yahweh met Moses, meaning to kill him, but Zipporah picked up a sharp flint, cut off her son's foreskin, and touched Moses with it, saying, "You are my blood-bridegroom." So Yahweh let Moses alone.' We notice here the hostile desert demon; the use of a flint, for metal was too recent to be permitted in magical rites; the protective touching of Moses (the Hebrew refers to touching his 'feet', a euphemism for the genitals); the reference to pre-marital circumcision. But exposure to the desert and to the tough discipline of its atmosphere could have a bracing effect on a man or a people coming from Egyptian civilization with its degrading mixture of luxury and oppression; and later the memory of purity in the wilderness could check the appeal of the lush pastures of Canaan.

Although the biblical accounts of the spiritual crisis of Moses in Midianite territory were written many centuries after the events, there is nothing unlikely in the heart of the story of the burning bush (Exodus 3). Moses notices that a bush seems to be on fire but it is not burnt up; this may be a reference to the discharge of atmospheric electricity known as St Elmo's fire. That shrub becomes to him holy ground. There he contrasts the freedom of the desert with the misery of the Hebrews in Egypt – and there he understands something of the presence and power of the desert god, Yahweh. He asks what is the name (in other words, what is the nature) of this god, and the answer comes: 'I AM; that is who I am.' An alternative translation of the Hebrew is: 'I will be what I will be.' The implications are clear enough in the biblical accounts of the religion which was founded there in the lonely wilderness. The reality of Yahweh, the only God who is ultimately real, will be known in his actions, not in any speculation about his nature. The reality will be revealed in history. And first it will be revealed as the misery of the Hebrews in Egypt is ended. These events will give a far stronger content to the name 'Yahweh' than any which may have been known among the Midianites.

The escape from Egypt has been surrounded by dramatic effects – by magic performed both by Moses and by Egyptian rivals, by plagues inflicted on Egypt, and by the parting of the sea so that between the wet walls the Israelites crossed on the dry ground. Some of these great stories can be related to less dramatic but more probable history. The 'plagues of Egypt' were to hand for the story-teller in normal events. The Nile in flood was full of mud which looked like blood, and the floods bred frogs and mosquitoes. Hail was rare but possible, and locusts were a more frequent plague. The hot, sand-laden wind from the desert (the present-day *Khamsin* or Darkness) produced boils or itchy skin. Many epidemics carried off the cattle or the children, and to this day smearing blood on the doorposts and lintel is a prophylactic rite practised by some Arabs.

The sea crossed by the refugees was clearly not the Red Sea but a 'Sea of Reeds' (Joshua 2:10). In other words, it was a freshwater marsh where the papyrus grew plentifully. Almost certainly it was fairly near the modern Suez Canal. Probably it was an arm of Lake Menzaleh near 'Pharaoh's store city', Rameses; or a little to the south, it may have been part of Lake Timsah or the Great Bitter Lake. A few scholars think that it may have been Lake Sirbonis on the Mediterranean to the east. In any such marsh the chariot-wheels of any Egyptian frontier guards pursuing the escapers could easily get bogged, particularly if a strong wind which had been drying the ground suddenly dropped.

But the reality, as it can be recovered after the discounting of what look like legends, remains truly marvellous – because of its consequences in the history of Israel and the world. Exodus 15: 21 preserves a song and puts it into the mouth of Miriam the sister of Moses. This song is regarded by the scholars as a very ancient expression of Israel's interpretation of its escape:

> Sing to Yahweh, for he has risen up in triumph;
> the horse and his rider he has hurled into the sea.

A later song, put into the mouth of Moses himself (Exodus 15), voices the response of Israel after centuries of reflection on all that had followed from the great escape:

> Who is like thee, O Yahweh, among the gods?
> Who is like thee, majestic in holiness,
> worthy of awe and praise, who workest wonders? . . .
> Yahweh shall reign for ever and for ever.

Other hymns which have survived from Ancient Israel's worship repeatedly give thanks for the Exodus. One example is Psalm 77:16–20, when the crossing of the Reed Sea is dramatized:

> The waters saw thee, O God,
> they saw thee and writhed in anguish;
> the ocean was troubled to its depths.
> The clouds poured water, the skies thundered,
> thy arrows flashed hither and thither.
> The sound of thy thunder was in the whirlwind,
> thy lightnings lit up the world,
> earth shook and quaked.

Thy path was through the sea, thy way through mighty
waters,
and no man marked thy footsteps.
Thou didst guide thy people like a flock of sheep,
under the hand of Moses and Aaron.

THE WILDERNESS

The long march through the wilderness was equally necessary in the formation of Israel. The account in *Exodus* (12:
37–38) admits that those who escaped from Egypt were a
mixed lot, including some who never became Israelites:
'The Israelites set out . . . and with them too went a large
company of every kind.' This crowd had to be turned into
an army and a church. As *Exodus* relates (chapter 16), they
needed to live together through the emergency of depending
for food on *manna*. (The Hebrew word means 'What is it?'
Modern experts agree that it was the resinous secretions of
plant lice on tamarisks.) The refugees needed to live together through the experience of depending for water on
small streams hidden in the rocks (Exodus 17: 1–7). They
had to marvel together at what seem to have been volcanic
phenomena – the pillar of fire at night (or was this the
glowing brazier which guides have often carried through
the desert?), the smoking mountain (19:18), the glory
which 'looked to the Israelites like a devouring fire on the
mountain-top' (24:17).

We cannot now discover exactly where they went, since
naturally they avoided the military and commercial road to
Palestine, which was guarded. Different traditions are
woven together in *Exodus*. Scholars have formed various
theories on the basis of these stories, but nothing is certain.
Chapter 17 of *Exodus* brings the refugees to the neighbour-
hood of Kadesh, an oasis which was the natural rallying
point for nomads wishing to enter the richer land of
Canaan to the north-east. This is soon after their escape
from Egypt, and before their journey to the 'mountain of

God'. But in the biblical narrative Kadesh is not entered until we come to the second half of *Numbers*, and the mountain is said to have been eleven days' journey from the oasis (Deuteronomy 1:2). We cannot even be sure of the name of the mountain. It is usually given as 'Sinai' but in the traditions called E and D (see chapter 8) it appears as 'Horeb'. Nor is it possible to be sure of its position.

If it was an active volcano, the mountain was almost certainly in north-west Arabia, beyond the gulf of Aqaba, for this is the only area in the whole region where volcanoes are known to have been active in historical times. The Midianites made this territory their home when they were not seeking other pastures for their flocks, and *Numbers* (10:29) tells us that 'Hobab son of Reuel the Midianite, his brother-in-law' reluctantly agreed to throw in his lot with Moses. This, together with the earlier description of a reunion with Jethro, seems to indicate a stay in this territory. Exodus 3:1 definitely locates 'the mountain of God' in a place where Moses could mind Jethro's flock.

The ancient Song of Deborah (Judges 5) refers to Yahweh as coming out of the land between Palestine and Arabia:

> I will raise a psalm to Yahweh the God of Israel.
> O Yahweh, at thy setting forth from Seir,
> when thou camest marching out of the plains of Edom,
> earth trembled; heaven quaked;
> the clouds streamed down in torrents.
> Mountains shook in fear before Yahweh, the lord of Sinai,
> before Yahweh, the God of Israel.

There is a similar reference in the very old Blessing of Moses (Deuteronomy 33:1-2). But in the fourth century AD Christian monks settled on Jebel Musa, an impressive peak a hundred miles south from this area, believing that it was Sinai, and even in modern times the Bible has usually been thought to suggest a position in the south of the peninsula of Sinai. There was a well-known route south to the copper mines which were worked under Egyptian direction, although the Israelites may have avoided this route, being nervous of the police.

All that we can know, and all that we need to know, is that during some years in the wilderness (forty was a conventional number) some of the tribesmen whose descendants later formed the people of Israel became devoted adherents of the religion of Yahweh – and therefore, at least potentially, 'my kingdom of priests, my holy nation' (Exodus 19:5). And later on they were able to draw into this highly distinctive religion other 'Hebrews' who joined them inside Canaan.

It cannot have been a short or simple process. It is significant that Aaron, the brother of Moses and in many of the stories his collaborator and spokesman, appears in one tradition as himself for a period an idol-worshipper (Exodus 32). A grandson of Moses was an idolater (Judges 18:30). A story in *Numbers* (chapter 11) also makes psychological sense. A 'mixed company of strangers' joined the Israelites and 'began to be greedy for better things'. The Israelites themselves found that once they had left Egypt absence had the usual effect on their hearts. 'Think of it!' they moaned. 'In Egypt we had fish for the asking, cucumbers and water-melons, leeks and onions and garlic.' Even Moses then lost his nerve. 'How have I displeased Yahweh that I am burdened with the care of this whole people? Am I their mother? Have I brought them into the world, and am I called upon to carry them in my bosom, like a nurse with her babies . . .?'

It is not surprising that we read of devices to maintain the flagging morale of the Israelites – devices which were approved in the religion of Yahweh, but which appear not unlike the heathen superstitions which Israel came to despise. One was the Ark, a sacred tent of the kind still being carried centuries later by tribesmen going to war in this area. It brought good luck and it localized the god – so when it was moved Moses was expected to say 'Up, Yahweh!' and when it halted he was expected to say 'Rest,

Yahweh!' (Numbers 10:35–36) as if Yahweh were a pet dog. Another morale-building device used by Moses was a bronze serpent looking for all the world like an idol (Numbers 21:8–9). This sacred object survived to feature in the Jerusalem temple, when the Israelites called it Nehushtan and burned sacrifices to it – until King Hezekiah, who 'did what was right in the eyes of Yahweh', broke it up (2 Kings 18:4).

But in that long march Israel's faith was formed. It was faith in Yahweh, whose character was set out in what later Jews called the Thirteen Attributes: 'a God compassionate and gracious, long-suffering, ever constant and true, maintaining constancy to thousands, forgiving iniquity, rebellion, and sin, and not sweeping the guilty clean away; but one who punishes sons and grandsons to the third and fourth generation for the iniquity of their fathers' (Exodus 34:6–7). And in Numbers 6:22–26 a blessing from this God is given for Aaron's use:

Yahweh bless you and watch over you;
Yahweh make his face shine upon you
   and be gracious to you;
Yahweh look kindly on you and give you peace.

That faith gave the people its identity. Here is a people so obscure in the development of ancient civilization that its founders appear only as the 'Hebrews' on the fringes. It is a people which boasts of its escape from forced labour in Egypt – but which is apparently not thought worth mentioning in any Egyptian record until its obliteration can be claimed in a few words of propaganda about a campaign in Canaan. It is a people which rather pathetically exaggerates its early numbers (Moses could command 603,550 'Israelites aged twenty years and upwards fit for service' according to Numbers 1:46). Yet this is in truth a people great – and unique.

The Israelites became a great people because the blessing which they attributed to the Moabite prophet Balaam

(Numbers 23) was really the view which, with good reason,
they took of themselves:

> I see a people that dwells alone,
> that has not made itself one with the nations . . .
> Yahweh their God is with them,
> acclaimed among them as king.
> What its curving horns are to the wild ox,
> God is to them, who brought them out of Egypt.

And so they could stumble into an understanding of
God's fatherhood which was to be of profound significance
for all mankind, as in the book of Hosea (11:1–4):

> When Israel was a boy, I loved him;
> I called my son out of Egypt . . .
> It was I who taught Ephraim to walk,
> I who had taken them in my arms . . .
> I had lifted them like a little child to my cheek . . .

The story of this people's birth is therefore important to
every people. Every people needs to ask itself what are its
equivalents of the Exodus of Israel from Egypt. Public
holidays, we may say, are needed not only for recreation
but also to unite a people in common memories and
common ambitions. In some sense, holidays make a people
holy. Every nation needs its shrines to symbolize its common
life – whether these are great churches or parliaments or
law courts or meeting places in the open air like the
sanctuaries which Israel took over from the Canaanites.
Such a place for corporate celebration can be in modern
times a sports arena or a city square or a park. Whether its
creed is remembered over a basket of produce, or over a
computer, or not at all, every nation needs to know what it
is escaping from, and where it is trying to go. Every nation
needs to be ready to make sacrifices for its freedom – and
for its ideals. And every nation needs to ask itself search-
ingly what its effective ideals are. Every nation needs to
make conscious efforts in order to keep this corporate life

strong and every nation needs to work at it repeatedly and frequently, for in the wilderness where it is very easy to die of thirst there is no short-cut to a healthy nationhood. Every nation needs its patriotic songs, its flags as the equivalent of the Ark of Israel, its paintings and statues as the equivalent of Nehushtan.

The idea that every nation has (or needs) its own liberation or Exodus is found within the Old Testament. Astonishingly, in the prophecy of Amos (9:7) the usually hated Philistines and Aramaeans – neighbours to the west and north who had waged many bitter wars against Israel – are said to have been led by Yahweh himself from their original homelands to their threatening positions on Israel's frontiers. Amos hears Yahweh asking:

> Did I not bring Israel up from Egypt,
> the Philistines from Caphtor, the Aramaeans from Kir?

The idea that 'the Exodus' needs to be repeated in new liberations may sound like a modern notion. But some six hundred years or so after Moses, a prophet taught just that message. He wrote with great daring:

> Thus says Yahweh,
> who opened a way in the sea
> and a path through mighty waters,
> who drew on chariot and horse to their destruction,
> a whole army, men of valour . . .
> Cease to dwell on days gone by
> and to brood over past history.
> Here and now I will do a new thing;
> this moment it will break from the bud.
> Can you not perceive it?
> I will make a way even through the wilderness
> and paths in the barren desert (Isaiah 43:16–19).

CHAPTER 4

The Growth of a People

THE OCCUPATION OF THE LAND

Every nation needs a land, an economy, and a government – and Ancient Israel was no exception. It grew as it acquired these sources of a nation's strength.

Every nation issues propaganda on such subjects, and again Ancient Israel was no exception. But its propaganda was included in the Bible, with the result that claims made about its territory, economy, and government more than a thousand years before Christ are still quoted in the twentieth century AD as sacred scripture. The modern world has reason to know that the Ancient Israelites' claim to occupy Canaan or Palestine by divine right has retained a great emotional power among Jews. Clear thought about this claim has become an urgent necessity not only for Jews but for all who are caught up in the modern drama of Zionism and Israel. And if clear thought can pierce these emotions, then it may be possible to find in modern study of the Old Testament some principles which can illuminate other nations' stories.

We turn first to the territorial ambitions of the Israelites. In *Genesis* (chapter 15) we read of a vision which led Abraham to 'put his faith in Yahweh, and Yahweh counted that faith to him as righteousness'. Although Paul based on these words a religious meditation with the theme that righteousness comes from faith in God's promises (Romans 4), the original setting was strongly political. The descendants of Abraham are to be as many as the stars in the sky, and to them 'I give this land from the River of Egypt to the Great River, the river Euphrates, the territory of the Kenites, Kenizzites, Kadmonites, Hittites, Perizzites,

Rephaims, Amorites, Canaanites, Girgashites, Hivites, and Jebusites.' The 'River of Egypt' mentioned here may be not the Nile itself but the 'Brook of Egypt', a wadi in the desert some fifty miles south-west of Gaza. But even so, there has only been one period in all history when such a vision has been even approximately fulfilled, and that was under David and Solomon soon after 1000 BC. Almost certainly the story in *Genesis* dates from that period. It celebrates the short-lived affluence of the Israelite empire.

In the next passage in *Genesis* where God makes a promise to Abraham (chapter 17), we read: 'I will fulfil my covenant between myself and you . . . generation after generation, an everlasting covenant, to be your God, yours and your descendants' after you. As an everlasting possession I will give you and your descendants after you the land in which you now are aliens, all the land of Canaan, and I will be God to your descendants.' This promise seems to have a different atmosphere. The generations are passing; the covenant between Israel and its God needs to be stressed again and again. And almost certainly this promise has a different source, some five hundred years after David and Solomon. It dates from a time when many Jews are exiles and aliens after the Assyrian and Babylonian conquests of Palestine, and when the Jews who have remained in Palestine are not one people politically. Claims running seven hundred miles from the Nile to the Euphrates have been abandoned, and the recovery of Jewish life in Palestine (a little land, about a hundred and fifty miles from north to south and half that distance from east to west) is a matter of defiant faith.

But whether in victory or in defeat, the people of Israel were clearly in love with their land. When they told the story of how Yahweh had revealed himself to Moses in the land of the Midianites, they insisted on a reference to the country of the Canaanites, Hittites, Amorites, Perizzites, Hivites, and Jebusites, a land flowing with milk and honey (Exodus 3:17). The milk was from goats; the honey was probably a syrup reduced from grape juice. When they told how the tribesmen had gathered in the surrounding desert for their attacks on this land, they pictured their ancestors' appetites being sharpened by the spectacle of grapes, pomegranates, and figs – and their ancestors' amazement being incre·sed by the sight of giants inhabiting the land (Numbers 13:21–33). When they told of the end of the life of Moses, they pictured the old man on the top of Mount Pisgah. To the east he would look over the desert. To the north and to the west he might see the land. His eye would move in delight across the Jordan, over Jerusalem and the hills, through the hills (somehow), down the fertile plain to the sea (Deuteronomy 34).

What was true about this land was that it was amazingly varied, a fit home for people in whose experience joy and despair were both so prominent. On Mount Hermon in the north the snows were eternal, but beneath it, along the 'Way of the Sea', passed caravans which a few days ago had been crossing the desert. The valley of Jezreel or Esdraelon in the centre was a rich granary, guarded by the fortress of Megiddo; but life was harder in hill-side towns such as Nazareth, a little to the north. In the south the Negeb was a barren steppe and the Dead Sea, 1280 feet below the Mediterranean, was surrounded by an eerie wilderness. The climate in the rift valley of the river Jordan, which flowed into the Dead Sea, was more or less tropical; but a few miles away was the hill country of Judah where the boy David looked after his father's sheep. The coast provided few harbours and they never became a seafaring people, but life in such a land sent their imaginations on long journeys.

Their love of their land led them to exaggerate its natural resources, as in the ecstatic accounts which they put into the mouth of Moses. 'Yahweh your God is bringing you to a rich land, a land of streams, of springs and underground waters gushing out in hill and valley, a land of wheat and barley, of vines, fig-trees, and pomegranates, a land of olives, oil and honey. It is a land where you will never live in poverty nor want for anything, a land whose stones are iron-ore and from whose hills you will dig copper' (Deuteronomy 8:7–9). 'The land . . . is a land of mountains and valleys watered by the rain of heaven. It is a land which Yahweh your God tends and on which his eye rests from year's end to year's end' (11:11–12).

But their love of this land endured when they discovered that much of it was scarcely more fertile than the wilderness they had left behind – and when, even in the plains, they experienced the lot of an agricultural labourer:

> You shall gain your bread by the sweat of your brow
> until you return to the ground (Genesis 3:17–19).

They accepted the fact that most of the pasture was so poor that the animals had to graze in one area in the winter and another in the summer. It made them liken the God of this land to a shepherd guiding his flock to green pastures – with a crook to rescue exhausted sheep who lay down to die, and with a large stick to use against wild animals (Psalm 23).

Their love of this land constituted their real claim on it. History seems to have delivered its verdict that they were wrong to believe that God had promised the land to them for ever; indeed, their own prophets said so when the land was conquered, the upper class deported, and the peasants made to serve foreign rulers and landowners. The 'everlasting' promises which they said God had spoken to Abraham and Moses turned out to be the Israelites' own dreams. But it seems not unreasonable to believe that, if the care of God for the human race is a reality, then there is a divine blessing on the natural wish of each people to possess its own territory in peace – and a particular blessing on the readiness of a people to gain their bread by their own sweat poured into the land.

The problem was that others already possessed, farmed, and enjoyed the land before the Israelites reached it. In two ways the invading tribesmen were lucky. To the east the Assyrian power was now in eclipse. To the west Egypt was also in decline. The Israelites entered a temporary vacuum in international power politics, and so they had their chance. However, Pharaoh Rameses III is now known to have reinstalled troops in the old garrison town of Beth-shan, and the bronze base of a statue of Rameses VI, who died in 1149 BC, has been discovered at Megiddo, also in the very centre of Canaan. We therefore now possess proofs that, despite the silence of the Old Testament on these topics, Pharaoh Merenptah's expedition was not the last Egyptian attempt to reassert control. And the land of Canaan which Egypt and Israel claimed was no vacuum.

It is known to have been a human habitation for some 600,000 years, since the Old Stone Age. The age of Israel's patriarchs was for Canaan the Middle Bronze Age. In Jericho, modern archaeology enables us to trace town life back to the Neolithic Age, and a tower has been unearthed (it stands about thirty feet high) which was built some 6800 years BC. No walled town older than Jericho has been discovered anywhere. Modern archaeology shows that the thirteenth century BC was an age when the Canaanites were heavily involved in international commerce and used many instruments of iron both for farming and for fighting. No distinctively Israelite remains are uncovered by the archaeologist's spade until a much later period; what we guess was Israelite building in this early period is a coarser copy of Canaanite work. It is significant that about 1020 BC 'no blacksmith was to be found in the whole of Israel' (1 Samuel 13:19).

To these discoveries by archaeologists in Canaan can now be added the finding of a library in the ruins of the ancient city of Ugarit, today called Ras Shamra, on the coast of Syria. The city was first excavated in AD 1929 and the library dates from about 1400 BC. It documents a civilization then already old. Although Ugarit was a Phoenician city, looking to the Mediterranean for much of its livelihood, its civilization was in essentials identical with that of the Canaanite city states to the south.

The Phoenicians have aptly been called the Japanese of the ancient world. Because they needed a simpler way of writing for commercial purposes, they invented a script very like our alphabet, probably in the seventeenth century BC. They were great shipbuilders; a ship which they made of their Lebanese cedar for a Pharaoh of Egypt about 2500 BC was found in AD 1954. Their name comes from a snail (in Greek *phoinix*). Mounds of the shells of these snails have been excavated; the mounds were industrial waste, for the snails were used to make a purple dye which was valued by the rich all round the Mediterranean. The word 'Canaan' seems to mean 'purple', although this is not certain. From the name of the Phoenician city of Byblos comes our 'Bible'; it was a proud city, and in a vivid narrative of about 1000 BC an Egyptian visitor to Byblos, Wenamun, complains of being insulted by the local ruler. In the whole Bible, no city except for Jerusalem itself is described more vividly than Tyre, the island-city with its luxury and its commerce and its boasts: 'I am perfect in beauty . . . I sit throned like a god on the high seas' (Ezekiel 26:1–28:19).

Such a civilization was not to be disposed of merely by repeating Yahweh's promises like incantations. Moreover, any weakness there may have been in the Canaanite or Phoenician city states also acted as an invitation to other peoples, whose own gods made similarly encouraging noises.

Israel's entry into Canaan seems to have more or less coincided with the settlement of other tribes, vaguely called 'Aramaean', in much of Syria to the north, behind the Phoenicians on the coast; with the arrival of still other tribes in the lands of Ammon, Moab, and Edom to the east of Canaan; and within Canaan itself with the arrival of the obscure peoples – the Perizzites, Hivites, and so forth – named alongside the Canaanites in the promises of the land to Abraham and Moses.

Most dangerous of all, the Israelites arrived in Canaan at about the same time as the 'sea people' known as the Philistines, who had spread from Crete to many desirable places around the Eastern Mediterranean. Like the Vikings pouring out of Scandinavia in a much later period, or like the European colonists in America, Asia, and Africa, these raiders seemed invincible; and they stayed to trade and to settle. The success which the Philistines achieved in 'Palestine' is remembered to this day in the name of the area. The names of three of their five chief cities are virtually the same today – Gaza, Ashkelon, and Ashdod – although the positions of Gath and Ekron have not been established with certainty. Such a people refused to drop dead as did (according to the Israelite story) their champion, Goliath.

The book of Joshua reports a quick and bloody conquest of Canaan, with three campaigns under Joshua's generalship; having crossed the Jordan from the east, in the centre (chapters 1–9), south (chapter 10), and north (chapter 11). But all the evidence points to the probability that such boastful reports – largely based, it would seem, on the traditions of the tribe of Benjamin – are exaggerated. The earlier books of the Old Testament give a clue to the real history when they tell us of the invading tribesmen's difficulties. They needed many years to build themselves up before they were able to enter Canaan – and then they failed in their first attempt, based on Kadesh (Numbers 20). They were refused permission to use the caravan route into Canaan known as the King's Highway; it ran from the gulf of Aqaba to the region of the Dead Sea, and so to the north. When they took an alternative route they still had to fight the Amorites and the tribesmen of Bashan (Numbers 21; Deuteronomy 3) before they could ford the Jordan from the east (Joshua 2).

The first chapter of the book of Judges seems, on the whole, a more sober account than the book of Joshua. 'Yahweh was with Judah and they occupied the hill-country, but they could not drive out the inhabitants of the

Vale because they had chariots of iron' – actually, chariots
of wood strengthened with iron. In Judges 1:27–35 we read
a series of admissions: at this place and that, the Israelites
'did not drive out' the Canaanites. In chapters 8 and 9 of
this book we read of treaties of alliance between the
Israelites and several Canaanite city states. Even in the book
of Joshua, mainly a collection of triumphant reports, we
read that the tribe of Dan was unable to occupy the area it
wanted, and had to rest content with a much inferior
territory in the far north, beneath Mount Hermon (19:
40–48). We also read a far-fetched story which boils down
to the fact that the Israelites made a peaceful agreement
with the inhabitants of Gibeon (chapter 9).

Modern archaeology has given only limited support to
the book of Joshua. Some cities in Canaan – Bethel, Debir,
Lachish, Gibeon, Shechem, Hazor – are known to have
been partially or wholly destroyed at the approximate time
when the Israelites are said to have been occupying the
land. Heavy layers of ash remain. Above them are the
remnants of crude buildings, while beneath them is evidence
of a more advanced civilization. But the absence of pottery
makes precise dating difficult, and some of the damage may
have been done by the Canaanites themselves (for their
cities were often at war with each other), or by the Philistines, or by the Egyptians. Sometimes the probable dating
of the damage tells against the Israelite claims. For example,
despite the book of Joshua (7:1–8:29) the city of Ai was
almost certainly already ruined (if its site was Et-Tell,
excavated in 1933); its very name means 'Ruin'. Recent
archaeology suggests that most of Jericho was probably also
then in ruins and without a city wall, despite the story that
the wall fell down when Joshua ordered the trumpets to be
blown (chapter 6).

There is no need to doubt Joshua's existence or his
heroism, but probably he was not quite the figure he was
later made out to be. He was not the commander-in-chief
of an invasion, like William the Conqueror in England. The

reference to his burial 'within the border of his own patrimony in Timnath-serah in the hill-country of Ephraim' (Joshua 24:30) may show that his family had already transformed themselves from nomadic Hebrews into land-owners before the Israelite tribes arrived from Egypt. Joshua may have been one of those who joined the invaders within Canaan. Whatever his origins, he is unlikely to have been given undisputed authority over such a motley collection as the tribesmen were at this stage. Probably when it had to fight, each group of Hebrews or Israelites fought with such allies as were able and willing to come to its help, and under the leadership of the person best able to inspire a fight.

The Song of Deborah (Judges 5), which clearly reflects such a way of responding to a crisis, dates from about 1125 and is one of the oldest parts of the Old Testament. It tells of a victory won over Canaanites in the plain of Jezreel or Esdraelon. It boasts of the leadership by a woman:

Champions there were none,
none left in Israel,
until I, Deborah, arose,
arose, a mother in Israel.

It gloats also over the killing of the Canaanite general, Sisera, by another woman, who pretended to shelter him as he fled from the battlefield:

Blest above women be Jael,
the wife of Heber the Kenite;
blest above all women in the tents.
He asked for water: she gave him milk,
she offered him curds in a bowl fit for a chieftain.
She stretched out her hand for the tent-peg,
her right hand to hammer the weary.
With the hammer she struck Sisera, she crushed his head;
she struck and his brains ebbed out.
At her feet he sank down, he fell, he lay;

at her feet he sank down and fell.
Where he sank down, there he fell, done to death.

But the Song of Deborah contains some interesting admissions. It hints that victory would have been impossible without astonishing luck. A thunderstorm bogged down the Canaanite chariots as the Egyptian chariots had been bogged down in the Reed Sea:

The stars fought from heaven,
the stars in their courses fought against Sisera.
The Torrent of Kishon swept him away . . .

This ancient battle-song shows that before Deborah's enthusiasm rallied the tribesmen they were scarcely a church or an army:

They chose new gods,
they consorted with demons.
Not a shield, not a lance was to be seen
in the forty thousand of Israel.

And it admits that some of the tribes would not be rallied. With contempt it names Reuben, Gilead, Dan, and Asher, all of whom refused to fight. Only ten tribes are mentioned, which may mean that the Song of Deborah dates from a time before there were twelve.

The rest of the book of Judges confirms the picture of an Israel easily demoralized, disorganized, and defeated. An invasion of Canaan by such tribesmen would have no chance of military success, had they not united in some emergencies under energetic leadership. Judges 2:6–16 sums up the process in the language of a later day. 'Another generation followed who did not acknowledge Yahweh and did not know what he had done for Israel . . . Yahweh in his anger made them the prey of bands of raiders and plunderers; he sold them to their enemies all around them, and they could no longer make a stand. Every time they went out to battle Yahweh brought disaster on them . . . Yahweh

set judges over them, who rescued them from the marauding bands.'

However, the Hebrew word traditionally translated into
English as 'judges' means in most places 'military leaders'.
Some 'judges' appear as breeders of Israelites rather than as
slaughterers of their enemies – Jair who 'had thirty sons,
who rode thirty asses' (10:4), Ibzan who 'had thirty sons
and thirty daughters' (12:8), and others. But the great
names are all military. So far from having an automatic
right to the obedience of all the tribes, such leaders had to
prove themselves and attract whom they could. The traditions of Israel also admitted that some of the bloodiest
battles in these years were fought between the tribes themselves – between the men of Gilead and Ephraim (12:1-6),
or between Benjamin and the rest (20:18-48).

There were, it is clear, many quiet years in this Israelite
occupation of Canaan; and years when 'the land was at
peace' are mentioned in the book of Judges. There is
another revealing passage in the book of Joshua (17:16–18).
The Joseph tribesmen complain that 'the Canaanites have
chariots of iron' which control the valleys. They are told:
'The hill-country is yours. It is forest land; clear it and it
shall be yours.' The same principle obtained in American
and Canadian history: it was work that won the West. No
doubt some violence was involved in the Israelite occupation of Canaan and in its defence against the Philistines (as
violence was involved in the white man's settlement of
North America). But we should not be deceived by the
militarist boasting of later generations into thinking that the
occupation of the land was mainly the result of a victorious
war. Mainly, this people grew as every people grows when
it has ceased to wander around hunting or breeding sheep.
It grew by working on the soil.

THE GROWTH OF THE ECONOMY

On this agricultural foundation every nation has to build a

fairly complicated economy if the varied needs of its members are to be supplied by specialist producers, craftsmen, and tradesmen. Unfortunately, however, the Old Testament does not give us much information about the economic nation-building of Ancient Israel.

The first peak of prosperity was reached under King Solomon, who died about 930 BC. He inherited from his father David peace in Canaan, the withdrawal of the Philistines to a small coastal strip, and a little empire controlling the neighbouring countries which had given Israel so much trouble – the Aramaean area around Damascus to the north (apart from the coastal strip occupied by the Phoenicians) and to the east Ammon, Moab, and Edom. Solomon was wise enough to acknowledge that he could not reimpose control on Damascus and Edom when they broke free. He was also wise enough to believe in a strong defence (archaeologists have excavated the military gateways he built for the three key fortresses of Hazor in the north, Megiddo in the centre, and Gezer in the south) – and in alliances for trade. His chief alliance was with the Phoenician, King Hiram of Tyre; this was the alliance that built the Jerusalem temple by a combination of Israelite forced labour, local stone, Lebanese timber, and craftsmen supplied by Hiram (1 Kings 5). One item in the bargain was that the Phoenicians were allowed to occupy part of Galilee (1 Kings 9:11). But many other links now bound Israel to the great world.

David's conquest of Edom had secured the port of Ezion-geber (the modern Eilat) on the gulf of Aqaba. Now Solomon, who may have also exploited the Egyptian copper mines nearby, developed the port. We read: 'King Solomon built a fleet of ships at Ezion-geber, near Eloth on the shore of the Red Sea, in Edom. Hiram sent men of his own to serve with the fleet, experienced seamen, to work with Solomon's men; and they went to Ophir and brought back four hundred and twenty talents of gold . . .' (1 Kings 9:26–28). Ophir was probably the modern

Somaliland. In the end, 'the king had a fleet of merchant-men at sea with Hiram's fleet; once every three years the fleet of merchantmen came home, bringing gold and silver, ivory, apes, and monkeys. Thus King Solomon outdid all the kings of the earth in wealth and wisdom, and all the world courted him' (1 Kings 10:22-23).

Among the rulers with whom Solomon developed social and trading relationships, the Queen of Sheba (in Arabia) is the most famous (1 Kings 10:1-15). We are told that he was devoted to 'seven hundred wives, who were princesses'. Part of the explanation is that these ladies – however many they may have been in real history – were married in order to embody an economic community. Among their charms were profitable connections within and outside the little empire, including a commercial treaty with Egypt (11:1-3). Such a harem must have been a conspicuous element in the small population of Jerusalem, but behind the glamour could be noticed an international trade in chariots and thoroughbred horses (10:28-29).

Solomon was the Louis XIV of Ancient Israel, and the opulence of his reign became legendary: 'no silver was used, for it was reckoned of no value in the days of Solomon' (10:21). In later periods, too, many of the Israelites prospered. A particularly affluent time was the period 886-853, when Omri and his son Ahab ruled their northern kingdom of Israel, now detached from Judah.

Omri made such an impression internationally that the Assyrians in their official inscriptions always referred to the kings of Israel as the 'House of Omri'. Even Jehu, who in fact exterminated Omri's dynasty, was to the Assyrians 'the son of Omri'. An Assyrian inscription tells us that Omri was so prosperous that he could employ two thousand chariots in addition to ten thousand foot soldiers when defying the emperor Shalmaneser III at the battle of Karkar in 853 BC. Archaeologists have excavated the stables which Ahab built for his cavalry at Megiddo and Hazor. They have also dug up the new fortress and city which this

determined ruler built on the bare hill of Samaria in order
to have a readily defensible capital. The 'ivory house'
which his son built was a landmark (1 Kings 22:39), and
many charred fragments of the ivory covering the stone or
wood of that place were unearthed in the excavation of
1932-3.

But such economic growth was viewed with suspicion or
regret by many Israelites. The glory of Solomon's court,
temple, and bureaucracy involved such tyranny and
extravagance that most of the people supported the
rebellion of General Jeroboam when Solomon's son Reho-
boam was so foolish as to think he could carry on in the
same style. The rebellion was blessed on behalf of Yahweh
by the prophet Ahijah: 'I am going to tear the kingdom
from the hand of Solomon' (1 Kings 11:31). And the
Marseillaise of this rebellion is preserved:

> What share have we in David?
>   We have no lot in the son of Jesse.
> Away to your homes, O Israel;
>   now see to your own house, David (12:16).

But in the Hebrew the word here translated as 'homes' is
the more primitive 'tents'; for the song was an echo of an
old freedom.

When in the north prosperity was rebuilt under the new
rulers on the basis of a rich agriculture, it corrupted and
divided the kingdom – according to commentators such as
Amos, who denounced the rich, idle women:

> Listen to this,
> you cows of Bashan who live on the hill of Samaria,
> you who oppress the poor and crush the destitute,
> who say to your lords, 'Bring us drink':
> the Lord God has sworn by his holiness
> that your time is coming
>   when men shall carry you away on their shields
>   and your children in fish-baskets (4:1-2).

According to Amos, the whole tribal tradition which looked to Joseph as a founder was in moral ruin at the height of its economic growth. The average Israelite owned neither bed nor chair, but the privileged few escaped into luxury:

> You who loll on beds inlaid with ivory
> and sprawl over your couches,
> feasting on lambs from the flock
> and fatted calves,
> you who pluck the strings of the lute
> and invent musical instruments like David,
> you who drink wine by the bowlful
> and lard yourselves with the richest of oils,
> but are not grieved at the ruin of Joseph . . . (6:4–6)

Such contempt for affluence is typical of the attitude of those who did most to shape Israel's moral traditions. Characteristic is the brevity with which the Old Testament deals with the forty-one-year-old reign in Samaria of Jeroboam II, the king who came second only to Solomon among the architects of Israelite prosperity and who presided over the boom which Amos disliked. A few sentences suffice for Jeroboam II. He 'did what was wrong in the eyes of Yahweh' (2 Kings 14:23–29).

Repeatedly the kingdoms of Israel and Judah were recalled from selfish and extravagant materialism to the stern religion of Yahweh – and were recalled from the emotional pleasures of the religious festivals to the practical demands of Yahweh's moral law in daily life. Amos expressed his contempt for the historic shrines:

> Come to Bethel – and rebel!
> Come to Gilgal – and rebel the more! (4:4)

> Resort to me, if you would live, not to Bethel;
> go not to Gilgal, nor pass on to Beersheba . . . (5:5)

In the southern kingdom of Judah, Micah asked with an equal contempt:

> What is the crime of Jacob? Is it not Samaria?
> What is the hill-shrine of Judah? Is it not Jerusalem?
> (1:5)

> Therefore, on your account
> Zion shall become a ploughed field,
> Jerusalem a heap of ruins,
> and the temple hill rough heath (3:12).

Amos was convinced that the Israelites' worship without 'justice' and 'righteousness' merely made Yahweh more and more angry:

> I hate, I spurn your pilgrim-feasts;
>   I will not delight in your sacred ceremonies.
> When you present your sacrifices and offerings
>   I will not accept them,
> nor look on the buffaloes of your shared-offerings.
> Spare me the sound of your songs;
> I cannot endure the music of your lutes.
> Let justice roll on like a river
> and righteousness like an ever-flowing stream (5:21-24).

And Amos made clear the chief demands of this 'righteousness'. They were demands made in daily life, in the nation's economic life:

> You that turn justice upside down
> and bring righteousness to the ground,
> you that hate a man who brings the wrongdoer to court
> and loathe him who speaks the whole truth:
> for all this, because you levy taxes on the poor
> and extort a tribute of grain from them,
> though you have built houses of hewn stone,
>   you shall not live in them,
> though you have planted pleasant vineyards,
>   you shall not drink wine from them (5:7-11).

Micah had a similarly plain message:

Shame on those who lie in bed planning evil and wicked
      deeds
   and rise at daybreak to do them,
      knowing that they have the power!
   They covet land and take it by force;
      if they want a house they seize it;
   they rob a man of his home
      and steal every man's inheritance (2:1-2).

Always the pressure of Israel's moral tradition was back
to the simplicity, honesty, and equality which had marked
the early years of the nation's story – or, at least, which
were believed to have marked them. Amos denouncing the
'cows' at the dinner tables of Samaria stood in the same line
as Elijah denouncing Ahab's seizure of the vineyard which
he wanted to enlarge the garden of his palace – the ancestral
field which little Naboth had obstinately refused to sell to
him (1 Kings 21). Ahijah, Elijah, Amos, Micah, and other
prophets pleaded that the old standards of brotherhood and
justice should never be sacrificed to the greed of the rich.
The ethical splendour of that stand became a theme of
Israel's conversations and scriptures, and it is no exag-
geration to say that it has moved every generation from
that day to this. What is not so often appreciated is that the
prophetic campaign for social justice entirely depended on
the belief that true and lasting prosperity came from
Yahweh, the God of Israel.

The Elijah who thundered against Ahab in Naboth's
vineyard was already in open conflict with his king on
religious grounds. Ahab had married Jezebel the daughter
of the king of Tyre, and in Samaria she had continued her
Phoenician religious practices enthusiastically, even fanatically, while she encouraged her husband to be a king. But
part of the conflict between the prophets of Yahweh and the
royal house was also due to the fact that Omri had determined to buy the goodwill of the Canaanites still numerous

in his kingdom by allowing them religious freedom. That Jezebel advocated the suppression of Yahwism enraged Elijah, but that Ahab tolerated Canaanite worship offended him no less.

The account of the conflict reaches its climax in the tremendous story of Elijah confronting the Canaanite 'prophets of Baal' on Mount Carmel by the sea (1 Kings 18). Exactly what happened cannot be recovered, but it is clear that it resulted in two massacres, first of many of the prophets of Baal, then in retaliation of many of the prophets of Yahweh. It then led to a revolution, when (encouraged by Elijah's disciple and successor Elisha) General Jehu waded to the throne through a sea of blood. Ahab's queen, his children, his nobles, his priests, his close friends, and any surviving prophets of Baal – all were slaughtered, most of them in Jezreel. At the time this seemed Yahweh's will: 'you have done well what is right in my eyes and have done to the house of Ahab all that it was in my mind to do' (2 Kings 10:30). In the next century the bloodbath of 842–41 sickened more sensitive consciences. The prophet Hosea named his eldest son Jezreel, for he heard the word of Yahweh: 'in a little while I will punish the line of Jehu for the blood shed in Jezreel' (1:4).

Behind the brutality and the atmosphere of fantasy which spoil many of the stories told about Elijah and Elisha there was, however, the reality of a serious conflict about a serious question. Whose ideas should dominate the nation's economic growth?

The Canaanite religion was elaborate, with many gods and goddesses including a trinity: a high but remote god (El), an active god, and a goddess who was his consort. But the heart of the religion was simple and powerful. The active god was Baal which means 'Master'; his proper name was Hadad, and essentially he was the weather god, his chief function being to preserve and increase the fertility of the land. After the long, hot, dry summer (from May to October) the land was hard, empty, and withered. The

possibility of ploughing now depended on the 'former rains'
(in October and November), and after the wet winter the
ripening of the crops depended on the 'latter rains' (in
March and April). These rains were regarded as the results
of Baal's sexual intercourse with his divine consort, and
were invoked by having sexual intercourse on earth –
either with fellow-worshippers (of both sexes, it seems) or
with sacred prostitutes. A great consumption of wine conquered any inhibitions there might be. All this took place
either in hill-shrines or in man-made 'high places' –
platforms of stone, some of which have been excavated by
the archaeologists.

When the religion of Yahweh confronted that religion of
Baal, much was at stake for the dignity of man. There is a
clear implication of this in the strange, old story of Noah
and his sons in *Genesis*. In another tradition Noah had been
'a righteous man, the one blameless man of this time'
(6:9). But here, after being saved from the Flood, he 'began
the planting of vineyards. He drank some of the wine,
became drunk and lay naked inside his tent. When Ham,
father of Canaan, saw his father naked, he told his two
brothers outside.' These two brothers were Shem and
Japheth, Shem being regarded as an ancestor of the
Semites and other Israelites. The brothers discreetly
covered Noah with a cloak, and later received Noah's
promise that as a reward Canaan would serve them as a
slave (9:20–25). Some incestuous and homosexual practices
in the course of orgies seem to be hinted at here.

Even when we discount the strong element of prejudice
in the Old Testament, we cannot on the evidence deny
the degradation of the Canaanite religion. When the
prophets of Yahweh clashed with the prophets of Baal, they
were proclaiming (however unworthily) some principles on
which mankind's progress depended. They were teaching
(however crudely) that a land is made fertile not by magic
but by honest work in co-operation with the bounty of
nature; that men and women prosper not by lowering them-

selves to the level of publicly-copulating animals but by subordinating their lusts to their human dignity; that men and women achieve the most fruitful union not by pouring their seed mindlessly into each other and into the earth but by honouring each other, by acknowledging each other's rights, and by working together under the discipline of justice; and that people get themselves into harmony with each other and with the mysterious power in nature – that 'peace' which the Israelites so loved, and called *shalom* – not by orgies but by careful, responsible behaviour inspired by a sober sense of a sacred purpose.

Had the battle of Elijah and Elisha against the religion of Baal ended in defeat, we can be sure that the religion of Yahweh would have been exterminated – if not by massacres ordered by Queen Jezebel, then by the seductiveness which is always exercised by magic, drugs, and bestiality. It would have been infinitely more difficult for later teachers or law-givers in Israel to attempt to raise their contemporaries to more truly humane standards of self-control and self-respect, and the permanent significance of the Israelites to humanity would have been no more than the permanent significance of the Canaanites.

We can be sure of that. But it is also fair to recognize a fact that lies beneath the surface of the Old Testament. For it was a fact that Ancient Israel incorporated into its own life many elements in the Canaanite civilization. In much the same way, the Roman empire was captivated by Greek culture and white Americans were enthralled by black music.

So far as we know, few of the Hebrews were literate before their arrival in Canaan; but the Hebrew language and literature were suggestively similar to Canaanite language and literature. The temple which Solomon had built in Jerusalem was built by Phoenician craftsmen on Phoenician models, and the God worshipped in it could be called 'Yahweh' or 'El'. Many of the psalms sung in it were, scholars think, sung to Canaanite tunes. Some tunes are listed in the Old Testament, including *The Hind of the Dawn* (22), *The Dove of the Distant Gods* (56), *Do Not Destroy* (57, 58, 59, 75), and *Lilies* (45, 69, 80) – although we do not know how many of these were Canaanite in origin, and all have been lost. Some of the words of the psalms are rich with Canaanite mythology (examples being 74:12–14 and 89:1–14). Many of the laws of Israel were copied from Canaanite practice. The economic life of Israel was transformed by contact with the more advanced Canaanites and with Phoenician traders. The daily life of Israel was greatly enriched by Canaanite culture. For example, its marriages were no doubt enriched by the uninhibited eroticism on display in the *Song of Songs*. All this constituted an immense danger to the religion of Yahweh; yet in the end, as the message of Yahweh's prophets slowly won its way, all that Israel adopted from Canaan was subordinated to this religion.

In *Deuteronomy* (8:11–18) a restrained prosperity is celebrated, but Yahweh is still to be worshipped humbly as the creator of all that is good:

Take care not to forget Yahweh your God and do not fail to keep his commandments, laws, and statutes which I give you this day. When you have plenty to eat and live in fine houses of your own building, when your herds and flocks increase, and your silver and gold and all your possessions increase too, do not become proud and forget Yahweh your God who brought you out of Egypt, out of the land of slavery; he led you through the vast and terrible wilderness infested with poisonous snakes and scorpions, a thirsty, waterless land, where he caused water to flow from the hard rock; he fed you in the wilderness on manna which your fathers did not know, to humble you and test you, and in the end to make you prosper. Nor must you say to yourselves, 'My own strength and energy have gained me this wealth', but remember Yahweh your God; it is he that gives you strength to become prosperous, so fulfilling the covenant guaranteed by oath with your forefathers, as he is doing now.

In the prophecy of Hosea, the continuing enticements of Canaanite religion were denounced:

New wine and old steal my people's wits:
    they ask advice from a block of wood
    and take their orders from a fetish;
for a spirit of wantonness has led them astray
and in their lusts they are unfaithful to their God.
Your men sacrifice on mountain-tops
    and burn offerings on the hills,
    under oak and poplar
and the terebinth's pleasant shade.
Therefore your daughters play the wanton
    and your sons' brides commit adultery (4:12–13).

Yet in this very book exceptionally bold use was made of the idea of waiting for the rain:

Come, let us return to Yahweh;
for he has torn us and will heal us,
    he has struck us and he will bind up our wounds;
    after two days he will revive us,
on the third day he will restore us,
    that in his presence we may live.
Let us humble ourselves, let us strive to know Yahweh,
whose justice dawns like morning light,
and its dawning is as sure as the sunrise.
It will come to us like a shower,
like spring rains that water the earth (6:1–3).

Hosea felt called by Yahweh to marry a loose-living woman who may have been a temple prostitute in the Canaanite religion – and to take her back when she has become an adulteress (1:2, 3:1–3). Thus the prophet's marriage, where many tragedies were overcome by forgiveness, became a drama of the inexhaustible love of Israel's God:

> I will woo her, I will go with her into the wilderness and
>   comfort her:
> there I will restore her vineyards . . .
> and there she will answer as in her youth . . .
> On that day she shall call me 'My husband'
>   and shall no more call me 'My Baal' (2:14–16).

In the book of Ezekiel, written more than two hundred years later, the account of the abominations of idol-worship within the doomed temple at Jerusalem reached a new intensity of indignation (Ezekiel 8). But here, too, the idea of Yahweh's marriage with Israel was expressed with a daring and a new eloquence of wonder and gratitude. 'Canaan is the land of your ancestry and there you were born,' says Yahweh through Ezekiel (16:3–8), and he continues:

> This is how you were treated at birth: when you were born, your navel-string was not tied, you were not bathed in water ready for the rubbing, you were not salted as you should have been nor wrapped in swaddling clothes. No one cared for you enough to do any of these things or, indeed, to have any pity for you; you were thrown out on the bare ground in your own filth on the day of your birth. Then I came by and saw you kicking helplessly in your own blood; I spoke to you, there in your blood, and bade you live. I tended you like an evergreen plant, like something growing in the fields; you throve and grew. You came to full womanhood; your breasts became firm and your hair grew, but still you were naked and exposed. Again I came by and saw that you were ripe for love. I spread the skirt of my robe over you and covered your naked body. Then I plighted my troth and entered into a covenant with you, and you became mine.

In the book of Isaiah (chapter 14) a 'song of derision over the king of Babylon' is included. It dates from Ezekiel's time or later. It uses Canaanite mythology, including the assembly of the gods on Mount Hermon in the north. But it uses this mythology in order to proclaim the triumph of Yahweh over his latest enemy:

> How you have fallen from heaven, bright morning star,
> felled to the earth, sprawling helpless across the nations!
>   You thought in your own mind,
>   I will scale the heavens;
> I will set my throne high above the stars of God,
>   I will sit on the mountain where the gods meet
>   in the far recesses of the north.
>   I will rise high above the cloud-banks
>   and make myself like the Most High.
> Yet you shall be brought down to Sheol,
>   to the depths of the abyss (14:12–15).

THE SAD NECESSITY OF GOVERNMENT

The growth of the nation resulted inevitably in that battle of ideas about the sources of its prosperity. The nation's growth also brought out into the open some basic questions about government.

Originally the tribesmen felt no need of a monarchy. So-called 'judges' led them in their fights with the Canaanites and others through the period from about 1200 to about 1020 BC. They are presented in the book of Judges somewhat in the style of the later kings; but it is clear that in fact their authority was far more flimsy. One of the most successful bandit-chiefs among these 'judges' was Gideon or Jerubbaal. His second name shows that he was not a consistent enemy of the Canaanite worship of Baal, and we are told that after his death the Israelites 'again went wantonly to the worship of the Baalim' (Judges 8:33). We are told, too, that after his death one of his sons tried to become king, and in the course of the attempt butchered all Gideon's other sons except one – who told a sarcastic story about a thorn-bush becoming king over the trees (Judges 9). This was not material of which a sacred monarchy could be made easily.

It was the pressure of the Philistines that eventually compelled these proud and quarrelsome tribesmen to accept a king. To the Canaanite 'cities', three hundred Israelite guerrillas might be alarming (as is claimed in Judges 7). Against desert tribesmen such as the Ammonites, an expedition might be effective if led by a chief capable of sacrificing his own daughter to the Yahweh who granted victory (Judges 11:28–40). But in battles against the well-armed and well-organized Philistines who had settled on the coast and who now wished to secure the rest of Canaan, an Israelite hero such as Samson could not win (Judges 13–16). Eventually Shiloh, which had become the main Israelite shrine, was destroyed by the Philistines, and the Ark of Yahweh which had been housed there was taken away in triumph (1 Samuel 4).

The traditions of Israel agreed that Samuel, who had been a prophet attached to the temple at Shiloh, anointed Saul the son of Kish, a Benjaminite, as the first king to lead the tribal militia against the Philistines. But in the first book of Samuel are preserved three significantly varied traditions about the circumstances in which the Israelite monarchy arose. These rival traditions may belong to the sources J and E (to be discussed in chapter 8). One, which seems to be the most authentic, is that Saul was acclaimed king at Gilgal when he had proved his military skill in defence against marauding Ammonites (chapter 11). Another tradition is a folk-tale that at Zuph Saul consulted Samuel as a 'seer' because he was looking for some lost property, and found himself anointed king at Yahweh's orders; here the atmosphere of frenzied excitement is probably authentic (9:1–10:16). The third tradition (8:1–22; 10:17–27) is the least enthusiastic. Told that

Israel must have a king like other nations, Samuel protests that this means rejecting Yahweh – and accepting a tyrant instead. Then Saul is chosen by lot, at Mizpah.

The authentic element in that third tradition is that Samuel soon fell out with the new king. The story that the first quarrel was over a sacrifice which Saul offered before a battle because 'the people were drifting away from me' (13:3-14) shows the causes of the split. In order to maintain his authority, any king in the ancient world had to build himself up religiously; it was the equivalent of a modern government's propaganda. The custodians of the traditional religion could easily be offended by this invasion of their territory.

In Israel, many battles of will had to be fought out between prophets and kings. The account of the first conflict leaves the modern reader sympathizing entirely with Saul – who did not massacre the Amalekites so completely as was ordered by Samuel, an exponent of the creed that the enemies of Yahweh must be exterminated (chapter 15). But later stories shift one's sympathy. A king who to acquire a religious hold on his subjects had to whip himself up into ecstasies could easily become the victim of a nervous breakdown, as seems to have been the case with Saul (16:14). A king who claimed to be also a priest and even a god could easily become the tyrant that Samuel feared; Solomon and a number of his successors proved that. Then the prophets of Yahweh had to defend a stable efficiency in government – and justice for the people.

In the Old Testament we find both ardent royalism and outspoken criticism of kings. The royalist propaganda is in places so strong that some modern scholars have agreed that the Israelites, like some neighbouring peoples such as the Babylonians, attached great importance to an annual enthronement festival in the Jerusalem temple, when on New Year's Day the king would perform various rites designated to renew his role as the representative of the people, as the bringer of blessings such as justice, peace and good crops, and as the bearer of divine authority. From the way that some scholars go on about this festival one would expect it to dominate the Old Testament, but unfortunately there is no uncontrovertible evidence that such a festival took place every new year among the Israelites.

The only surviving description of a coronation of a king in the temple relates to 837–36 BC, when the young Joash was crowned (2 Kings 11). When his father Ahaziah had been murdered, his grandmother Athaliah had seized power. It was the only occasion in the history of Judah after David's time when the royal power was held by a woman or by one not descended from David, but Athaliah had been born a princess in the northern kingdom where dynastic loyalties were weaker.

Joash had been hidden as a baby with a nurse in a bedroom in the temple buildings, when the other princes were murdered; and 'he remained concealed with her in the house of Yahweh for six years, while Athaliah ruled the country.' Then Jehoiada the priest, who had supervised this extraordinary concealment, decided that the time had come to produce the boy-king and to dispose of the usurper. The temple policemen were issued with 'King David's spears and shields, which were in the house of Yahweh'. Thus guarded by museum exhibits, the priest 'brought out the king's son, put the crown on his head, handed him the warrant, and anointed him king. The people clapped their hands and shouted, "Long live the king." ' His wicked grandmother, brought on to the scene by the shouts, 'found the king standing, as was the custom, on the dais, amidst outbursts of song and fanfares of trumpets in his honour'. When the wicked old queen had been disposed of, and Jehoiada had announced a new covenant between Yahweh, the king, and the people, they escorted Joash 'through the Gate of the Guards to the royal palace, and seated him on the royal throne'.

Despite its lack of clear evidence about an annual enthronement festival, the Old Testament shows that the

Israelite kings, or some of them, claimed a sacred authority not entirely unlike the position of the Pharaohs in Egypt. Some of the Old Testament's psalms may have been among the songs sung before King Joash. One repeats Yahweh's decree about a king:

> 'You are my son,' he said;
>   'this day I become your father.
>   Ask of me what you will:
>   I will give you nations as your inheritance,
>   the ends of the earth as your possession.
>   You shall break them with a rod of iron
>   you shall shatter them like a clay pot' (2:7–9).

Another psalm seems to be a prayer at a coronation:

> O God, endow the king with thy own justice,
>   and give thy righteousness to a king's son,
> that he may judge thy people rightly
>   and deal out justice to the poor and suffering.
> May hills and mountains afford thy people
>   peace and prosperity in righteousness.
>   He shall give judgement for the suffering
>   and help those of the people that are needy;
>   he shall crush the oppressor.
>   He shall live as long as the sun endures,
>   long as the moon, age after age.
> He shall be like rain falling on early crops,
>   like showers watering the earth.
> In his days righteousness shall flourish,
> prosperity abound until the moon is no more.
> May he hold sway from sea to sea,
>   from the River to the ends of the earth (72:1–7).

Another psalm is a song at the king's marriage with a princess of Tyre:

> Your throne is like God's throne, eternal,
>   your royal sceptre a sceptre of righteousness.

You have loved right and hated wrong;
so God, your God, has anointed you
　　above your fellows with oil, the token of joy.
Your robes are all fragrant with myrrh and powder of
　　aloes,
　　　　and the music of strings greets you
　　　　from a palace panelled with ivory.
A princess takes her place among the noblest of your
　　women,
　　　　a royal lady at your side in gold of Ophir (45:6–9).

And one psalm adds to the military might of a king the
perpetual youth of a prodigy and the perpetual holiness of
a priest:

　　Yahweh said to my lord,
　　　'You shall sit at my right hand
　when I make your enemies the footstool under your feet.'
　When Yahweh from Zion hands you the sceptre, the
　　　　symbol of your power,
　　　march forth through the ranks of your enemies.
　At birth you were endowed with princely gifts
　　　and resplendent in holiness.
　You have shone with the dew of youth since your mother
　　　bore you.
　Yahweh has sworn and will not change his purpose:
　　　'You are a priest for ever,
　　　in the succession of Melchizedek' (110:1–4).

David became the model king in the psalms used in the
Jerusalem temple, which was the royal chapel of the House
of David. There they sang with Yahweh himself:

I have discovered David my servant;
　I have anointed him with my holy oil.
My hand shall be ready to help him
　and my arm to give him strength.
No enemy shall strike at him
　and no rebel bring him low;

I will shatter his foes before him
  and vanquish those who hate him.
My faithfulness and true love shall be with him
and through my name he shall hold his head high
                                              (89:20–24).

And they repeated the divine promises to the House of David:

Yahweh swore to David
  an oath which he will not break:
'A prince of your own line
  will I set upon your throne.
If your sons keep my covenant
  and heed the teaching that I give them,
their sons in turn for all time
  shall sit upon your throne' (132:11–12).

In the first book of Samuel (chapters 16–26) charming stories are told about the rise of David. A sheep-owner's eighth son, brought up in the obscure village of Bethlehem, this handsome young man is said to have been anointed king by the great prophet Samuel. We are told that he attracted King Saul's and the people's attention when with a stone from his shepherd's sling he killed the Philistine champion Goliath. Elsewhere a report is given that 'Elhanan son of Jair of Bethlehem killed Goliath of Gath' – which may indicate that David's original name was Elhanan, although later traditions explained that Elhanan was another man, who killed another champion who was only the brother of Goliath (2 Samuel 21:19; 1 Chronicles 20:5).

David is said to have become the king's armour-bearer and son-in-law and a brilliantly professional soldier (a trade unknown in Israel before the monarchy). Three times (1 Samuel 18:7; 21:11; 29:5) the chant is recorded:

Saul made havoc among thousands
but David among tens of thousands.

And the stories of how the jealous Saul threw David out of his court, how David escaped Saul's vengeance, and how David spared Saul's life, are retold with great skill and with great credit to David (1 Samuel 17–27).

But just as archaeologists have dug up Saul's palace at Gibeah and found it only a modest little fort, so modern scholars have probed these famous tales of David and have uncovered many traces of Ancient Israel's somewhat sordid problems. We can now begin to see the political realities beneath the glamour of the royal psalms.

Fleeing from Saul's rage, David learned for himself how fragile was the monarchy he was to inherit. 'Men in any kind of distress or in debt or with a grievance gathered round him' (22:2). Eventually he threw in his lot with the Philistines as a mercenary soldier (chapter 27). The reason why he did not fight as an ally of the Philistines in the battle on Mount Gilboa where Saul and Jonathan were killed was that the Philistines did not trust him and sent him away (chapter 29).

After Saul's suicide David climbed to the throne of a united kingdom – but he had learned how to climb from those harsh experiences under Saul. First he got himself anointed king of his own tribe, Judah, with the Philistines' consent. Then he launched a civil war against the rest of Israel which had rallied to Saul's son, Ishbaal. He pleaded his innocence of the murders of Ishbaal and his general, Abner; but the murders happened, and David gained from them. With the continuing acquiescence of the Philistines, he was invited to be king over all Israel. Himself a former mercenary, he now hired a bodyguard of foreign mercenaries. Sending them silently up the water shaft, he seized Jerusalem, a mountain stronghold which had remained in Jebusite hands. He made it his own city as well as the capital of his kingdom. Then he used his knowledge of the Philistines' military tactics to turn against those who had formerly been his employers and patrons.

All this took him ten tense and bloody years (2 Samuel

2–5). And although the Philistine threat to Israel was finally broken by David, fellow-Israelites could use against him and his successors the methods by which he had obtained power. His son Absalom called out the tribal militia against him, and might have overthrown him had not David kept control of his mercenaries (2 Samuel 15:1–19:8). On the death of Solomon a professional soldier, Jeroboam, succeeded in making himself king over all Israel apart from Judah (1 Kings 12–13).

David and Solomon equipped their state with an army, a civil service, and a court the like of which Israel had not known before. It is clear that Philistine, Phoenician, and above all Egyptian models were used; Solomon married a Pharaoh's daughter. The tradition preserved in the Bible is ambivalent in its attitude to this tenth-century achievement. On the one hand, the military heroes and the leading bureaucrats who served the glorious kings are listed proudly, and there is a great emphasis on the splendour of the Jerusalem temple and palace. On the other hand, the methods which made Solomon's opulence possible – the use or threat of ruthless violence; copying foreign models which involved welcoming foreign religions; exalting the king over his subjects, and his will over their customs; imposing heavy taxation and forced labour on the Israelites; dividing the country into twelve new tax districts which cut across the old tribal boundaries – all are denounced. Adoram, the man who had organized the labour gangs under Solomon, was stoned to death (1 Kings 12:18).

In the 1950s archaeologists excavated the palace which King Jehoiakim built at Ramat Rahel on the road between Jerusalem and Bethlehem, at the turn of the seventh and sixth centuries BC. It must have been a fine building. The only thing wrong with it was that the little state of Judah, press-ganged into labouring on it, could not afford such royal luxury, least of all when the Babylonian empire was known to be likely to destroy the state. The prophet

Jeremiah (22:13–15) commented on that latest folly of the
kings:

> Shame on the man who builds his house by unjust means
>   and completes its roof-chambers by fraud,
>   making his countrymen work without payment,
>   giving them no wage for their labour!
> Shame on the man who says, 'I will build a spacious house
>   with airy roof-chambers,
> set windows in it, panel it with cedar
>   and paint it with vermilion'!
>   If your cedar is more splendid,
>   does that prove you a king?

And Jeremiah contrasted the tyranny of Jehoiakim with the
conduct of his father, Josiah:

> Think of your father: he ate and drank,
> dealt justly and fairly; all went well with him.
>   He dispensed justice to the lowly and poor;
> did not this show he knew me? says Yahweh.

It is clear from the Old Testament that many retained a
faith in kings, particularly in the House of David which was
believed to have received everlasting promises from Yahweh.
In the nation's most stormy or barren periods the hope
endured, as in Isaiah (32:1–2):

> Behold, a king shall reign in righteousness
>   and his rulers rule with justice,
>   and a man shall be a refuge from the wind
>   and a shelter from the tempest,
>   or like runnels of water in dry ground,
> like the shadow of a great rock in a thirsty land.

But the Old Testament also shows that some of the most
prominent teachers of the Israelites were reduced to despair
about the monarchy. They preferred to tell how Gideon
had declared in the heroic days: 'I will not rule over you,
nor shall my son; Yahweh will rule over you' (Judges 8:23).

In the end they openly said that the whole experiment of having earthly kings had been a mistake, indeed a sin. Hosea (8:4) claimed to be the voice of Yahweh:

> They make kings, but not by my will;
>   they set up officers, but without my knowledge.

We may conclude that this people's growth as a nation involved the necessary evil of strong government. The historians of Israel acknowledged the necessity, ending the book of Judges with this condemnation of the chaos: 'In those days there was no king in Israel and every man did what was right in his own eyes.' But equally, the historians followed the prophets in making the evil plain. What they wrote about their kings was seldom flattering, seldom even polite. And that is why the history-writing of Ancient Israel has been for all subsequent generations something more than a collection of great stories. It has been a clarion call against tyranny (as it was for Cromwell's Englishmen or for the Americans of New England). And it has been an education in political realism and maturity.

CHAPTER 5

The Crisis of a People

ISRAEL'S SELF-CRITICISM

In the ancient world each people had in addition to its land, its economy, and its government an asset which it claimed was the greatest, and the source of all the others: its god. And the god of that people was expected to busy himself in its interests.

A clear illustration of the link between land and god comes in the book of Judges (11:23-24). Jephthah is trying to persuade the Ammonites to stop attacking Israelite territory, and is recalling Israel's victory over the Amorites. 'Yahweh the God of Israel drove out the Amorites for the benefit of his people Israel. And do you now propose to take their place? It is for you to possess whatever Kemosh your god gives you; and all that Yahweh our God gave us as we advanced is ours.'

Another example of the attachment of a god to a country comes in the story of Naaman the Aramaean general who has recovered health by following the instructions of an Israelite prophet Elisha (2 Kings 5). Naaman has been cured of his skin disease through washing in the River Jordan. Now he must return to his own country, and that must mean worshipping his country's god, Rimmon, with his king. But in gratitude he wishes when back home to offer his own sacrifices to Yahweh, and for this to be possible he asks Elisha to provide two mules' load of Israelite earth.

The crisis of Israel came when this attachment of its God to its land was broken. In 722-21 BC the city of Samaria, the last remnant left of the northern kingdom of Israel founded by Jeroboam on Solomon's death, fell to the Assyrian army. On 16 March 597, and again at some date in the summer of

586, Jerusalem – David's city, the beloved 'Zion', in recent
centuries the capital of the southern kingdom of Judah –
fell to the Babylonian army. Psalm 79 preserves the sense of
utter dismay:

> O God, the heathen have set foot in thy domain,
>   defiled thy holy temple
> and laid Jerusalem in ruins.
>   They have thrown out the dead bodies of thy servants
>   to feed the birds of the air;
>   they have made thy loyal servants carrion for wild
>   beasts.
> Their blood is spilled all round Jerusalem like water,
>   and there they lie unburied.
> We suffer the contempt of our neighbours,
>   the gibes and mockery of all around us.

And Psalm 137 records the bewilderment of the exiles:

> Our captors called on us to be merry:
>   'Sing us one of the songs of Zion.'
> How could we sing Yahweh's song
>   in a foreign land?

Yet it was in this exile that the religious legacy of Ancient
Israel to mankind was assembled – for it was a legacy of
self-criticism.

In the modern world, even a patriot can admit that his
country can bring disaster on itself by defying the laws
which make for peace and prosperity. In the ancient world,
one of the ways of absorbing the shock of disaster was to
attribute it to the wrath of the country's god. In AD 1868,
some thirteen miles east of the Dead Sea, a stone was found
which had been inscribed about 830 BC on the orders of
Mesha, king of Moab. The inscription confesses past
Israelite victories over Moab: 'Omri, king of Israel,
oppressed Moab for many days, because Kemosh was
angry with his land.' But Mesha attributed his own
victories over Israel to the god's changed attitude: 'I slew

all the people of the town, a spectacle for Kemosh and Moab . . . Kemosh drove out the king of Israel before me . . .' Mesha did not mention the sacrifice to Kemosh of his own son and heir, which the tradition of Israel affirmed was the cause of their army's retreat in consternation (2 Kings 3:26–27).

The explanation of disaster by the belief that the country's god was angry was often made in Israel, as elsewhere. It comes in the accounts of the people's wanderings under Moses. About 400 BC the theme of the book of Joel is that the harvest and vintage are 'desperate', and there has been a plague of locusts, because the worship of Yahweh has been neglected. But it was the strange glory of Ancient Israel to be uniquely powerful in expressing the conviction that the work of God was to be seen in an extraordinarily disastrous series of events – nothing less than the deaths of the kingdoms of Israel and Judah.

Once empires so powerful and ruthless as Assyria and Babylon began to take an interest in their little land, the tribesmen of Israel could scarcely hope to remain untouched. The strength and ambition of Assyria began to revive in the time of Solomon – and that would have ended Israel's own little attempt at an empire, even if Solomon's kingdom had remained united. But the danger in which the Israelites stood from the nearby empires was increased by their own divisions. Not only was there the split between Israel and Judah. Within each petty kingdom, there was a split between rich and poor. They had, in fact, only two realistic hopes. They might escape notice by avoiding the wars and plots of these imperial centuries, and by paying tribute without seeming so troublesome that the imperial government would have to exert detailed control. And they might escape internal disintegration by building up a brotherhood between all classes on the basis of their common religion and their common heritage of law and justice. We cannot be sure that such a policy could have brought success; it was so seldom tried. Yet the tragic history of the Israelites gives some hints of what might have been if only . . .

Had the Israelites kept up their defences while giving no trouble, and had they maintained their unity and morale, they might have formed a kind of Switzerland, for even a mighty empire might well have rested content with the acknowledgement of its superiority and with a financial tribute from a people so formidable yet so harmless. An emperor was almost always preoccupied; the hill country around Jerusalem was of little interest to the empires; and the richer plains of Palestine towards the coast were mainly of interest as a corridor. To the Egyptians, this was the route to the timber of Syria and to the fertile lands around the Tigris and Euphrates. To the Assyrians or Babylonians, this was the way to the wealth along the banks of the Nile.

Despite the military strength and ruthlessness of these empires, the fortified cities of Palestine were not easy to conquer. The Egyptians made no lasting military impression on the land during all the history of Ancient Israel. Tiglath-Pileser III was the most aggressive of the Assyrian emperors, as his own complacently arrogant inscriptions record. But he left Israel alone when he overran Syria in 738 BC, and left the capital and its surroundings alone when he conquered the rest of the kingdom five years later. It took a siege lasting three years before Samaria fell in 722–21, and the Assyrians failed to capture Jerusalem twenty years later. The Babylonians did take Judah's capital, but even they knew it would not be a walk-over and so after their decisive victory over Egypt at Carchemish (605) they let six years pass before beginning their siege.

Had the Israelite kings been more discreet, an empire might well have been content to let them remain in peace as vassals – an inglorious position which they did in fact occupy for more years than the Old Testament makes clear on a casual reading. The words of Isaiah (30:15) were the words of a true statesman:

Come back, keep peace, and you will be safe;
in stillness and in staying quiet, there lies your strength.

But as Isaiah continues: 'You said, No.' 'You make plans
. . . you weave schemes' (30:1). For some of these petty
kings were crazily provocative, like biting mosquitoes.

The Assyrian invasion of 733 was provoked by the alliance
of Israel with the little state of Damascus against Assyria,
an alliance which they tried in vain to get Judah to join
(2 Kings 16:5). The Assyrian conquest of Samaria in the
720s was similarly provoked. 'When the king of Assyria
heard that Hoshea was being disloyal to him, sending
messengers to the king of Egypt . . . and withholding the
tribute which he had been paying year by year, the king of
Assyria arrested him and put him in prison. Then he invaded the whole country and, reaching Samaria, besieged
it for three years' (17:4–5). The Assyrian invasion of Judah
twenty years later was also provoked. Diplomats from the
rising king of Babylon, then conducting an intrigue against
the Assyrians, had been welcomed in Jerusalem (20:12–19).
Now the Assyrians came to call Judah to account. So
'Hezekiah king of Judah sent a message to the king of
Assyria at Lachish: "I have done wrong; withdraw from
my land, and I will pay any penalty you impose upon me" '
(18:14).

Hosea (7:11) offers a biting comment on such intrigues:

Ephraim is a silly senseless pigeon,
now calling upon Egypt, now turning to Assyria for help.

And Isaiah (31:3) gives an accurate warning about the outcome of such games of power politics:

The Egyptians are men, not God,
their horses are flesh, not spirit;
and . . . the helper will stumble and he who is helped will
fall,
and they will all vanish together.

Nebuchadnezzar's invasion of Judah was also provoked, for 'Jehoiakim became his vassal; but three years later he broke with him and revolted' (2 Kings 24:1). Almost incredibly, the man then chosen by the Babylonians to be a puppet king in Jerusalem, Zedekiah, also 'rebelled against the king of Babylon' (24:20), with the result that the Babylonians set fire to the temple, the palace, and much of the city, after a siege lasting eighteen months (25:1–21). Finally the governor installed over what was left of Jerusalem, Gedaliah, was murdered (25:22–26). At the head of the murderers was Ishmael, 'who was a member of the royal house' and the last of these would-be George Washingtons.

Had the tribes of Israel been united, they would have presented a stronger front to such dangerous times. Very soon after the division between the northern and southern kingdoms, invading Egyptians taught them the lesson that a divided house falls. Pharaoh Shishak sent an expeditionary force which entered Jerusalem, 'removed the treasures of the house of Yahweh and of the royal palace, and seized everything, including the shields of gold that Solomon had made' (1 Kings 14:25–28). An Egyptian inscription at Karnak boasts of this campaign. But the lesson was not learned; the division between north and south could not be healed. They were still capable of fighting a pitched battle in the 780s (2 Kings 11:8–16). Fifty years later the Israelites 'marched on Jerusalem, but could not force a battle'. This was the occasion when Isaiah exhorted King Ahaz in Jerusalem to stand firm because soon the northern kingdom would be desolate – and when he foretold God's punishment of this civil war: 'Yahweh will whistle for the fly from the distant streams of Egypt and for the bee from Assyria' (chapter 7).

The divisions inside each kingdom were no less suicidal. In the thirty years before Samaria fell to the Assyrians, six kings reigned over it; of these, three were assassinated. The prophecies of Amos, Hosea, Isaiah, Micah, and Jeremiah indicated deep and dangerous social conflicts when they denounced the exploitation of the poor by the rich. Indeed, Micah (3:2–3) said that the ruling class of Judah were like cannibals:

> You flay men alive and tear the very flesh from their
>   bones;
> you devour the flesh of my people,
> strip off their skin,
>   splinter their bones;
> you shred them like flesh into a pot.

Much of the commentary of the prophets on the history of these kingdoms has the bitter theme: nations so feckless, so divided, and so unjust, deserve to die.

THE PROPHETIC ATTACK

About 750 BC, the book of Amos begins with attacks on Damascus, Gaza, Tyre, Edom, Ammon, and Moab. These condemn Israel's neighbours for their offences against each other; thus Gaza and Tyre are denounced for returning refugees to Edom, Edom is denounced because 'they hunted their kinsmen down', and Moab is denounced because 'they burnt the bones of the king of Edom to ashes.' Such passages hint that the moral implications of Israel's religion could be one of the foundations of international law. But even more impressive is the Israelite prophet's sudden attack on his own country. We can imagine how, when first uttered, it seemed sensational.

> For crime after crime of Judah
>   I will grant them no reprieve,
> because they have spurned the law of Yahweh . . .

> For crime after crime of Israel
>   I will grant them no reprieve,
> because they sell the innocent for silver
>   and the destitute for a pair of shoes . . .

Chapter 3 drives home the wrath of Yahweh:

> As a shepherd rescues out of the jaws of a lion
>   two shin bones or the tip of an ear,
> so shall the Israelites who live in Samaria be rescued
> like a corner of a couch or a chip from the leg of a bed.

A few years later Hosea (13:7–8) compared God with a wild animal, so enraged is Yahweh with the sins of his people:

> I will be like a panther to them,
> I will prowl like a leopard by the wayside;
> I will meet them like a she-bear robbed of her cubs
>   and tear their ribs apart . . .

And in the south Micah (1:3–5) expecting Jerusalem to become a heap of ruins like Samaria, compared Yahweh with an erupting volcano:

> Look, Yahweh is leaving his dwelling-place;
> down he comes and walks on the heights of the earth.
> Beneath him mountains dissolve
>   like wax before the fire,
>   valleys are torn open,
> as when torrents pour down the hill-side –
> and all for the crime of Jacob and the sin of Israel.

So Micah 'must howl like a wolf, mourn like a desert-owl' (1:8).

His contemporary Isaiah denounced those 'who add house to house and join field to field', and whose houses were the scenes of drunken feasts (5:8–12). Unlike Micah, Isaiah believed that Jerusalem would be spared – but he, too, saw the Assyrian army as being sent by Israel's God:

> So he will hoist a signal to a nation far away,
>   he will whistle to call them from the end of the earth;
>   and see, they come, speedy and swift;
>   none is weary, not one of them stumbles,

not one slumbers or sleeps.
None has his belt loose about his waist
  or a broken thong to his sandals.
Their arrows are sharpened and their bows all strung,
  their horses' hooves flash like shooting stars,
  their chariot-wheels are like the whirlwind.
Their growling is the growling of a lioness,
  they growl like young lions,
which roar as they seize the prey
  and carry it beyond reach of rescue (5:26–29).

The sustained attack which Jeremiah delivered on his own city before it fell to the Babylonians constitutes the most deeply moving example of the Israelite capacity for self-criticism. To most of those who first heard it, it was treachery. But to later generations, Jeremiah's prophecy was nothing less than the word of God. In chapter 36 we are told that in 605 BC Jeremiah dictated his key prophecies since 627 to make a scroll (written by his faithful secretary, Baruch); and the scroll was read by a courtier named Jehudi to Jehoiakim in his winter apartments with the fire burning in a brazier in front of him. 'When Jehudi had read three or four columns of the scroll, the king cut them off with a penknife and threw them into the fire in the brazier. He went on doing so until the whole scroll had been thrown on the fire ... [But] the word of Yahweh came to Jeremiah: Now take another scroll and write on it all the words that were on the first scroll ...' And so the integrity of this astounding man lit a greater fire.

'You keep saying, "This place is the temple of Yahweh, the temple of Yahweh, the temple of Yahweh!" This catch-word of yours is a lie; put no trust in it. Mend your ways ...' That was the message of Jeremiah (7:3–4) – if necessary alone:

Prophets and priests are frauds,
  every one of them;

they dress my people's wounds, but skin-deep only,
  with their saying 'All is well' (8:10–11).

Often Jeremiah was in despair about his people:

Can the Nubian change his skin,
  or the leopard its spots?
And you? Can you do good,
  you who are schooled in evil? (13:23)

The heart is the most deceitful of all things,
  desperately sick; who can fathom it? (17:9)

The poignancy of his book is doubled by the fact that he
often despaired of himself: 'Why . . . is my pain unending,
my wound desperate and incurable?' (15:18) 'O Yahweh,
thou hast duped me, and I have been thy dupe . . . A curse
on the day when I was born!' (20:7–14) 'Deep within me
my heart is broken' (23:9). A poem which is a nightmare
of a waste land records his anguish as his nation goes down
in ruin (4:11–5:17):

I hear the sound of the trumpet,
  the sound of the battle-cry.
Crash upon crash,
  the land goes down in ruin . . .

I saw the earth, and it was without form and void;
  the heavens, and their light was gone.
I saw the mountains, and they reeled;
  all the hills rocked to and fro.
I saw, and there was no man,
  and the very birds had taken flight.
I saw, and the farm-land was wilderness,
  and the towns all razed to the ground . . .

While his country was being threatened or invaded by
the terrible Babylonians, Jeremiah urged surrender as a
religious duty – and did so consistently, whether in palace
or prison. 'I will summon all the tribes of the north, says

Yahweh: I will send for my servant Nebuchadrezzar king of Babylon' (25:9). 'If any nation or kingdom will not serve Nebuchadrezzar king of Babylon or submit to his yoke, I will punish them with sword, famine, and pestilence, says Yahweh, until I leave them entirely in his power' (27:8). When King Zedekiah sent for Jeremiah from prison and asked him whether there was any word from Yahweh to a city which was then enjoying a brief interval in the horror of the Babylonian siege, Jeremiah replied: 'There is – you shall fall into the hands of the king of Babylon' (37:17).

So saying, Jeremiah was the climax of a great succession which dared to speak on behalf of Yahweh *against* Israel.

ISAIAH THE PROPHET

What response could the Israelites make to this prophetic challenge? Only twice in the two centuries which witnessed the fall of these two kingdoms is it said that the true prophets of Yahweh were honoured.

The first occasion was at the end of the eighth century BC, the age of Isaiah. He acquired prestige as the man who promised safety to Jerusalem in two crises (first when the city was surrounded by the Israelites from the north, and then when the more formidable war machine of Assyria moved to crush it) – and as the man who twice saw his promises come true. That is how Isaiah features in the second book of Kings, where he is simply the patriot who declares that the beloved city cannot be violated by any invader:

> He shall not enter this city
>   nor shoot an arrow there,
> he shall not advance against it with shield
>   nor cast up a siege-ramp against it.
> By the way on which he came he shall go back;
>   this city he shall not enter.
>   This is the very word of Yahweh.

I will shield this city to deliver it,
for my own sake and for the sake of my servant David
(19:32–34).

In this edifying narrative the good King Hezekiah turns to
Yahweh in a prayer which in its theology is supremely
confident: 'O Yahweh, God of Israel, enthroned on the
cherubim, thou alone art God of all the kingdoms of the
earth . . .' (19:15).

In his own book, moreover, Isaiah seems to promise
Hezekiah's son a reign of prosperity and peace:

> The people who walked in darkness
> have seen a great light:
> light has dawned upon them,
>   dwellers in a land as dark as death.
> Thou hast increased their joy and given them great glad-
>   ness;
> they rejoice in thy presence as men rejoice at harvest,
> or as they are glad when they share out the spoil;
>   for thou hast shattered the yoke that burdened them,
>   the collar that lay heavy on their shoulders,
>   the driver's goad, as on the day of Midian's defeat.
>   All the boots of trampling soldiers
>   and the garments fouled with blood
> shall become a burning mass, fuel for fire.
>
> For a boy has been born for us, a son given to us
>   to bear the symbol of dominion on his shoulder;
>   and he shall be called
>   in purpose wonderful, in battle God-like,
>   Father for all time, Prince of peace.
> Great shall the dominion be,
>   and boundless the peace
> bestowed on David's throne and on his kingdom,
> to establish it and sustain it
>   with justice and righteousness

from now and for evermore.
The zeal of Yahweh of Hosts shall do this (9:2–7).

But we may wonder what was the real significance of such
patriotic emotion. An Assyrian inscription of 691 claims
that ten years earlier Hezekiah had capitulated to their
army, which had conquered forty-six walled towns in
Judah and had shut him up in Jerusalem 'like a bird in a
cage'. According to the Assyrians, Hezekiah had paid a
large tribute and had done homage 'slavishly'. The biblical
story admits that Hezekiah paid to Sennacherib, king of
Assyria, a tribute so heavy that the temple and the treasury
were both stripped of all their silver (2 Kings 18:13–16).
It is impossible to be sure what actually happened. Some
scholars believe that there were two Assyrian invasions, the
first of which devastated Judah but the second of which
ended in a rapid retreat shortly before Sennacherib's death
in 681, thus giving rise to the belief that Jerusalem was
invulnerable. During this second invasion Hezekiah may
have been helped by 'Tirhakah King of Cush' (2 Kings
19:9), who became ruler of Egypt about 689. There is,
however, no actual evidence of two Assyrian invasions. A
reference by the Greek historian Herodotus to a plague of
rats inflicting the Assyrian army on the frontiers of Egypt
may mean that the army was struck by an epidemic carried
by rats, but if so it is less dramatic than the biblical story:
'That night the angel of Yahweh went out and struck down
a hundred and eighty-five thousand men in the Assyrian
camp; when morning dawned, they all lay dead' (2 Kings
19:35).
The outcome of these now mysterious events was that
Judah was once more an Assyrian vassal-state, unable to
take part in the power politics of the period. Hezekiah's son
Manasseh turned out to be little more than an Assyrian
puppet (see page 212). But evidently Isaiah's comprehensive warning when Jerusalem was surrounded by
enemies (chapter 1) did not lead to any lasting change of

heart. On the contrary, Isaiah is recorded as being in despair about Jerusalem's entire leadership:

Be warned: the Lord, Yahweh of Hosts,
is stripping Jerusalem and Judah
   of every prop and stay,
   warrior and soldier,
judge and prophet, diviner and elder,
   captains of companies and men of rank,
   counsellor, magician, and cunning enchanter (3:1–3).

It was the theme of Isaiah that only faith, justice, and righteousness would be a 'corner-stone of granite' for Jerusalem: 'have firm faith, or you will not stand firm' (7:9). A leadership which had laid no such corner-stone could only expect to be swept away in a storm of death, in which they would find Yahweh himself conducting a holy war against Israel, however 'strange' or 'outlandish' it might seem (28:16–22).

Because Isaiah was such a great prophet, the work of other prophets was added on the same scroll, constituting the present 'Book of Isaiah'. The foundation of this school of prophets is alluded to in Isaiah 8:16–18:

   Fasten up the message,
seal the oracle with my teaching;
   and I will wait for Yahweh
who hides his face from the house of Jacob;
   I will watch for him.
See, I and the sons whom Yahweh has given me
   are to be signs and portents in Israel,
sent by Yahweh of Hosts who dwells on Mount Zion.

Since Isaiah had so many 'sons' in that sense, it is now impossible always to be sure which prophecies of encouragement or doom are his, and which originated with his disciples. But the strange names which he gave to his sons show that the doom was a large part of his message: 'A-

remnant-shall-return' (7:3) and 'Speed-spoil-hasten-plun-
der' (8:1–4).

Isaiah saw a storm coming. Only when that storm had
raged freely would Jerusalem know what remained.

> Listen! it is the thunder of many peoples,
> they thunder with the thunder of the sea.
> Listen! it is the roar of nations
> roaring with the roar of mighty waters.
> When he rebukes them, away they fly,
> driven like chaff on the hills before the wind,
>   like thistledown before the storm (17:12–13).

JOSIAH THE REFORMER

The other occasion when true prophecy was honoured,
according to the Old Testament, was under King Josiah. In
the year 622–21 a book was discovered in the temple at
Jerusalem, and was adopted by the king as the basis of a
reforming programme. The account in 2 Kings 22:3–13
deserves study:

> In the eighteenth year of his reign Josiah sent Shaphan
> son of Azaliah, son of Meshullam, the adjutant-general,
> to the house of Yahweh. 'Go to the high priest Hilkiah,'
> he said, 'and tell him to melt down the silver that has
> been brought into the house of Yahweh, which those on
> duty at the entrance have received from the people, and
> to hand it over to the foremen in the house of Yahweh,
> to pay the workmen who are carrying out repairs in it,
> the carpenters, builders, and masons, and to purchase
> timber and hewn stones for its repair. They are not to be
> asked to account for the money that has been given them;
> they are acting on trust.
>
> The high priest Hilkiah told Shaphan the adjutant-
> general that he had discovered the book of the law in the
> house of Yahweh, and he gave it to him, and Shaphan
> read it. Then Shaphan came to report to the king and

told him that his servants had melted down the silver in the house of Yahweh and handed it over to the foremen there. Then Shaphan the adjutant-general told the king that the high priest Hilkiah had given him a book, and he read it out in the king's presence.

When the king heard what was in the book of the law, he rent his clothes, and ordered the priest Hilkiah, Ahikam son of Shaphan, Akbor son of Micaiah, Shaphan the adjutant-general, and Asaiah the king's attendant, to go and seek guidance of Yahweh for himself, for the people, and for all Judah, about what was written in this book that had been discovered. 'Great is the wrath of Yahweh,' he said, 'that has been kindled against us, because our forefathers did not obey the commands in this book and do all that is laid upon us.'

It is clear that 'this book' had largely been compiled in the northern kingdom before the fall of Samaria, in order to embody the insights of the prophetic movement led by men such as Elijah and Amos. Modern study was begun in 1805 by a German scholar, Wilhem de Wette, who demonstrated in some detail that the book (or rather, an enlarged version of it) appears in the Old Testament under the title *Deuteronomy*. Later we shall consider the laws in this book, and also the historical writing which it inspired; here it is enough to see what happened when, whether by accident or design, it had been discovered.

It was a time when, with the decline of Assyrian influence, the Jerusalem temple was already being repaired for the worship of Yahweh, and the discovery of the book was made the occasion of a drastic reform (2 Kings 23). All sacrifices were prohibited outside the Jerusalem temple. The law-book had charitably ordered that local priests deprived of their function by this monopoly should be welcomed as extra staff with equal pay in the temple (Deuteronomy 18:6–8), but evidently this was too much for the Jerusalem priests (2 Kings 23:9). The motive behind this reform is clear. It is to cleanse the land not only of Canaanite, Assyrian, and other heathen 'abominations', but also of any local Israelite worship which might be polluted or tempted by such foreign ways. The solution was to centralize all sacrifices under the direct control of the kings and priests in the capital.

But as with the popularity of Isaiah, so with the reform of Josiah; it went only skin deep. Modern historians have shown that it was part of a general recovery of independence in the vassal-states of an Assyrian empire which was now breaking up. The last of the great Assyrian emperors, Asshur-bani-pal (whose library at Nineveh has been excavated and has provided us with most of our knowledge of the literature of ancient Mesopotamia), died in 633. Under Josiah, Zephaniah had prophetic visions of Jerusalem being searched by Yahweh with a lantern, to chastise the rich drunkards as the day of wrath arrived (1:12–18). But he also had visions of Nineveh made desolate:

> Flocks shall couch there,
>   and all the beasts of the wild.
> Horned owl and ruffed bustard shall roost on her capitals;
>   the tawny owl shall hoot in the window,
>   and the bustard stand in the porch.
> This is the city that exulted in fancied security,
> saying to herself, 'I am, and I alone' (2:14–15).

The Assyrians were succeeded by the Babylonians in the control of the Middle East. These were the Neo-Babylonians, who revived the glories of the Old Babylonian empire which had been brought to an end by the Hittites some nine hundred years before. The Neo-Babylonians were also known as 'Chaldaeans' from the name of an Aramaean group which had settled in the area some four hundred years before, and which had revitalized the Old Babylonian stock.

Responding to the rise and fall of empires, the prophets

Nahum (see page 228) and Habakkuk now declared that
Yahweh was raising up the 'Chaldaeans' to punish the
Assyrians. Habakkuk taunted Nineveh:

> Because you yourself have plundered mighty nations,
>   all the rest of the world will plunder you (2:8).

This prophet had no illusions about the Babylonians:

> Terror and awe go with them;
> their justice and judgement are of their own making.
> Their horses are swifter than hunting-leopards,
>   keener than wolves of the plain;
>   their cavalry wait ready, they spring forward,
>   they come flying from afar
>   like vultures swooping to devour the prey.
> Their whole army advances, violence in their hearts;
>   a sea of faces rolls on;
>   they bring in captives countless as the sand.
>   Kings they hold in derision,
>   rulers they despise;
>   they despise every fortress,
>   they raise siege-works and capture it (1:7-10).

But the prophet's faith was that Yahweh was at work,
gradually disclosing his power until one day the earth
would be 'full of the knowledge of the glory of Yahweh as
the waters fill the sea' (2:14). It was not a reckless faith, but
the prophet was sure of it and of its security: 'the righteous
man will live by being faithful' (2:4).

However, history continued to crush the hopes of Judah.
Because Josiah's reform was bound up with the fall of the
Assyrian empire, it largely perished when events grew less
favourable.

For a time Josiah was able to exercise authority over all
the territory of the former kingdom of Israel (2 Kings
23:19), but in 609 he involved himself disastrously in power
politics. Pharaoh Necho II was on his way to defend the
Assyrians against the Babylonians, attempting to preserve

the balance of power in the Middle East. Josiah 'went to meet him; and when they met at Megiddo, Pharaoh Necho slew him' (2 Kings 23:29). The account in 2 Chronicles (35:20–27) expands that cryptic sentence, but only briefly, by explaining that the Pharaoh had no wish to fight the king, but 'Josiah would not be deflected.' It adds that, wounded by the Egyptian archers, Josiah died in the chariot taking him back to Jerusalem, and that 'all Judah and Jerusalem mourned for him. Jeremiah also made a lament for Josiah; and to this day the minstrels, both men and women, commemorate Josiah in their lamentations.'

Jeremiah later encountered the people's reaction against Josiah. All that puritanism had only led to one more disaster. The Egyptian invaders had been succeeded by the Babylonians; the turning to Yahweh had not paid off. The people protested to the prophet that when they had sacrificed to foreign gods they 'had food in plenty, and were content' – but 'from the time we left off burning sacrifices to the queen of heaven and pouring drink-offerings to her, we have been in great want' (44:15–19).

Jeremiah also experienced in himself a disillusionment with Josiah's method of imposing reform by the totalitarian censorship of public worship. The prophet lost patience both with the throne and with the altar. The sons and successors of Josiah with whom he had to deal aroused in him contempt rather than hero-worship. The God in whom he came to trust had a mind above any possibility of being placated by temples or sacrifices (7:11–28).

Neither Isaiah as the counsellor of King Hezekiah, nor King Josiah himself, was able to halt the disintegration of the little kingdom of Judah, the remnant of the Israelite state. What endured from years of accelerating doom was not any success which any king could command but the naked faith expressed in Habakkuk's prayer:

Although the fig-tree does not burgeon,
  the vines bear no fruit,

the olive-crop fails,
   the orchard yields no food,
   the fold is bereft of its flock
      and there are no cattle in the stalls,
   yet I will exult in Yahweh . . . (3:17–18)

THE REMAINING HOPE

As disasters overwhelmed the two kingdoms of Israel and
Judah, these prophets of doom were honoured. It is one of
the outstanding facts in the whole story of this astonishing
people. Like any other people being severely criticized, they
resented and tried to silence their critics. But in the end they
honoured them. They did not kill them; even Jeremiah was
not executed. Instead, they eventually included these
prophets' warnings among their holy scriptures.

When the fall of the northern kingdom had fulfilled the
warnings of Amos and Hosea, evidence about the witness of
those prophets was pieced together in Jerusalem. The title
of the book of Hosea is: 'The word of Yahweh which came
to Hosea son of Beeri during the reigns of Uzziah, Jotham,
Ahaz, and Hezekiah, kings of Judah, and during the reign
of Jeroboam son of Jehoash king of Israel.' This clearly
implies that the book was edited by a Jerusalem scribe for
whom it was natural to put the kings of Judah first, and for
whom the history of the northern kingdom was less important; in fact, most of Hosea's work was done during the
reigns of six successors of Jeroboam II.

When Jerusalem had itself been set on fire, the prophets'
words were still treasured – not only because their warnings
had come true but also because they pointed to the one
hope remaining. The book of Jeremiah contains many
passages of consolation to Jerusalem (notably chapters
30–33) and many warnings to foreign nations that their
own punishment was coming (notably chapters 46–51). It
is clear that some of these passages are by hands later than
Jeremiah's – including the hand of his secretary Baruch

(who enjoyed such a high reputation in later Judaism that a number of writings were fathered on him, among them the laments, exhortations, and consolations now in the Apocrypha as the book of Baruch). But the story is told in chapter 32 of how during the terrible last days of the kingdom of Judah, Jeremiah bought a field near his ancestral village, Anathoth. It was to be a sign that 'houses, fields, and vineyards will again be bought and sold in this land'; and we can believe that Jeremiah really did it, because he really felt so ordered by his God.

When all kings fail, Jeremiah's God says: 'I will myself gather the remnant of my sheep' (23:3). And when the city falls, and all the fabric of the society where the Israelites have taught each other and encouraged each other is destroyed, this God will make a new agreement with the people, one by one. On the ruins of Jerusalem Yahweh will build a community of the spirit. Jeremiah heard this promise as the word of God: 'I will set my law within them and write it on their hearts. I will become their God and they shall become my people. No longer need they teach one another to know Yahweh; all of them, high and low alike, shall know me, says Yahweh, for I will forgive their wrongdoing and remember their sin no more' (31:33–34).

It is amazing that those exiled from Jerusalem to Babylon kept their faith in Yahweh. Because of that, they or their descendants were able to accomplish a spiritual reconstruction.

It is true that they were not the only orthodox Jews in the world, although they often thought they were. The ten tribes of the centre and north were not lost completely when the northern kingdom was overrun by the Assyrians. Many Jews from this area remained orthodox Jews in exile, as the story of *Tobit* testifies. In Palestine, too, the area later called 'Samaria' was not so heretical as the Jews in Jerusalem to the south (or, later on, in Galilee to the north) asserted. The Samaritans who gradually broke away and built their own temple certainly believed that they were conservatives, for they were loyal to the pure religion of Yahweh embodied in the Bible's first five books (the Pentateuch). They derived their name from *samerim*, meaning 'keepers' of the Law.

But it is no accident that now we have to speak of 'the Jews' (the people of Judah) rather than 'the Israelites'. The group deported from Jerusalem and Judah to Babylonia was far more creative religiously than were the exiles from the northern kingdom, and Jerusalem when it was rebuilt had a religious vitality unmatched by the Samaritans.

Many signs show how near was total disaster. For a long time after the Assyrian conquest of the northern kingdom, the whole of Samaria was viewed as being thoroughly polluted – an attitude shown vividly in 2 Kings 17 and in the Christian gospels. From its Assyrian occupation, the adjacent Aramaean territory became known for ever as 'Syria'. After the arrival of the Assyrians, the ex-Israelites (whether in exile or still in their homes) began using Aramaic, not Hebrew, as their everyday language. The explanation is that the Assyrian empire, and later its Babylonian and Persian successors, found it convenient to use this international language which might be called a sister, but never a daughter, of Hebrew. Previously it would have been the case that while the ambassador of the Assyrian emperor could speak Aramaic, as could the leading officials of the court in Jerusalem, 'the people on the city wall' would have known only Hebrew (2 Kings 18:26). But after the Assyrian conquest even Hebrew, preserved for sacred purposes, was now normally written in a new way, using the Aramaic square script. After the arrival of the Babylonians, the Jews took to using the Babylonian names of the months, beginning the new year in the spring instead of the autumn.

But after years of uncertainty Jerusalem was restored as the centre of Judaism; as a little Jewish state, and as a place to which all Jews could look; as the beating heart of faith in Yahweh. And essentially this reconstruction was accomplished before the Jerusalem temple was fully restored. It was accomplished in hundreds of synagogues attended by the exiles, or by the people left behind in the devastated homeland.

Unfortunately no evidence has survived to show the origins of the synagogues in any detail, but this institution which was to be so vital for Judaism across many centuries clearly emerged as a response to the destruction of the temple. In a home, or in a special building, faithful Jews gathered not to sacrifice any animal or bird but to hear their traditions proclaimed, to sing their psalms, and to pray. A great impetus was given to the collection and editing of prophecies, laws, and histories. Gradually the selection of holy writings to be read and expounded became traditional, and so the 'canon' or content of the Jewish scriptures came to be fixed. Gradually, too, more and more importance was attached to the day on which this worship took place, the seventh day of the week, the Sabbath. Elaborate precautions against any distraction from the worship developed. The Sabbath was already a day of rest (the Babylonian day of rest was called *Shappatu*), but now the rest became strictly defined. To worship and to rest on the Sabbath became a badge of being a Jew – a badge which could be worn far from Jerusalem.

For a man, another badge was circumcision. A number of peoples around Israel had shared this custom; circumcision is known to have been practised among the Egyptians about 3000 BC. But it so happened that the Philistines could be hated as 'the uncircumcised'; it also so happened that the custom was unknown in Mesopotamia, so that during their exile under the Assyrians and Babylonians the Jews attached more and more importance to circumcision as marking them off from 'the nations', the Gentiles. In the first century AD, after a great debate, the Christian Church was to decide that circumcision was not needed before Gentiles could become Christians, and Paul's letters passionately expressed his conviction that it could be an excuse for arrogance before God and man. But during the exile circumcision became – like the synagogue, the scriptures, and the Sabbath – a way of maintaining the worship of Yahweh when the traditional religious institutions of Israel were all destroyed. Every Jew's body became a walking temple.

Enormous consequences in the spiritual history of mankind followed this reconstruction of Judaism in exile. Two years before the destruction of Jerusalem by the Babylonians, the prophet Zarathushtra (in Greek Zoroaster) appeared in Chorasmia, now the borderland between Iran and Afghanistan. He preached 'the Wise Lord' (*Ahura Mazdah*) as the one true God, and in the centuries following Zoroastrianism deservedly secured a great influence. But today the number of Zoroastrians in the world is little more than a hundred thousand (the Parsees of India). And what the Jews did after the fall of Jerusalem continues to shape Judaism, Christianity, and Islam.

Jeremiah's enemies had said that they could do without him, for 'there will still be priests to guide us, still wise men to advise, still prophets to proclaim the word' (18:18). Now Jerusalem's exiles found that they could do without kingdom or temple and still find creative leadership from priests, teachers, and prophets proud to stand in the tradition of Jeremiah. So Jeremiah's own boast (9:23-24) came true with a fullness he did not live to see:

> Let not the wise man boast of his wisdom
>   nor the valiant of his valour;
> let not the rich man boast of his riches;
> but if any man would boast, let him boast of this,
>   that he understands and knows me.
> For I am Yahweh, I show unfailing love,
> I do justice and right upon the earth;
>   for on these I have set my heart.

CAN THESE BONES LIVE AGAIN?

The last king of Judah to enjoy a long reign in peace had
been Azariah or Uzziah (probably from 769–68 to 741–40). It
had been in the year of his death – and he had died 'a leper'
– that Isaiah had experienced in the Jerusalem temple the
vision of Yahweh that was to last through years of fruitless
preaching to a deaf people (chapter 6). Then Yahweh had
been seen 'seated on a throne, high and exalted, and the
skirt of his robe filled the temple'; the angels or cherubim
of Yahweh had been heard 'calling ceaselessly to one
another, "Holy, holy, holy is Yahweh of Hosts"'; and the
glory of Yahweh, of which the whole earth was full, had
filled the temple, touching the prophet's mouth as with a
glowing coal.

About a century and a half later another prophet 'was
among the exiles by the river Kebar, the heavens were
opened and I saw a vision of God.' It is characteristic of
Ezekiel that in his vision he was given a scroll to eat
'written all over on both sides with dirges and laments and
words of woe'. He, too, was a prophet of doom – a victim
of the first Babylonian deportation in 598, sure that the
complete ruin of Jerusalem was impending. But above all
he was a prophet of God's glory and mercy, so that when
he ate the scroll 'it tasted as sweet as honey' (2:9–3:3).

The divine glory and mercy were now imagined with a
wealth of picture and phrase without equal in the history of
Israelite prophecy. Ezekiel saw a storm-wind, 'a vast cloud
with flashes of fire and brilliant light about it; and within
was a radiance like brass, glowing in the heart of the
flames.' In the fire he saw 'the semblance of four living
creatures in human form', their 'appearance . . . was as if
fire from burning coals or torches were darting to and fro
among them.' Above them was 'a vault glittering like a
sheet of ice, awe-inspiring'. Above the vault was a throne;
and 'high above all, upon the throne, a form in human
likeness'. Yet from this throne of glory came the voice of

mercy: 'Man, stand up, and let me talk with you' (chapter
1).

A God so glorious and so merciful could do anything to
discipline and then to save his people. Ezekiel (chapter 17)
told a parable of an eagle which took just a twig from a
noble cedar-tree, and from that twig made another cedar
grow in a far-off city:

> A great eagle
> with broad wings and long pinions,
> in full plumage, richly patterned,
>   came to Lebanon.
> He took the very top of a cedar-tree,
> he plucked its highest twig;
> he carried it off to a land of commerce,
>   and planted it in a city of merchants.

And he seemed to hear Yahweh saying to the exiles that he
could just as well carry *his* twig back to Israel:

> I, too, will take a slip
> from the lofty crown of the cedar
>   and set it in the soil;
> I will pluck a tender shoot from the topmost branch
>   and plant it.
> I will plant it high on a lofty mountain,
>   the highest mountain in Israel.
> It will put out branches, bear its fruit,
>   and become a noble cedar.
> Winged birds of every kind will roost under it,
>   they will roost in the shelter of its sweeping boughs.

Ezekiel saw that individuals cleansed and empowered by
such a vision could start the reconstruction of a Jewish
community, even while in exile. He felt called as an individual – the most eloquent author yet to appear in the
history of Israel – to reach other individuals with the
divine warning and promise. In another vision he saw the
God of Israel finally deserting Jerusalem: 'the glory of

Yahweh rose up and left the city' (11:23). But to individuals
who responded after this destruction of the state, new life
was offered. The individual need not be suffocated by the
corporate guilt or sucked down into the corporate doom.
'It is the soul that sins, and no other, that shall die; a son
shall not share a father's guilt, nor a father his son's' (18:
20). For Yahweh, so far from being permanently angry,
had 'no desire for any man's death' (18:32).

This assurance was not reached easily. At one moment,
the fate of an exile in an unclean land seemed like having to
bake bread with human dung (4:12–13). At another, it
seemed that Yahweh might deliberately have lured Israel
into sinning (20:23–26). Or it seemed wrong to weep for his
dead wife when his whole people was dying (24:18–24). For
days and years of exile, bewildered and despairing, Ezekiel
stayed silent. But then 'fugitives came to me from Jerusalem
and told me that the city had fallen' (33:21). And he spoke.

Ezekiel filled out Jeremiah's image of Yahweh the Good
Shepherd with a tenderness which showed that he himself
was a pastor (chapter 34). He filled out Hosea's image of
Israel being raised from the dead with an intensity which
showed that his own heart, in a valley of dry bones, had
died and come back to life (37:1–14):

> The hand of Yahweh came upon me, and he carried
> me out by his spirit and put me down in a plain full of
> bones. He made me go to and fro across them until I
> had been round them all; they covered the plain, count-
> less numbers of them, and they were very dry. He said
> to me, 'Man, can these bones live again?' I answered,
> 'Only thou knowest that, Yahweh my lord.' He said to
> me, 'Prophesy over these bones and say to them, O dry
> bones, hear the word of Yahweh. This is the word of
> Yahweh to these bones: I will put breath into you, and
> you shall live. I will fasten sinews on you, bring flesh upon
> you, overlay you with skin, and put breath in you, and
> you shall know that I am Yahweh.'

I began to prophesy as he had bidden me, and as I prophesied there was a rustling sound and the bones fitted themselves together. As I looked, sinews appeared upon them, flesh covered them, and they were overlaid with skin, but there was no breath in them. Then he said to me, 'Prophesy to the wind, prophesy, man, and say to it, These are the words of Yahweh: Come, O wind, come from every quarter and breathe into these slain, that they may come to life.' I began to prophesy as he had bidden me: breath came into them; they came to life and rose to their feet, a mighty host.

He said to me, 'Man, these bones are the whole people of Israel. They say, "Our bones are dry, our thread of life is snapped, our web is severed from the loom." Prophesy, therefore, and say to them, These are the words of Yahweh: O my people, I will open your graves and bring you up from them, and restore you to the land of Israel. You shall know that I am Yahweh when I open your graves and bring you up from them, O my people. Then I will put my spirit into you and you shall live, and I will settle you on your own soil, and you shall know that I Yahweh have spoken and will act. This is the very word of Yahweh.'

Out of his own suffering this prophet drew the promise of a new heart and a new spirit in the individual (36:24–28), the glory returning to the City of God (chapters 40–48). As is the way with exiles seeking consolation, he drew up plans for the great day of return. He planned the ideal temple, and he pondered the reforms which would be needed after the homecoming. Not only would sacrifices have to be confined to the temple in Jerusalem; among all the priests, only the loyal 'sons of Zadok' (a group about whose origins we cannot be sure) could be trusted with the charge of Yahweh's altar (chapter 44). Not only should the princes of Israel maintain law and justice; they should never oppress the people again, and should be content with a greatly reduced estate (45:7–12).

It was a dream: a pure river was to spring up beneath the Jerusalem temple and was to sweeten the Dead Sea (47: 1–12). But this was a dream with power for the future. It was appropriate that when in AD 1909 another group of Jews ended their exile and built a city, they named it Tel Aviv after the name of Ezekiel's place of exile (3:15).

THE SONGS OF AN EXILE

Although at the time Ezekiel's dream seemed to belong to the distant future, suddenly history took a new turn. Babylon fell to the Persian King Cyrus in 539. In the book of Jeremiah (50:2) a song of hope is included – and if this song came from Jeremiah's time, it must have seemed a far-fetched hope:

Declare and proclaim among the nations,
keep nothing back, spread the news:
　Babylon is taken.

Now it came true. And so a prophet arose whose work was put on the same scroll as Isaiah's but whose name we do not know. He was the greatest of all Israel's prophets, and his was a voice of exultant joy:

Comfort, comfort my people;
　– it is the voice of your God;
speak tenderly to Jerusalem
　and tell her this,
that she has fulfilled her term of bondage . . . (40:1–2)

It is easy to be so carried away by the delight of this prophet's poetry that one fails to notice the argument. Actually the argument is simple. Cyrus has been called and anointed by Yahweh to do his work (45:1–7). The music here chimes with Cyrus' own claims (which have survived) that many gods, including the Babylonian gods themselves, had sent him into the Babylonian empire as the great

liberator. To the Jewish prophet, however, the fall of
Babylon proves that the Babylonian gods were mere idols,
while Israel's God is the Creator whose energies can never
be exhausted and whose purposes can never be defeated
(40:12–41:29; 45:8–48:22). And the present generation
of Jews has been summoned as witnesses; it is as if a case
were being tried in a court of law (43:9–13). They are to
witness that Yahweh has never forgotten Israel (49:14–26).
For the exiles are to be allowed back home!

This prophet of the Exile probably wrote the poem now
included in the book of Isaiah as chapter 35:

> Then shall blind men's eyes be opened,
>   and the ears of the deaf unstopped.
> Then shall the lame man leap like a deer,
>   and the tongue of the dumb shout aloud;
> for water springs up in the wilderness,
> and torrents flow in dry land.
> The mirage becomes a pool,
>   the thirsty land bubbling springs;
>   instead of reeds and rushes, grass shall grow
>   in the rough land where wolves now lurk.
> And there shall be a causeway there
> which shall be called the Way of Holiness,
>   and the unclean shall not pass along it;
> it shall become a pilgrim's way,
>   no fool shall trespass on it.
> No lion shall come there,
> no savage beast climb on to it,
>   not one shall be found there.
> By it those he has ransomed shall return
>   and Yahweh's redeemed come home;
> they shall enter Zion with shouts of triumph,
> crowned with everlasting gladness.
> Gladness and joy shall be their escort,
> and suffering and weariness shall flee away.

We know from Persian evidence that it was the policy of Cyrus and his successors to relax the iron grip of the Babylonian emperors on their provinces. Deported people who might give trouble in exile were allowed to move back to their own lands; and to secure goodwill local customs, including religious customs, were tolerated and subsidized. It was a successful policy; the Persian empire lasted for almost exactly two centuries until it was conquered by Alexander the Great. But the policy was interpreted in far more glowing terms by this poet-prophet.

In his eyes, the return of the Jewish exiles – such an astonishing reversal of fortune (44:24–28) – must be acknowledged by the whole earth as the vindication of Israel's God. All the suffering of this people would have its reward as the nations applauded Yahweh for his new act. In this way this people would be 'a light to all peoples, a beacon for the nations' (42:6). To this God 'every knee shall bend' (45:23), for

> Yahweh has bared his holy arm
>   in the sight of all nations,
> and the whole world from end to end
> shall see the deliverance of our God (52:10).

In the sixth century BC, only a few exiles seem to have trickled back to Jerusalem; much of the city, including the temple, was allowed to remain in ruins. The conversion of the world did not take place. But over the centuries this prophet's vision of God has come to seem, in more and more eyes, the only true vision if God is true. It is the vision of one, holy, transcendent God: 'monotheism'. 'To him nations are but drops from a bucket' (40:15). This is the power in all the stars (40:26). This is 'the everlasting God, creator of the wide world' (40:28). 'I alone, I am He' (43:25).

This God makes fearful demands on those who serve him. In four 'Songs of the Suffering Servant' which are inserted into his book, this great prophet and poet describes one who seems to be sometimes an individual, sometimes the embodiment of Israel. The first song is about the modesty, the gentleness, and the patience of 'my servant' (42:1–4). The second compares the servant of God with an arrow hidden out of sight in the quiver, yet promises that 'when they see you kings shall rise' (49:1–7). The third says that the servant is a listener before he becomes a teacher with skill to console the weary – and a silent prisoner, insulted and tortured, before he is helped by God (50:4–11).

The fourth song (52:13–53:12) is the most famous portrait of this servant of God – obscure, ugly, 'tormented and humbled by suffering', despised, led like a dumb sheep to execution, given 'a burial-place among the refuse of mankind'. Onlookers had reckoned that this miserable man had been 'smitten by God'; yet they have come to see that 'the chastisement he bore is health for us', that 'after all his pains he shall be bathed in light', and that 'after his disgrace he shall be fully vindicated.' In this song the servant is compared with the animal killed in sacrifice – innocently bearing the penalty of the guilt of others, uncomplainingly dying so that others may be healed. The servant is also seen as the priest of mankind: he 'interceded for their transgressions'. It is a portrait which Christians have always accepted as a picture of Jesus (see page 22); but first it was a portrait of 'the Jew'.

This prophet has not escaped the question why a God so glorious has called his chosen people to such a history, his servant to such suffering. The prophet's answer is one which we may contrast with the teaching given by two sages who were his contemporaries (at least approximately) in far-off Asia. Gautama the Buddha taught not about God or gods but that desire is the cause of suffering, and non-existence the remedy. Confucius taught about a 'heaven' serene above the affairs of men. But the prophet of the Jewish exile proclaimed a God involved in the desire, the work, and the suffering:

Thus speaks Yahweh who is God,
   he who created the skies and stretched them out,
   who fashioned the earth and all that grows in it,
who gave breath to its people,
   the breath of life to all who walk upon it . . .

   Long have I lain still,
I kept silence and held myself in check;
now I will cry like a woman in labour,
   whimpering, panting and gasping . . . (42:5,14)

Listen to me, house of Jacob
   and all the remnant of the house of Israel,
a load on me from your birth, carried by me from the
      womb;
   till you grow old I am He,
   and when white hairs come, I will carry you still;
I have made you and I will bear the burden . . .
                            (46:3–4)

CHAPTER 6

Rebuilding a People

THE SECOND TEMPLE

The last five centuries of the history of the Jews before the
birth of Jesus can be treated as a mere epilogue to the Old
Testament. The events are less dramatic than in the six
centuries between the Exodus and the Exile. The material
describing them is far less plentiful, partly because there
is now no political entity to be called 'Israel'. Yet these five
centuries saw the birth of Judaism, the religion of the Jews;
and it was Judaism that fed the mind of Jesus the Jew – and
that influenced Mohammed. For any Jew or Christian or
Muslim, these five centuries are better treated as a prologue.

A decree which the Persian emperor, Cyrus, issued in
538 BC is included in the Old Testament (Ezra 6:3–5). It is
given in Aramaic, which was the normal language of the
Persian administration (and which, in a slightly different
form, was also the normal language of Jesus). Its authenticity, although far from certain, seems possible.

> In the first year of King Cyrus, the king issued this
> decree concerning the house of God in Jerusalem: Let
> the house be rebuilt as a place where sacrifices are offered
> and fire-offerings brought. Its height shall be sixty cubits
> and its breadth sixty cubits, with three courses of massive
> stones and one course of timber, the cost to be defrayed
> from the royal treasury. Also the gold and silver vessels
> of the house of God, which Nebuchadnezzar took out of
> the temple in Jerusalem and brought to Babylon, shall be
> restored; they shall all be taken back to the temple in
> Jerusalem, and restored each to its place in the house of
> God.

However, little action seems to have resulted immediately. We are told that the decree was filed away, Cyrus died eight years after issuing it, and none of the civil servants in Babylon could find it when some twenty years later an inquiry arrived addressed to a new emperor, Darius, by officials in that part of the Persian empire (Ezra 5:8–17). Those officials had been told that the foundation stone of a new temple in Jerusalem had been laid by 'a man named Sheshbazzar' (a Babylonian name) who had been entrusted with this task by Cyrus. But the work of reconstruction had not been strenuous until recently; and so the officials asked for instructions. After a moment of bureaucratic consternation, eventually the decree of Cyrus was found in the royal residence in the province of Media, at Ecbatana, and Darius renewed the royal authority for the temple's reconstruction (Ezra 6:6–12). At length a new temple was consecrated in 515.

The story of the rebuilding of the temple shows how difficult it was to stir up enthusiasm. The building was not large (sixty by sixty cubits, the cubit being the distance between the elbow and the knuckles of the clenched fist), and the royal treasury was to meet all costs, yet there was this delay. The explanation seems to be that the eloquence of the prophet whose poems we have been studying (Isaiah 40–55) failed to persuade his first hearers or readers to take effective action. Presumably most of them had been born in exile, and many of them were well off – why should they all return with enthusiasm to an unknown and uncomfortable Palestine? And the Jews remaining in Jerusalem had been demoralized by the deportation of the whole upper class.

But the Old Testament also records how prophets continued to do battle for the honour of Yahweh. Their predecessors' work had been accepted as a true verdict on the history of Israel; the Persian officials are said to have reported the Jewish conviction that 'because our forefathers provoked the anger of the God of Heaven he put them into the power of Nebuchadnezzar the Chaldaean, king of Babylon, who pulled down this house' – the essence of the prophetic message. Now fresh prophets arose.

They were stimulated by the excitement which arose when there was confusion in the Persian empire on the death of the emperor Cambyses in 522. Rebellions had to be dealt with before Darius I secured the throne. It was in 520 that a prophet named Haggai proclaimed as the word of Yahweh in Jerusalem: 'I will shake heaven and earth, sea and land, I will shake all nations; the treasure of all nations shall come hither and I will fill this house with glory . . . Mine is the silver and mine the gold, says Yahweh of Hosts, and the glory of this latter house shall surpass the glory of the former' (2:6–9).

Haggai's message was 'to Zerubbabel son of Shealtiel, governor of Judah, and to Joshua son of Jehozadak, the high priest'. To Zerubbabel, the grandson of Jehoiachin, king of Judah, he added words which were definitely political: 'I will overthrow the thrones of kings, break the power of heathen realms, overturn chariots and their riders; horses and riders shall fall by the sword of their comrades.' Haggai promised that Yahweh would take Zerubbabel and 'wear you as a signet-ring'. These words are clearly an invitation to take advantage of the Persian civil war and to seize power in Jerusalem.

But Zerubbabel disappears from history. Certainly Darius soon established control; the governor in Jerusalem either toed the line or was removed. Not long after Haggai's inflammatory message another prophet, Zechariah, arose to preach a gospel of peace. 'The whole world is still and at peace' (1:11). 'This is the word of Yahweh concerning Zerubbabel: Neither by force of arms nor by brute strength but by my spirit! says Yahweh of Hosts. How does a mountain, the greatest mountain, compare with Zerubbabel? It is no higher than a plain' (4:6–7). Yet there is to be no holy war. Jerusalem has no need of defensive walls, for Yahweh will be a wall of fire round it (2:1–5). The exiles are to return to it in peace, and are to be joined by others. 'When ten men from nations of every language pluck up courage, they shall pluck the robe of a Jew and say, "We will go with you because we have heard that God is with you" ' (8:23).

After the brief episode of Zerubbabel, the leadership in Jerusalem lay in the hands of the priests. Indeed, the text of Zechariah as we have it reads: 'put the crown on the head of Joshua son of Jehozadak, the high priest . . . Here is a man named the Branch' (6:11–12). It seems that the original text referred to Zerubbabel as the Branch of the tree of David, for we read: 'he . . . will be seated on his throne and govern, with a priest at his right side' (6:13). But the alteration of the name was significant for the future. The royal house of David was never again to rule in Jerusalem.

THE ACHIEVEMENT OF NEHEMIAH

Darkness now descends on the history of the city and the temple. The only evidence which comes from Jerusalem during the next seventy years (during which the Persians failed in their attempt to conquer Greece) seems only to emphasize how dark the time is.

This evidence is the book of Malachi, meaning 'my messenger'. We do not know this prophet's name, but we can see that he feels called to act 'like a refiner's fire, like fuller's soap' (3:2) – and even then he feels that no prophet less than another Elijah will do (4:5). For the Jerusalemites have wearied Yahweh (2:17). They have offended their God by offering as sacrifices in the temple blind, lame, or diseased animals which they themselves would despise as food (1:6–14); by tolerating a slack priesthood (2:9); and by divorcing their Jewish wives in order to marry foreigners (2:10–16). This prophet is aware of the loyalty to Yahweh of Jews now dispersed in many lands. 'From furthest east to furthest west my name is great among the nations. Everywhere fragrant sacrifice and pure gifts are offered in my name . . .' But that proud thought makes him more depressed about the profanation of Yahweh's name by the Jews of Jerusalem (1:11-12).

Elijah did not come to Jerusalem. But Nehemiah did – in 445. His brief autobiography has been preserved (1:1-7:73 and parts of chapters 11-13). As an exiled Jew he had risen high at the Persian court under Artaxerxes I. He tells us: 'I was the king's cupbearer, and one day, in the month Nisan, in the twentieth year of King Artaxerxes, when his wine was ready, I took it up and handed it to the king, and as I stood before him I was feeling very unhappy. He said to me, "Why do you look so unhappy?" . . . I . . . answered, "The king will live for ever. But how can I help looking unhappy when the city where my forefathers are buried lies waste and its gates are burnt?" ' (2:1-3).

Nehemiah obtained from his royal master authority to rebuild the walls of Jerusalem; no doubt Artaxerxes reflected that such a fortified city might be a convenient defence against Egypt, now in revolt against Persian rule. And Nehemiah's memoirs proudly describe how he achieved his task. He dismissed Zechariah's belief that walls were not necessary in Jerusalem: that was pacifist sentimentality. Walls were needed – and walls were built. In an equally practical manner he did something about the life within the walls, making the citizens cancel their debts to each other. There must be brotherhood. Evidence that Nehemiah had once again made Judah a political unit has been provided by the discovery of coins of the late fifth or early fourth century, stamped YHD.

Nehemiah then reported back at court, and his authority was renewed. In a second mission (probably beginning in 433) he did his utmost to carry forward the reconstruction of the little state along the lines advocated by Ezekiel and the other sensitive exiles (chapter 13). Discipline was enforced in the temple, and the Sabbath in the streets. When Nehemiah found that some Jews had married foreign

women and that half their children could not speak
Hebrew, 'I beat them and tore out their hair.'

He tells us that he was in constant tension with Sanballat
and Tobiah, the governors of the Persian colonies of
Samaria and Ammon. He recounts the tricks with which
they tried to stop the rebuilding of the walls of Jerusalem.
They did not stop short of inciting bandit-raids on the city.
Political as well as personal rivalries were involved, for
before Nehemiah's independent commission a defenceless
Jerusalem had been merely one town in the colony of
Samaria – and now it recovered a certain political importance. But we know from the correspondence of the Jewish
temple at Elephantine in Egypt that Sanballat named his
sons Delaiah and Shlemiah; these names, like Tobiah's,
indicate adherence to the religion of Yahweh. Indeed,
Nehemiah himself informs us that the high priest Eliashib
allowed Tobiah the use of a room attached to the temple,
and also allowed his own grandson to marry Sanballat's
daughter – acts which drove Nehemiah to fury.

Such clashes with fellow-worshippers of Yahweh show
how necessary it had become to produce a more organized
answer to the question of this religion's identity. To this
question, the exercise of Nehemiah's strong personality was
not an adequate reply. In far-off Elephantine, the easy-
going worshippers of 'Yahu' and his bride (see pages 184-5)
thought that they could appeal for help to Jerusalem and
to Samaria at the same time, as another of their surviving
letters shows. Judaism needed to be defined.

The Samaritans built their own sanctuary on Mount
Gerizim for the worship of Yahweh, near the ancient
shrine of the tribes of Israel at Shechem; but we do not
know when. The earliest surviving mention of this Samaritan sanctuary refers to the 160s (2 Maccabees 6:2). The
Jewish historian Josephus, writing in the first century AD,
says that the Samaritans got permission from Alexander the
Great to build their temple in 333. He gives 'Sanballat' as
the name of the governor of Samaria then. What we can be

sure of is that at some date between 440 and 330, the embittered relations between the Jews of Judah and the Samaritans became a final schism. Step by step the situation was created which a Samaritan woman describes in John's gospel: 'Our fathers worshipped on this mountain, but you Jews say that the temple where God should be worshipped is in Jerusalem' (4:20).

THE MISSION OF EZRA

Another mission to Jerusalem probably began in 398 (although the date is far from certain). The work of Nehemiah was now greatly strengthened by a no less determined but more learned reformer, the priest Ezra.

He also obtained royal authority, the emperor now being Artaxerxes II, and the relevant decree is included in the Old Testament (Ezra 7:12–26). We also possess the brief memoirs in which Ezra describes his journey back to Jerusalem where he ended up 'dumbfounded' by the scandals (Ezra 7:28–9:4). And we have an account which many scholars accept as largely authentic of the reading of 'the book of the law of Moses' which Ezra had brought with him (Nehemiah 8).

There is no agreement among modern scholars about exactly which part of the Old Testament was read by Ezra on New Year's Day 'from early morning till noon'. Probably it was the *Law of Holiness* (see page 190); perhaps it was the 'priestly' history linked with this law in the Pentateuch (see page 214). But the details of the scene are exact: the crowd in the square by the Water Gate, Ezra on a wooden platform, his assistants interpreting him when he paused (probably they translated from his Hebrew into the people's Aramaic), and the dinner-time dismissal. 'You may go now,' said Ezra; 'refresh yourselves with rich food and sweet drinks, and send a share to all who cannot provide for themselves; for this day is holy to our Yahweh. Let there be no sadness, for joy in Yahweh is your strength.'

The reforms on which Ezra concentrated were those which Nehemiah had already tackled – purity in the temple, Sabbath keeping, an end to mixed marriages, the regular remission of debts. Indeed, some modern scholars think that Ezra came to Jerusalem *before* Nehemiah, and others that he worked alongside him. The two books in the Old Testament bearing these great men's names were edited by 'the Chronicler', who tells us about Ezra first. But a letter discovered in Elephantine seems to demand the earlier date for Nehemiah, and Nehemiah's authentic memoirs never mention Ezra. Ezra's work makes more sense if we see it as a follow-up to Nehemiah's – as a successful attempt to enforce reform on the systematic basis of 'the book of the law of Moses', not on the basis of Nehemiah's will power. On this dating, Ezra was a contemporary of Socrates (who was condemned to death in Athens in 399 BC).

Whatever his dates Jewish tradition is right to regard Ezra as one of its key figures. Essentially what he did was to base the Jewish identity on the 'law of Moses' which had been developed in the Babylonian exile. Even the Samaritans, who abhorred his memory, accepted the *Law of Holiness* and the Pentateuch which he or his disciples made authoritative; by the time of Jesus of Nazareth, the Jewish rabbis taught that Ezra and the other 'Men of the Great Assembly' had accomplished the formation of *all* the holy scriptures, although modern scholars conclude that the process was not complete for another 250 years. The prestige attached to the name of Ezra was also reflected in the Jewish tradition which identified him with the Chronicler, who probably worked about 350 BC (see page 216). And as the Koran records (9:30), Mohammed was under the impression that 'the Jews say Ezra is the Son of Allah.'

Two books often found in the Apocrypha (although not in the Roman Catholic version) were also ascribed to him. In fact, however, both these books date from considerably later. The so-called 'first book of Esdras' is very largely a translation into Greek of various material available to us elsewhere. The opening description of the reformed Passover under King Josiah, for example, is copied from the second book of Chronicles. Much of the rest of the material repeats the books of Ezra and Nehemiah in the Old Testament. The most interesting fresh section is a story of a debate between three pages at the court of Darius (3:1–5:3). The first praises the strength of wine; the second extols the power of the king himself; the third first speaks of the attractiveness of women, and then claims that truth is mightiest, for 'hers are strength and royalty, the authority and majesty of all ages. Praise be to the God of truth!' The third page, who wins the debate, is named here as Zerubbabel, who is rewarded with his commission to rebuild Jerusalem – but originally this story was Persian. This 'first book of Esdras' finishes in mid-sentence: 'They gathered together.'

Another book in the Apocrypha called 'the second book of Esdras' contains seven visions which Ezra is supposed to have had in Babylon in 556 BC. But clearly it was written after the fall of Jerusalem to the Romans in AD 70. The whole book is a poignant attempt to recover the security of Jewish faith under the impact of that near-final shock. As it wrestles with the nation's latest death, it is a kind of corporate *Job*. As it looks forward to a miraculous new age when wrongs will be righted, it grows out of the same soil as the early Christian belief in the coming kingdom of God; but it does not belong to Ezra's age of determined reconstruction for Judaism on earth. In the form in which this book appears in our Apocrypha, both the prologue and the epilogue (chapters 1, 2, 15, and 16) translate Christian additions from the Latin. The Jewish text seems to have reached its present form about AD 120.

So neither of these 'books of Esdras' provides any information about the historical Ezra.

FAITH IN A DARK AGE

Before we dismiss Ezra as a dull legalist, we need to remind ourselves of the psychological realities of life in Jerusalem after its reconstruction. It was a community often depressed and conscious of its guilt. As one of its hymn-writers complained:

> We cannot see what lies before us, we have no prophet
>> now;
>> we have no one who knows how long this is to last
>>> (Psalm 74:9).

Or as another of this community's teachers (whose poems were honoured by being included in the book of Isaiah) wrote:

> We look for light but all is darkness,
>> for the light of dawn, but we walk in deep gloom.
> We grope like blind men along a wall,
>> feeling our way like men without eyes;
> we stumble at noonday as if it were twilight,
>> like dead men in the ghostly underworld.
> We growl like bears,
> like doves we moan incessantly . . . (59:9–11)

It was a community still tempted, as its ancestors had been, to placate heaven and to communicate with the dead by heathen practices – 'offering sacrifice in gardens, burning incense on brick altars, crouching among graves, keeping vigil all night long' (65:3–4). But before we call that guilt morbid, we need to notice in the poems of the 'Third Isaiah' how regularly sins against justice in society are more important than sins against purity in the temple.

It was a time when heaven seemed very high above Jerusalem, and the glories of the past seemed a long way off. We read the prayer:

> Look down from heaven and behold

from the heights where thou dwellest holy and glorious.
> Where is thy zeal, thy valour,
>> thy burning and tender love?
Stand not aloof; for thou art our father,
though Abraham does not know us nor Israel acknowl-
> edge us (63:15–16).

But this was also a time when this high God was believed to
dwell in the humble and the broken-hearted – not merely
with them, but *in* them:

> Thus speaks the high and exalted one,
> whose name is holy, who lives for ever:
>> I dwell in a high and holy place
>>> with him who is broken and humble in spirit,
>>> to revive the spirit of the humble,
>>> to revive the courage of the broken (57:15).

It was a time when the birth-pangs of a new age seemed
to be very prolonged:

> Shall a woman bear a child without pains?
> give birth to a son before the onset of labour?
>> Who has heard of anything like this?
>> Who has seen any such thing?
> Shall a country be born after one day's labour,
> shall a nation be brought to birth all in a moment?
>> (66:7–8)

But this was also a time of faith that the power of Yahweh
was not exhausted:

>> For behold, I create
> new heavens and a new earth.
>> Former things shall no more be remembered
>> nor shall they be called to mind.
>> Rejoice and be filled with delight,
>>> you boundless realms which I create . . . (65:17–18)

It was a time which never forgot the tragedy, whose God was a God never remote from the tragedy:

It was no envoy, no angel, but he himself that delivered
them;
he himself ransomed them by his love and pity,
lifted them up and carried them
through all the years gone by (63:9).

But it was also a time when the consolations of this God were known. To Jesus of Nazareth, a poem written in this time was the best summary of his own mission (Luke 4:18–19):

The spirit of the Lord Yahweh is upon me
because Yahweh has anointed me;
he has sent me to bring good news to the humble,
to bind up the broken-hearted,
to proclaim liberty to captives
and release to those in prison;
to proclaim a year of Yahweh's favour
and a day of the vengeance of our God;
to comfort all who mourn,
to give them garlands instead of ashes,
oil of gladness instead of mourners' tears,
a garment of splendour for the heavy heart.
They shall be called Trees of Righteousness,
planted by Yahweh for his glory.
Ancient ruins shall be rebuilt
and sites long desolate restored;
they shall repair the ruined cities
and restore what has long lain desolate (61:1–4).

We can now perhaps look more sympathetically at the laws which, thanks to Nehemiah and Ezra, were the strength of this Jewish community.

CHAPTER 7

A People's Laws

WHAT IS LAW?

For strictly orthodox Jews the laws included in the Old Testament remain the Maker's book of instructions, and being a Jew means obedience without question or complaint. 'The Law has been revealed from heaven; nothing is to be added to it or taken away from it.' Those are the very words of the great Moses Maimonedes, giving the essentials of the Jewish faith in the twelfth century AD. Although in practice it proves impossible to be completely obedient to all the regulations – some of them cannot be kept in modern conditions, while others were changed within the Old Testament – still the ideal is there: keeping the Law.

Non-Jews tend to think that it must all be a great burden. And so, it seems, it often has been. The most irksome restrictions are dietary. Only animals which are four-legged, cud-chewing, and of cloven hoof are permitted – and only they when they have been specially slaughtered (the throat is cut so as to drain all the blood). Everything that lives in the water is impure apart from fish with scales and fins. Very many Jews brought up traditionally have rebelled against the old regulations and have tried to work out a reformed or liberal version of Judaism, so that outwardly at any rate they might conform to their neighbours' customs.

This rebellion goes on in our time. The argument is obvious. If Elijah was allowed to eat meat brought to him by ravens without asking whether it was properly slaughtered ('flawlessly fit' or *glat kosher*), as is stated in 1 Kings 17: 6, why should a Jewish housewife in twentieth-century New York be compelled to use different cooking utensils for meat and milk because Exodus 23:19 orders: 'You shall not boil a kid in its mother's milk'?

At a deeper spiritual level, there have been many Jews who have experienced the detailed Law as a barrier between them and God – or, at any rate, as something less important than a direct, loving relationship with God. Paul's letters in the New Testament contain many expressions to the effect that keeping the Law meticulously brought him little or nothing except a sense of sin – so that the key word in Christianity was for him *grace*, the gracious acts of God doing what the Law could never do. Whether or not they have become Christians, many Jews have been brought to a point not unlike Paul's.

It is, however, a great mistake to think that all Jews have such attitudes. Many have taken a great pride in their legal inheritance. In *Deuteronomy* this pride is expressed. 'When they hear about these statutes, they will say, "What a wise and understanding people this great nation is!" What great nation has a god close at hand as Yahweh our God is close to us whenever we call to him? What great nation is there whose statutes and laws are just, as is all this law which I am setting before you today?' (4:6–8). Devout Jews have many customs to show their love of the Law. The classic passage is also in *Deuteronomy* (6:6–9). 'These commandments which I give you this day are to be kept in your heart; you shall repeat them to your sons, and speak of them indoors and out of doors, when you lie down and when you rise. Bind them as a sign on the hand and wear them as a phylactery on the forehead; write them up on the doorposts of your houses and on your gates.'

The Old Testament contains many other examples of people expressing joy that they have been chosen to keep God's Law. It was like a uniform which they wore with pride. This is the theme of the longest psalm, Psalm 119. Here each section begins with a different letter of the Hebrew alphabet, and every one of the eight verses in that section begins with the same letter, but the thought as a whole does not sound artificial. 'In thy commandments I find continuing delight . . . Make me walk in the path of thy commandments, for that is my desire . . . I have cherished thy decrees all my life long . . . The law thou hast ordained means more to me than a fortune in gold or silver . . . Grant me life, as thy love is unchanging, that I may follow all thy instructions . . . Thy word is revealed, and all is light.'

The same theme inspires a shorter psalm:

> The law of Yahweh is perfect and revives the soul.
>> Yahweh's instruction never fails,
>> and makes the simple wise.
> The precepts of Yahweh are right and rejoice the heart.
>> The commandment of Yahweh shines clear
>> and gives light to the eyes.
>> The fear of Yahweh is pure and abides for ever.
> Yahweh's decrees are true and righteous every one,
> more to be desired than gold, pure gold in plenty,
>> sweeter than syrup or honey from the comb.
>> It is these that give thy servant warning,
>> and he who keeps them wins a great reward (19:7–11).

That, very briefly, is the Jewish attitude to the religious law – a mixture of rebellion against the restrictions with a moving delight in the heritage. But the question remains what the Jewish religious law can possibly mean to those of us who are not Jews by birth. Do these regulations, so ancient and so complicated, hold any meaning for people who never for one second consider themselves obliged to obey all of them literally?

Most non-Jews have dismissed the whole subject. These parts of the Old Testament are, it is said, 'mere law' – and we believe instead in 'the Gospel'. Or if we are less willing to identify ourselves with Christianity, we call these things 'legalism' and we rate them lower than the claims of 'humanity'. But such an attitude of total boredom and rejection misses something of real and permanent value.

A little portrait of 'the man who is righteous' is given by a priest and prophet, Ezekiel (18:5–9). At first glance his idea of virtue seems remote. He refers to the Canaanite orgies at mountain-shrines, for example; and that is not our problem. But let us look more closely! 'Consider the man who is righteous and does what is just and right. He never feasts at mountain-shrines, never lifts his eyes to the idols of Israel, never dishonours another man's wife, never approaches a woman during her periods. He oppresses no man, he returns the debtor's pledge, he never robs. He gives bread to the hungry and clothes to those who have none. He never lends either at discount or at interest. He shuns injustice and deals fairly between man and man. He conforms to my statutes and loyally observes my laws. Such a man is righteous: he shall live, says the Lord Yahweh.'

In effect Ezekiel is saying that to be righteous means this: reverence before the true source of all life, accompanied by the rejection of all that is unworthy of worship; honour for marriage and tenderness to a woman; justice for the poor; respect for debtors and the destitute; the refusal to make a profit out of distress; constant fair dealing. If that is the essence of the Old Testament's moral demand and legislation, it surely does not deserve to be dismissed by anyone in any age without examination.

However, an intelligent understanding of the legislation in the Old Testament also requires a willingness to see how the detailed changing laws responded to various situations in the life of the people. For modern scholars are agreed that these laws come from a number of sources. Since Moses was regarded as the great law-giver in Ancient Israel, almost all the laws were attributed to him just as psalms were ascribed to David and proverbs to Solomon. Moses was represented as speaking to generations yet unborn, as in *Deuteronomy*: 'It is not with you alone that I am making this covenant and this oath, but with all those who stand here with us today . . . and also with those who are not here with us today' (29:15).

By the time when the New Testament was written almost

the whole of the written legislation of Ancient Israel had solidified as 'the Law of Moses'. In the gospel of John (10:34; 15:25), even psalms are quoted as 'the Law'. In theory at any rate, every regulation now possessed the same authority, so that a vast amount of ingenuity had to be exercised by the teachers of the Law in reconciling all the regulations with each other and with practical problems. But the New Testament also shows how Jesus of Nazareth and Paul of Tarsus wrestled with the difficulties inflicted by this tradition on the intelligence and the conscience. Was the whole Law equally authoritative? Was some of it (such as the provision for divorce) only given as a temporary concession to the hardness of men's hearts? Was some of it not meant to be obeyed literally, such as the complete prohibition of work on Saturday (the Sabbath)? Was some of it meant mainly to arouse the sense of sin, rather than to guide life? Jesus, Paul, and the early Christians not only felt compelled to separate the 'Law of Moses' from the more elaborate traditions developed by the teachers of the Law. They also felt obliged to exercise their judgement on the 'Law of Moses' itself.

Essentially the same task is ours. We must discriminate. There is no other way of seeing what were the purposes of these laws, and what are the points of contact with our own needs.

LAWS FOR FARMERS

We therefore make a brief study of five collections of laws in the Old Testament, against their historical backgrounds. The first collection was put together in the tenth century BC, probably under Solomon. It is the only collection of laws given to us by the historical tradition called J (see page 201). Found in Exodus 34: 10–26, it has a striking unity – for it consists entirely of echoes of the great battle against the Canaanite fertility cults in Palestine.

'You shall demolish their altars . . . You shall not pros-

trate yourselves to any other god . . . You shall not make
yourselves gods of cast metal.' These were battle-cries; and
the mysterious prohibition 'You shall not boil a kid in its
mother's milk' probably prohibits the imitation of a
practice in Canaanite magic.

Other laws give the positive side. Three 'pilgrim-feasts'
are mentioned 'when all your males shall come into the
presence of Yahweh', to sacrifice at a shrine. There is
'Unleavened Bread', when any remnant of the old leaven
for baking is to be thrown away as a sign that the winter is
over. There is 'Weeks' or the firstfruits of the wheat crop
(later more familiar from Greek as 'Pentecost' and in
Hebrew as *Shavuos*). There is 'Ingathering' or the harvest
festival when the last of the grapes becomes wine and the
last of the other fruit is stored safely. There is also a brief
reference to the pilgrim-feast of Passover, without explanation.

In addition to such celebrations with his neighbours
before his God, the farmer is to make regular sacrifices of
wealth and time to Yahweh. 'Every first birth of the womb
belongs' to God, and is to be sacrificed – although an
animal is to be killed instead of the first-born son, and a
sheep instead of the first-born ass. And a day is also to be
sacrificed regularly. 'On the seventh day you shall cease
work; even at ploughing time and harvest you shall cease
work.'

Another small collection of laws similarly brings before
us the daily life of the Israelite farmer (Deuteronomy 27:
15–26). This collection, however, concerns not public acts
of worship but private behaviour.

It takes the form of curses to be uttered on malefactors
when the tribes of Israel gather for their festival at Shechem
(see page 70). Although in its present form this collection
is included in *Deuteronomy*, a book edited some six hundred
years BC, it may well be five hundred years older. It curses
the man who 'carves an idol or casts an image . . . in secret',
but that is the only curse which deals with what we call

religion. Some of the curses prohibit incest; another is directed against 'him who lies with any animal'. The man 'who slights his father or his mother' is blasted. So is the man 'who moves his neighbour's boundary stone'. So is the man who misdirects a blind man or who withholds justice from the alien, the orphan, and the widow. The man who strikes another is condemned even though it is 'in secret'; so is the man who takes a reward to kill another, even before a murder occurs. The people who framed these curses worshipped a God who knew the heart's secrets.

THE BOOK OF THE COVENANT

A more substantial collection of laws is called by modern scholars the *Book of the Covenant*. It is found in *Exodus* (chapters 20–23) and belongs to the historical tradition called E (see page 206). It was put together not later than the eighth century BC. Like the collections which we have already noticed, it reflects the ordered life of agriculture. It is, however, likely that some of these laws do go back to Moses in the wilderness, or to the early 'judges' who led the settlement in Palestine. Certainly it starts with a reminder of those days: 'I am Yahweh your God who brought you out of Egypt . . .' .

The Ten Commandments which form the preface to this collection proclaim many of the same prohibitions that we have already met. 'You shall have no other god' – and therefore no carved image (of any god, or to be on the safe side, of any man, bird, animal, or fish that might be taken as a god). 'Remember to keep the sabbath day holy.' 'Honour your father and your mother.' 'You shall not covet your neighbour's house' – or his wife, slave, or property. Other commandments are equally firm: no wrong use of Yahweh's name in oaths, no false evidence against your neighbour, no murder, no adultery, no theft. In no way is the fellow-Israelite to be cheated or damaged. Why not? He worships the same God!

The *Book of the Covenant* shows the simple, moral character of this worship – with altars made of earth or rough stones in many local shrines, 'wherever I cause my name to be invoked'. It shows also how strong was the demand for fair dealing and brotherhood among the worshippers. If the first collection which we considered preserves echoes of the battles of Elijah against the Canaanite fertility cults, we may say that this collection is on the same moral level as the prophetic books of Amos and Hosea. A fellow-Israelite who needs a loan is to be given one without interest. If he has pawned his cloak, it is to be returned by sunset, 'because it is his only covering'. If he has got so deeply into debt that he has had to accept enslavement he is to be freed after six years, with his wife – unless 'the slave should say, I love my master.' Such laws of Ancient Israel destroy the whole network of exploitation which elsewhere has so often enabled rich farmers to make debtors and serfs of their poorer neighbours.

Just as impressive is the respect for the honour of all Israelites shown in the regulations about crime. Of course the *Book of the Covenant* is not unique in this attitude. In *Genesis* (9:6) is preserved a formula which some scholars believe was recited as the death sentence for murder was being carried out:

> He that sheds the blood of a man,
> for that man his blood shall be shed;
> for in the image of God
> has God made man.

But a study of the *Book of the Covenant* is of special interest here. Scholars have been able to trace many fairly close parallels between these regulations and earlier law-codes of the Ancient Middle East. It is clear that the Israelites copied much of the law, as well as much of the religion, of the Canaanites; and no doubt other laws came from other external sources. But some important features of Israel's criminal law were definitely in contrast with other codes –

for example, with the famous Code of Hammurabi, king of Babylon, promulgated in 1791 BC and discovered by a French archaeologist in AD 1901. And these features stress the equal dignity of all the Israelites.

No mention is made of a king or of a state to enforce the laws gathered in the *Book of the Covenant*. They are to be enforced by the Israelite tribesmen acting together. We could call such a society a democracy, were it not so plainly a theocracy, a people putting themselves under the government of God.

There are no class distinctions in Israel's laws. Although Hammurabi protected his aristocrats and his ordinary citizens differently, in the *Book of the Covenant* one man's loss deserves exactly the same compensation as every other man's. There is a stern emphasis on justice for the weak. 'You shall not wrong an alien, or be hard upon him; you were yourselves aliens in Egypt. You shall not ill-treat any widow or fatherless child. If you do, be sure that I will listen if they appeal to me; my anger will be roused and I will kill you with the sword; your own wives shall become widows and your children fatherless.'

In Israel's laws no general use was made of the punishment of mutilation. It was tempting for ancient legislators to use this punishment, for most malefactors did not have enough money to pay any sizeable fine and most societies could not afford to maintain elaborate prisons. But in Ancient Israel chopping off a limb of a thief was rejected as an infringement of human dignity. It is unfair to view the famous *lex talionis* as an example of primitive brutality. 'Wherever hurt is done, you shall give life for life, eye for eye, tooth for tooth, hand for hand, foot for foot, burn for burn, bruise for bruise, wound for wound.' That law is, on the contrary, an example of rough justice to deter the hot-tempered Israelites from doing physical damage to each other – for each is a man in the image of God. And it says: only *one* eye, only *one* tooth!

Very often in these regulations we glimpse a society

which is too rough to be humane as modern civilization understands that term, but which certainly is a brotherhood to a degree seldom seen in the ancient world – or in the modern. When a man takes to his bed as a result of a brawl, the man who hit him 'shall pay for loss of time and shall see that he is cured'. When a man's ox or ass strays and is found by an enemy, that enemy is to take it back to him. When a virgin is seduced she is to be married with a proper bride-price, or her father is to receive the bride-price as compensation. But when a man kills another without intent, he is not to be executed as a murderer; 'the slayer may flee to a place which I will appoint for you.' And when a man fatally injures a burglar, he is not to be reckoned a murderer – if the burglar broke in by night. There is no penalty of death or mutilation for theft. Such laws of Ancient Israel were more humane than the laws of England at the beginning of the nineteenth century AD. Unfortunately, however, the word 'brotherhood' is accurate in a limiting sense. Women had few legal rights in Ancient Israel – fewer than in Babylon or Egypt.

But we have still not mentioned the most important point about this *Book of the Covenant* as it can be seen in the light of modern scholarship. It is a covenant or agreement like a treaty between an emperor or other overlord and his vassal-king in a satellite state. It begins with a reminder of why the lesser king depends on the greater ('I am Yahweh your God who brought you out of Egypt . . .'). It states clearly what the lesser king may and may not do. It warns of the penalties for any breach of this treaty, and it promises rewards for obedience. A treaty dictated by an overlord – that is the character of this whole collection of detailed and diverse laws.

Modern scholars have drawn attention to the fact that some of the laws are categorical ('You shall . . .' or 'You shall not . . .'), while others are 'casuistic' or expressed in terms of possible cases ('When a man . . .'). The categorical laws are the more solemn and religious; during an act of worship a direct order is being given by God's representative, without any ifs or buts. The other class of laws ('When a man . . .') grows, rather, out of daily experience; if some problem arises, this is the way to deal with it. It is likely that most regulations in the latter category were taken over from customs which the Israelites found established in Canaan. But both categories have been joined in this *Book of the Covenant*. From first to last, all these laws to preserve the Israelite brotherhood are presented as the decrees of the divine emperor.

THE CODE OF DEUTERONOMY

About half of the laws gathered in the *Book of the Covenant* are repeated in the *Code of Deuteronomy* (meaning the 'second law'). Since AD 1805 this code has been recognized as the nucleus of the book discovered in the Jerusalem temple in 622–21 BC (see page 143). It was later included after some editing in *Deuteronomy* (chapters 12–26). The publication of this book caused the religious revolution under King Josiah, but its ideals outlived Josiah.

The most striking innovation is that far more severe measures are taken against heathen worship. This code is meant to be, at long last, the decisive blow in the centuries-old struggle against Canaanite religion. It also replies to the recent invasion of the Jewish heritage by the religion, as well as by the armies, of the Assyrian empire. It takes some steps which we must call desperate, but modern archaeology has supplied evidence which helps us to understand the mood of these laws.

In many Palestinian sites, including some near the Jerusalem temple, little statues have been found – sexually suggestive statues, for they are the symbols of the nude mother-goddess of fertility. They are souvenirs of the worship which these laws tried to ban for ever. At Elephantine in the south of Egypt the records of a Jewish temple have been found, mostly dating from the fifth century.

These records show that at Elephantine regular sacrifices were offered both to 'Yahu' (Yahweh) and also to goddesses bearing the Canaanite names Ishum-bethel, Anath-bethel and Herem-bethel. One goddess actually has the name Anath-yahu, which seems to indicate that she was regarded as Yahweh's wife. In other words, at Elephantine the religion of Yahweh had become little different from the heathen worship of many gods, worship with a sexual content. But there is much evidence in the Old Testament that heathen worship took place in the Jerusalem temple itself. King Ahaz is criticized as having rearranged the temple in the Assyrian style (2 Kings 16:10–20) – and is said to have sacrificed his own sons in heathen rites in the nearby Valley of Hinnom (2 Chronicles 28:3). The altar was removed by his successor, but Ezekiel tells us that he saw in the temple 'figures of reptiles, beasts, and vermin, and all the idols of the Israelites', with 'women sitting and wailing for Tammuz' (a fertility rite) and 'men prostrating themselves to the rising sun' (chapter 8).

The *Code of Deuteronomy* strictly forbids all sacrifices except in 'the place which Yahweh your God will choose out of all your tribes to receive his name that it may dwell there'. This place is not named. If, as modern scholars believe, the Code was compiled largely in the northern kingdom, the original intention was presumably to give the monopoly to one of the northern shrines. In that case the obvious place is Shechem, named as the setting for the recitation of laws (11:26–32; chapter 27). However, by the time that the book was published after the fall of the northern kingdom, only one real possibility remained: Jerusalem itself, already the centre of the worship patronized by the House of David and the holy city of Isaiah's prophecy.

This prohibition of local sacrifices reflects the reformers' despair at the possibility of ending the temptations and scandals involved. Even now, the prohibition was not effective outside Palestine: the temple at Elephantine shows that, and was probably not unique. In Palestine the veto was obeyed for a time, so far as we know. When the Jerusalem temple lies in ruins, we meet eighty men from Shechem, Shiloh, and Samaria. 'They had shaved off their beards, their clothes were rent and their bodies gashed, and they were carrying grain-offerings and frankincense to take to the house of Yahweh' (Jeremiah 41:5) – surely one of the most pathetic of all pilgrimages to Jerusalem. But in the end the *Code of Deuteronomy* proved unrealistic at this point, even within Palestine. Every village came to have its own synagogue where no sacrifices were performed but where a sincere piety was nourished and expressed. *Deuteronomy* had left a religious vacuum which the synagogue filled. And even that was not enough. As we have seen (page 167), at an uncertain date the Samaritans, who for largely political reasons disliked going on pilgrimage to Jerusalem, built their own temple for sacrifices on Mount Gerizim, very near the old shrine at Shechem. The centralization of worship in Jerusalem had turned out to be all too disastrously a policy of despair.

The same despair is seen in other measures against heathen worship. Already Exodus 22:20 had decreed: 'Whoever sacrifices to any god but Yahweh shall be put to death.' But the *Code of Deuteronomy* demands in remorseless detail the extermination of all who worship heathen gods. A prophet who 'calls on you to follow other gods' incurs the death penalty for so preaching; and all the peoples living in the land before the Israelites are simply to be destroyed. The only excuse that can be offered nowadays for this policy of genocide is that it seemed at the time to be justified as the only hope of preserving the pure worship of Yahweh not only against the lures of Canaanite magic and fertility cults but also against the power and propaganda of the Assyrian empire. Our only consolation for the presence of such a savage commandment in the Bible is that it was never carried fully into effect. In practice the Jews have always had to live alongside neighbours of other origins. They have never been able to make themselves clean by a bloodbath,

any more than their neighbours have been able to reach a
final solution by Auschwitz.

The second great difference between the *Code of Deuteronomy* and the earlier *Book of the Covenant* is happier. For
Deuteronomy enters greater depths as it describes the
society that Yahweh wants Israel to be: 'You are the sons
of Yahweh your God . . . You are a people holy to Yahweh
your God.'

Like the earlier codes, this *Code of Deuteronomy* lists the
festivals in the farmer's year. But they have ceased to be the
festivals of the home and the tribe; instead, 'three times a
year all your males shall come into the presence of Yahweh
your God in the place which he will choose.' These festivals
are to have their centres firmly in the temple, and their
themes firmly in the nation's holiness.

The two spring festivals of Passover and Unleavened
Bread are now joined together and are made into 'Yahweh's
Passover', a temple sacrifice commemorating the deliverance of Israel from Egypt. At each Passover meal after the
sacrifice, a son of the family is to ask the meaning of the
feast. The formula to be used in reply, recalling the Exodus,
is set out (6:20–25). Passover was, it seems, originally a
family feast when a lamb of the new flock was eaten and
blood was smeared over the tent as a magical practice to
ward off evil from the family and the flock. Unleavened
Bread was associated with the time when 'you went out
from Egypt' as early as Exodus 34:18, but that feast seems
to have originated as neighbouring farmers gathered to
celebrate the barley harvest. Now the *Code of Deuteronomy*
nationalizes both days and makes them one, with one
spiritual meaning.

The plan in *Deuteronomy* that all male Israelites should
worship together in the Jerusalem temple at Passover was
never realistic. But it had a permanent effect. For centuries
before Jesus was crucified outside Jerusalem at Passover-
time, the city would be crowded with pilgrims to this feast;
and more than nineteen centuries after that crucifixion, all

devout Jews still observe the rites of Passover at home according to the *Code of Deuteronomy*. If they have to keep the feast outside the holy city, they end by voicing the hope: 'Next year in Jerusalem!'

The ideal of the holy nation is pursued in detailed regulations about what food may be eaten as 'clean'. Some of these regulations seem to be fairly new; for example, it is thought that the prohibition of pork may have originated in the fact that the Canaanites often sacrificed boars and consumed the flesh. Some regulations, old or new, are hygienic. Others are so ancient that no explanation can be given why a certain food is forbidden or 'taboo'. The insistence that 'You must strictly refrain from eating the blood, because the blood is the life' may have been hygienic in origin; more probably, however, it is an attack on the Canaanite idea that the power of an animal could be absorbed by eating its more or less raw carcass (a common notion in ancient magic).

Other regulations witness to a growing sense of the dignity of individual Israelites. Floggings are never to exceed forty strokes; 'otherwise . . . your fellow-countryman will have been publicly degraded.' The sense of an individual's responsibility is clearer. 'Fathers shall not be put to death for their children, nor children for their fathers; a man shall be put to death only for his own sin.' At other places *Deuteronomy* becomes positively tender. 'When a man is newly married, he shall not be liable for military service or any other public duty. He shall remain at home exempt from service for one year and enjoy the wife he has taken.' 'When you make a loan to another man, do not enter his house to take a pledge from him' – and never accept a millstone in pawn; it is too precious to its owner. When you build a new house put a parapet along the roof to prevent accidents.' This tender spirit extends to birds and animals. 'When you come across a bird's nest by the road . . . do not take both mother and young.' 'You shall not muzzle an ox while it is treading out the corn.'

Some laws in this code show that affluence has brought its evils. More careful provision has to be made for divorce – but a man who has to marry a girl he has seduced is never free to divorce her. There has to be a law about the remission of money debts at the end of every seventh year, and another to provide for the appointment of professional judges. Provision is made for the election of a king, but it is a grudging provision. 'You shall appoint over you a man of your own race . . . He shall not acquire many horses, nor, to add to his horses, shall he cause the people to go back to Egypt' – in other words, back to slavery. 'He shall not acquire many wives and so be led astray; nor shall he acquire great quantities of silver and gold for himself.' In the circles behind the *Code of Deuteronomy* the age of Solomon was never idealized. They knew too much about kings.

To the men who compiled these laws, the growing complications in the life of society seemed to call not for a growing cynicism or ruthlessness, but for growth and elaboration in the application of honest justice. The fervour with which they preached this message almost burns the page. 'You shall not pervert the course of justice or show favour, nor shall you accept a bribe; for bribery makes the wise man blind and the just man give a crooked answer. Justice, and justice alone, you shall pursue, so that you may live and occupy the land which Yahweh your God is giving you.'

The *Code of Deuteronomy* goes deeper than the *Book of the Covenant* because it tries to reach the heart. It is to be read aloud at a great festival of all Israel every seven years. Its laws call for the response of the heart: 'Be careful to observe them with all your heart and soul.' They echo Elijah and Amos, and probably they echo Hosea, Micah, and Isaiah. One passage contrasts the Canaanite soothsayers with the true prophets. Moses assures the future: 'Yahweh your God will raise up a prophet from among you like myself, and you shall listen to him' – a promise which came to have a special meaning for the early Christians. The law-giver here tackles the question: how are we to distinguish between the true prophet and the false? The answer is simple. 'When the word spoken by the prophet . . . does not come true, it is not a word spoken by Yahweh.' When that passage was written, Israel had learned how to distinguish true prophecy from false by the lessons of some tragic history.

These laws, like those prophets, constantly bear witness to the vigorous, dominant activity of Yahweh. Like the *Book of the Covenant*, the *Code of Deuteronomy* includes the Ten Commandments – but in a slightly different version, and separated from the main collection of laws.

The existence of two versions shows that the original was expanded in two ways, and the most interesting difference concerns the reason given for rest on Saturday (the Sabbath day). In Exodus 20:11 we read: 'for in six days Yahweh made heaven and earth, the sea, and all that is in them, and on the seventh day he rested.' Not for *Deuteronomy* the idea of God or anyone else resting! In Deuteronomy 5:15 we read: 'Remember that you were slaves in Egypt and Yahweh your God brought you out with a strong hand and an outstretched arm, and for that reason Yahweh your God commanded you to keep the sabbath day.' The God of *Deuteronomy* is incessantly at work looking after his people, and it is for this reason that he has a right to be worshipped incessantly and exclusively.

This code of laws supplies its own summary: the *Shema*, quoted by Jesus (Mark 12:30) as the summary of man's whole duty to God and recited by all devout Jews daily. 'Hear, O Israel, Yahweh is our God, one Yahweh, and you must love Yahweh your God with all your heart and soul and strength.'

THE LAW OF HOLINESS

The last collection of laws which we shall study comes from the time when the prophet's warnings to the northern and southern kingdoms had all been fulfilled, and the upper class of the Jews was in exile. This collection, first recognized as such in 1877, is called the *Law of Holiness*. It is preserved after some editing in *Leviticus* (chapters 17–26), and is closely associated with the historical tradition called P (see page 214).

The key fact about these laws is that they were compiled by exiled priests. Although the kingdoms of Israel and Judah are no more, in the vision of these exiles the land is clothed with the beauty of holiness. 'You shall be holy because I, Yahweh your God, am holy' – that refrain is repeated. The holiness embraces the practical life of a layman. Here, indeed, is the one law which is used by Jesus to sum up the whole duty of man to man: 'You shall love your neighbour as a man like yourself.' And it is instructive to notice the context of this law. It comes immediately after a warning not to seek revenge or cherish anger against a fellow-Israelite – the 'neighbour' whom these priests have in mind. And in practical neighbourliness, a little earlier the farmer has been told not to reap right to the edges of a field, nor glean the fallen grapes, so as to leave something for the poor. A little later a man who has had sexual intercourse with another man's slave-girl is told how to make expiation. But very clearly the main concern of the *Law of Holiness* is purity in the worship of Yahweh.

In keeping with the *Code of Deuteronomy*, this worship is centralized in the Jerusalem temple – or rather (since the convention has to be maintained that it is Moses who is speaking) in the 'Tent of the Presence' or the 'Tabernacle of Yahweh' in the wilderness. Any Israelite who slaughters an ox, sheep, or goat and does not bring it to this tent 'shall be held guilty of bloodshed . . . and shall be cut off from his people'. At the tent he is to hand the animal over to a priest; the practice of a layman sacrificing, for which there is evidence earlier in the Old Testament, is now strictly forbidden. The Levites, formerly priests at the local shrines,

are now put firmly in their places as assistants to the
Zadokite clan who are given a monopoly of the priesthood.

As we have seen, the *Code of Deuteronomy* transformed the
spring festivals into 'Yahweh's Passover' in Jerusalem.
Now the *Law of Holiness* regulated the autumn feast of
Tabernacles. It had been a merry harvest festival when the
Israelites had camped out beneath the trees whose fruit
they were gathering and had sampled the new wine. In
these new laws it became another pilgrimage to the holy
city. The booths were no longer to be fruit-pickers' huts;
they were to be sacred reminders of the tents which Israel
had used in the wilderness under Moses. Fortunately,
however, the joy of Tabernacles (in Hebrew *Sukos*) has
been preserved by Jews into our own time, and a spray of
citron, palm, myrtle, and willow leaves is carried by the
worshipper in the synagogue. This is the feast which Jesus
keeps in Jerusalem in chapters 7 and 8 of John's gospel.

In the *Law of Holiness* a new day was added to the
religious year: the Day of Atonement (*Yom Kippur*). Its
introduction very clearly illustrates the growth of the sense
of guilt. It is to be a day of fasting and prayer by sinners:
'you shall mortify yourselves and do no work because it is a
day of expiation.' Two he-goats are to be taken. One,
chosen by lot, is to be burned as a sacrifice to Yahweh: it is
the 'sin-offering'. The other is to be driven into the wilderness, taking away the sins of the people: it is the 'scape-
goat'.

Such laws take on a further significance once we ponder
the fact (or at least the probability) that at the time when
the *Law of Holiness* was compiled the Jerusalem temple lay
in ruins. An exile's homesickness produces a longing to be
together in worship – to be together, and at last to be pure,
liberated from the uncleanness and guilt felt everywhere in
a foreign land. The *Law of Holiness* brings out poignantly
the problem of preserving Israel's purity and identity now
that the Jews had to mix with many peoples in exile. 'I am
Yahweh your God: I have made a clear separation between

you and the nations, and you shall make a clear separation between clean beasts and unclean beasts.'

From the homesick priest's longing to offer in the Jerusalem temple the pure sacrifices of a holy people grows the dream of a holy land – a land of brotherhood under the holy God.

Previous collections of laws had freed Israelite slaves every seven years ('man or woman' adds the *Code of Deuteronomy*). But now this *Law of Holiness* completely prohibits the enslavement of Israelites. 'When your brother is reduced to poverty and sells himself to you, you shall not use him to work for you as a slave. His status shall be that of a hired man or a stranger lodging with you.' And in the year of 'jubilee' (so called from the Hebrew for 'trumpet') he, too, is to return to his father's land.

An even more dramatic trumpet-call for equality can be heard in what the *Law of Holiness* says about landownership. Every fiftieth year, when the trumpets sound every Israelite is to return to the field tilled by his ancestors, his once more without payment. Between such jubilees the Israelite is to be free to sell this land, but always the next-of-kin is to have the first option. Never is there to be hard bargaining by next-of-kin or stranger, and always when any sale is made it must be subject to the return of the land in the jubilee. The God of Israel watches over all transactions as the only ultimate owner of his holy land: 'no land shall be sold outright, because the land is mine.'

This was an extension of a law in the *Book of the Covenant*, repeated in the *Code of Deuteronomy*: the sabbath year for the land. Every seventh year the land was to lie fallow. The farmer was neither to sow nor to reap, but was to live off the extra harvest promised every sixth year. We should say that the aim of this law was not to exhaust the soil. The *Law of Holiness* declared that it was to acknowledge the landownership of Yahweh.

The evidence suggests, however, that these laws about the holy land were ideals never completely established. A reference to 163–62 BC (1 Maccabees 6:49–53) is the first clear record of the enforcement of the sabbath year of rest for the land – and it resulted in a lack of provisions. Even those stern reformers, Nehemiah and Ezra, make no mention of any attempt to enforce the law of the jubilee year. However, we are told that the people agreed with Nehemiah to 'forgo the crops of the seventh year' (10:31), and according to Josephus both Alexander the Great and Julius Caesar remitted taxes in this sabbath year.

This *Law of Holiness* put in unmistakable language the consequence of Israel's past failures to live up to such ideals of purity and brotherhood. The consequence was exile. These priests hear the thunder of Yahweh: 'If you . . . defy me, I will defy you in anger, and I myself will punish you seven times over for your sins. Instead of meat you shall eat your sons and your daughters . . . I will pile your rotting carcasses on the rotting logs that were your idols . . . I will scatter you among the heathen . . . And I will make those of you who are left in the land of your enemies so ridden with fear, when a leaf flutters behind them in the wind, they shall run as if it were the sword behind them; they shall fall with no one in pursuit . . . You shall meet your end among the heathen . . .'

But that horrifying account of a people's total breakdown is not quite the end. We read: 'If then their stubborn spirit is broken and they accept their punishment in full, I will remember my covenant with Jacob and my covenant with Isaac, yes, and my covenant with Abraham, and I will remember the land.' This *Law of Holiness* – in its tragic atmosphere so different from the earlier laws – belongs to the same world as Jeremiah and Ezekiel.

THE MEANING OF THE LAWS

This, then, was the Law in the Old Testament. But everything we have learned points to the wrongness of thinking about it too simply as 'the Law'. Not only does it come

from different dates and circumstances – at one time limiting the enslavement of Israelites and at another prohibiting
it altogether. It also touches many matters which no modern
law could notice. The first code which we examined did
public battle for Yahweh against the Canaanite fertility
gods; and even if a modern legislature could be persuaded
to deal with religion in such a manner, it certainly could
never enact the second code, cursing those whose thoughts
were evil. The *Book of the Covenant*, the *Code of Deuteronomy*,
and the *Law of Holiness* are all, as we have seen, a strange
mixture of legislation and preaching; the legal reflection of
prophecy, the manifesto of a reformation, the Utopia of
exiled priests. Although the phrase 'the Law' has no doubt
come to stay, a better name for the whole collection is the
Hebrew term *Torah*, which is still used by Jews for this
purpose. The term is not easily translated, but its meaning
is nearer 'Teaching' than 'Law'.

Liberal Jews, and non-Jews such as Christians and
Muslims, are agreed that the religious and moral regulations in this *Torah* do not all possess a permanently binding
authority; and orthodox Jews have through the centuries
devoted immense piety, learning, and ingenuity to interpreting and applying them afresh in changing circumstances. Only a fanatical minority in the modern state of
Israel wishes to resurrect the civil and criminal laws. Yet
all these biblical laws, of all kinds, have a meaning if we
see them as evidence of the spiritual and moral struggles of
different generations in Ancient Israel's history – and as a
challenge to order our own societies in accordance with
certain basic principles.

This *Torah* was surely right to mix the personal and the
social. It permanently rebukes the tendency to confine
morality to private life, leaving business and politics to the
laws of the jungle; and to confine religion to spiritual
insights and emotional experiences, throwing the institutions of society to the wolves. The *Torah* enacts one law which
in every generation needs repeating to starry-eyed idealists:

a law against escapism. It seeks justice in every part of the struggle of man in society. It affirms that, to be healthy, human life needs to be ordered in all its expressions on a basis which takes account both of the brutality and of the glory of human nature.

The *Torah* also rebukes the cynics. Any people needs a unity of purpose, a dedication to a goal beyond the day-to-day conflicts and compromises. This corporate goal needs to be expressed in rituals as well as in speeches, in laws as well as in art or music. If religion or politics or economics cannot provide a strong sense of corporate identity, then a society will have to try to be content with enthusiasm for sport or entertainment – but a unity of purpose it simply must have. The people of Ancient Israel had such a unity, being driven forward by their conviction of their destiny as the people of God. Yahweh had brought them out of Egypt and had made a treaty with them. He had given them their land with all its fertility, but as they used the land they regarded him as its only owner in the last analysis. They felt called to be a holy people in a holy land, although they were ruthless in describing their failures. And at least occasionally, they had a glimpse of a God who gave an exodus to every people, even to the Philistines and Aramaeans (see page 94); and a moral law to every people, even to Edom or Moab (see page 135), even to all the sons of Noah (see page 215).

That was a long time ago. But in the twentieth century all strong societies still rest on a fundamental agreement about purposes and values. Communists certainly believe so – and do their utmost to build new societies on the basis of the Marxist creed. One of the supreme questions of the twentieth century is whether there is any viable alternative to Communism as the inspiration of a strong modern society. The Old Testament is a reminder that religion has been extremely powerful in expressing the purposes and values of past societies; and our knowledge of the modern world shows that religion has by no means lost all this historic power. For those who refuse to accept that a strong society must be Godless, the task is to work out modern equivalents of the Old Testament Law.

If that seems a frightening task, we need to learn one last lesson from those so-called 'laws'. The men who framed them did not hesitate to grapple with areas which might very easily have been considered as beyond Yahweh's reach. These laws, practical or ideal, drove into the farmer's daily life the acknowledgement of Yahweh as the sole fertilizer and owner of the land – first in defiance of the established and seductive Canaanite religion, then in defiance of all the trends concentrating landownership in the hands of the rich. Every area of life was claimed for Yahweh, from sex to birds' nesting. And this *Torah* refused to stop at people's public behaviour. It attempted to probe secret malice and to pierce the heart with the commandments of God. Finally, it refused to accept as decisive the destruction of the whole framework of national life. In defeat and exile it carried on. In the centuries of Judaism after the Old Testament period it still carried on, producing varied schools and movements of rabbis to apply the Law to new problems, evoking an immense richness of oral teaching which from time to time would be ordered and sifted in a new written code. This Jewish tradition of law-making austerely condemned the Israel that had been – but it still dreamed of the Israel that might be, delighting to create fresh institutions with their accompanying laws. At its best it has been, and it is, a tradition dedicated to behaviour, the other three-quarters of religion; and to justice, the other three-quarters of love.

CHAPTER 8

A People's Histories

THE INTERPRETATION OF THE PAST

That Napoleon failed to unite Europe because he lost a series of battles, of which the most notable was Waterloo, is a matter of fact. Whether this was a good thing or a bad thing is a matter of opinion. It is certain that Captain Cook discovered New South Wales, at least so far as the Royal Navy was concerned. But what 'Australia' means is a question on which opinions will differ and change. So every generation needs its new biography of Napoleon and its new history of Australia – and would need it, even if historical research did not progress.

Every people sees its past in the light of its present, and by that interpretation is helped to build its future. The story of America, for example, has usually been told in terms of the frontier and the manifest destiny of the United States, and countless Americans have drawn pride from that telling of their story. When the American dream enters a period of disillusionment, the past is interpreted again; now history is seen from the point of view of the man at the bottom of the pile, even from the point of view of the Red Indian. The presentation of British history has similarly been in terms of the growth of the United Kingdom and of the British Empire at heaven's command. When the map of the world has been redrawn, and when the wish of the English, the Scots, the Welsh, and the Irish to stay together is in open dispute, the history books are rewritten. In many nations history has often been presented as a series of episodes in the lives of monarchs, or as one long example of the rise of the middle class – until there is a shift of power in society, and now, like the crowds in Red Square, the text books cheer the armed march past of the proletariat.

The Old Testament shows the Israelites and Jews interpreting and reinterpreting their past in the light of changing
events. In that they were no exception to the general rule of
large-scale history-making. What was exceptional about
the authors of the Old Testament, however, was the religious passion which they brought to the business. To them,
giving an account of the past was a duty which they owed
to Yahweh and his people, precisely because it was in the
history of his people that Yahweh had revealed who he was.
The Old Testament is accordingly a rich library of history
books, in many places telling us as much about their
authors as about the events they narrate. It was appropriate
that when the Jewish rabbis classified their scriptures into
'the Law, the Prophets, and the Writings', they did not
group the histories with the 'Writings' such as the psalms
and the wisdom literature. These historians were called
'the Former Prophets'.

An essential tool in the modern understanding of the
Old Testament is the knowledge that large parts of it are
the work of five major historians – the Yahwist, the Elohist,
the Deuteronomist, the Priest, and the Chronicler.

Unfortunately it is not possible to give these historians
more attractive names. We do not know what their proper
names were; nor do we know how many people have contributed to the making of the material finally assembled by
the editor whom we meet as the historian. We discern that
there is this distinctive material because the final editor has
left distinctive characteristics in it. One tradition calls God
'Yahweh'; the second calls him 'Elohim'; the third is
marked by the same attitudes as *Deuteronomy*; the fourth has
the same outlook as the priestly *Law of Holiness*; the fifth
comes after the codification of 'the Law' and the regulation
of the Jerusalem temple by Ezra.

For many centuries, the understanding that there were
five different historical traditions in the Old Testament was
lost. The recovery of this knowledge was one of the great

triumphs of German scholarship in the nineteenth century. When we ask why the composition of the Old Testament was so little understood for so long – although it was very often studied with great care and reverence – there are several explanations. It all became sacred literature, so that its real author was believed to be God and men thought it blasphemous to probe the ways in which its human authors had set to work. But even had Jews or Christians probed questions of authorship with modern instruments of scholarly investigation, they would have found not five personalities of individual historians, great authors to set beside Herodotus, Thucydides, Tacitus, Gibbon, and Macaulay. They would have found five traditions to which very large numbers of people had contributed, often by word of mouth. Indeed, a main tendency of twentieth-century Old Testament scholarship has been to correct the emphasis of the nineteenth-century scholars on literary 'sources'; present-day investigators concentrate more on the *oral* tradition before a word was written down, and on the *communal* nature of all this history-making.

Another reason why the process of history-making was forgotten is that the Old Testament is the work of editors who wove the various traditions together. We can understand why such a harmony of various histories was for so long regarded as a single narrative. Fortunately, however, the editorial skill of those who compiled the Old Testament which we possess did not extend to destroying all traces of the separate traditions. Only on a casual or uncritical reading does what they edited read like one story. Closer examination detects innumerable places where separate – indeed, sometimes contradictory – traditions have been joined. The cracks are still there as clues to the process.

Fortunately, too, three of these historians – the Yahwist, the Elohist, and the Priest – prefaced their histories of Israel with some stories about the dawn of history. These chapters are not 'history' in the modern sense. But each of these men retold the ancient sagas, or added new ones, in a way which

was thoroughly characteristic of his own tradition. In
telling about what happened once upon a time, he showed
himself.

THE J TRADITION: EMPIRE AND UNDERSTANDING

The earliest historian whom we shall consider here is called
the Yahwist or J, but he is no isolated individual. This is a
school or tradition of history-making, edited in the tenth or
ninth century BC in identifiable circumstances.

Just as the success of England in the Elizabethan Age
prompted Shakespeare's historical plays and a library of
historical books which Shakespeare and his contemporaries
enjoyed, and just as the empire of Augustus inspired Virgil
and Livy, so the empire-building of David and Solomon
sparked off a new pride. Stories were gathered in order to
tell how the people of Israel had risen to this height. They
were old stories, but often clumsily old: they needed to be
retold with a young zest or elegance. Twentieth-century
scholars have sometimes felt able to detect some distinct
sources within this tradition – as Shakespeare's plays can
be taken apart to show the sources. One passage in J seems
to praise the nomadic life rather than agriculture; another
story seems to be told from the layman's point of view, not
the priest's; and so suggestions are made that here is
evidence of a source earlier than the rest of the Yahwist's
work. Whatever we make of such guesses, we must avoid
the error of thinking of one author building his history on
his own original research into the evidence. This history is
the creation of a whole people over whole centuries; and it
belongs to the camp fire, not to the library. It belongs to a
people which, like Shakespeare's audience in the Globe or
Virgil's hearers at recitals in Rome, drank in their past and
felt themselves heroes.

The Yahwist is so called since he uses Israel's own name
for God. Because in places the emphasis seems to be on the
south rather than the north, it has been suggested that this

book was compiled in the kingdom of Judah rather than in that of Israel, but the evidence is not strong. If (as seems probable) J originally began with an account of the creation of the world this has been lost, and if (as is equally likely) J's original climax was the conquest of the Promised Land and the establishment of the monarchy, the narrative here has been so submerged beneath later writing as to be difficult or impossible to recognize. But enough remains to enable us to detect J's attitude as he uses the old material which he has gathered from the tradition of his people.

Some of the material is very old and comes from Mesopotamia, as we see when we are told that the four rivers flowing from the garden of Eden include the Tigris and the Euphrates. The garden is vaguely imagined to be among the mountains whose snows fed the great rivers of Mesopotamia. But next to this archaic map is an account of the creation and fall of Adam and Eve; and this account shows the psychological insights of the relatively sophisticated tenth or ninth century BC. Not for nothing do 'Adam' and 'Eve' come from Hebrew words meaning 'man' and 'life'; for J's stories are really about human existence.

To be sure, some of the material consists of ancient, widespread myths and even puns – the making of *adam* from the 'dust of the ground' (*adamah*); the breathing of life into the nostrils; the making of the woman from the man's rib; the magic garden ('paradise' comes from the Persian word for 'garden', and *eden* in Hebrew means 'bliss'); the sinister snake; the divine veto on man's attempt to know as much as the gods; man's disobedience, the divine wrath. But J's psychological insights add new points to these ancient stories. We notice that although woman is said to derive her being through man, in emotional reality man depends on woman, for Eve virtually tells Adam what to do. We notice how the crucial rebellion against authority comes with deciding for oneself what is right and what is wrong. That is what Eve suggests Adam should do – although originally the forbidden tree in the garden seems to have been a tree of knowledge, and 'knowing both good and evil' probably meant knowing both what is useful and what is harmful. We notice how the rebellion was made because evil was 'pleasing to the eye and tempting to contemplate'. Since sexual intercourse is the most vivid kind of knowledge – the Hebrew of Genesis 4:1 means literally 'the man knew his wife Eve' – we notice that the growth of sexual shame follows sin: 'they discovered that they were naked.' It is unlikely to be a coincidence that all these psychological insights into the influence of women, into the lure of rebellion, into beauty, sex, and shame are also prominent in the narrative of the succession to King David; that history was written at about the same time as J, quite possibly by one of the group behind J (see pages 53-7). Probably we are looking at Adam through the eyes of the contemporaries of Solomon.

It is entirely characteristic of J that the primitive, often crude tradition is mixed with the deep psychological insights. Thus Yahweh is heard 'walking in the garden at the time of the evening breeze'. But when Yahweh calls to man 'Where are you?' a deeper level is penetrated – the level where a man is addressed by his conscience inescapably, the level where in response a man blames a woman and she blames the power of evil. This Yahwist retells ancient explanations about why snakes have no legs, why women have labour pains, why men have to work so hard on the land, why nomadic shepherds are the enemies of settled farmers ('Abel was a shepherd and Cain a tiller of the soil'). But the stories contain insights into the sorrows of human existence – sorrows increased by men's habit of murdering each other, as Cain murders Abel. Behind the stories are to be found ancient attitudes – for example, that the sacrifices of Abel (a nomad like the original Hebrews) please Yahweh more than those of Cain (the ancestor of farmers such as the Canaanites). But here are also precious insights into the mercy of Yahweh. For man's sake this God of grace becomes a matchmaker ('It is not good for the man to be alone. I will provide a partner for him'), a tailor ('Yahweh made tunics of skins for Adam and his wife'), and a policeman ('Where is your brother Abel?'). Yahweh avenges the innocent man's blood which cries to him from the ground, but at the same time protects the murderer. Cain is condemned to be a desert outlaw ('you shall be a vagrant and a wanderer on earth'), yet is not completely outlawed (he is not to be killed); for Yahweh is his creator, too. In the end Cain becomes himself a Hebrew under Yahweh's protection.

In the primitive story, angels and a 'sword whirling and flashing' prevent man from ever returning to the happiness and innocence of Eden. But J assembles this traditional material in a way which is not innocent – which is, in fact, full of implied comments on civilization. The descendants of Adam include Jabal 'the ancestor of herdsmen who live in tents' and Jubal 'the ancestor of those who play the harp and pipe', with Tubal-cain 'the master of all coppersmiths and blacksmiths'. The first murderer was also, we are told, the first man to build a city. All human life is potentially there as Adam and Eve stumble into history; and all human life is still in touch with Yahweh (4:17–26).

We are given the old legend of intermarriage between the 'sons of the gods' and the 'beautiful daughters of men', with the comment that mingling of the divine and the human, this royal race of demi-gods, was nevertheless only 'mortal flesh' (6:1–4). We are given, too, the ancient myth of the flood, probably originating in the flooding of the Euphrates and the Tigris although similar myths are known in many other parts of the world. This myth has survived in a Babylonian version called the *Gilgamesh Epic*, discovered in AD 1853 and dating from before 1800 BC. But as this Yahwist retells the old story, his own insights go deep. To him, 'the loathsomeness of all mankind has become plain to me, for through them the earth is full of violence' – yet Yahweh still loves the righteous Noah. In his continuing courtesy Yahweh even closes behind them the door of the

Ark where Noah and his family take refuge. When the Ark comes to rest in the mountains of Armenia (where the Euphrates and the Tigris originate), it is a new chance for mankind. The old song is quoted in its beautiful simplicity:

> While the earth lasts
> seedtime and harvest, cold and heat,
> summer and winter, day and night,
> shall never cease.

But this song about the regularity in nature is accompanied by an insight into Yahweh's ever-new forgiveness of man in history: 'Never again will I curse the ground because of man, however evil his inclination may be from his youth upwards' (8:21,22).

Then J uses another old legend, which told of men building a tower to reach heaven – only to have their work stopped by jealous gods. Since the tower is here called Babel, this version of the legend seems to have arisen around the *ziggurat* or tower built in Babylon by Hammurabi and for long in ruin (it was to be restored by Nebuchadnezzar). But again there is the insight. Yahweh has stopped the building of the heaven-storming tower by breaking men's unity of purpose and speech: 'they will not understand what they say to one another' (11:1–9). But when readers are given 'the table of the descendants of Shem' (11:10–31), they are meant to draw for themselves the conclusion that Yahweh has not finally taken offence – and that he has been specially patient with all the 'Semites'. God is in his heaven, uniquely holy, uniquely strong, and man is always only mortal flesh; yet God has mercy on man.

Supremely is Yahweh merciful to Abraham and his descendants. This Yahwist (12:3) quotes the old song about Israel:

> Those that bless you I will bless,
> those that curse you, I will execrate.

All the families on earth
will pray to be blessed as you are blessed.

And he presents this divine blessing on a people in terms of
Abraham's personal relationship with Yahweh (12:8). He
tells many stories about the patriarchs and Moses, about the
settlement of Canaan, and about the later history, gathering
the stories from the traditions of different shrines and different tribes. But he is a great unifier, a creative artist whose
work has, for all its richness, a final unity – and some have
not hesitated to use about his editorial skill the word
'genius'. For throughout the material can be found the
theme of Yahweh's mercy. One of J's greatest stories says
that his mercy would have led Yahweh to spare Sodom if
that wicked city had contained only ten good men (Genesis
18:16–33). Yahweh's mercy certainly did lead him to
establish the throne of David and Solomon. The brief-
lived Israelite empire is clearly what the Yahwist has in
mind when he gives the enthusiastic prophecy of Balaam
that 'a star shall come forth out of Jacob' and smite Moab,
Edom, and Seir (Numbers 24:15–19); or when he declares
that 'all the families on earth will pray to be blessed as you
are blessed' (Genesis 12:3). The God who had mercy on
Adam, Cain, Noah, and Abraham is the God who has led
David into an imperial glory.

THE E TRADITION: THE PROPHETS' PAST

The second of these historical traditions in the Old Testament is called E because its editor, the Elohist, usually calls
God 'Elohim'. It dates from the ninth or eighth century BC
and comes from the northern kingdom, Israel.

It is probably a reflection of the continuing Canaanite
influence in Israel that God is called by this name which
Canaanites and Israelites could have in common. But that
implies no disloyalty towards Yahweh. On the contrary,
the activity in Israel of great prophets of Yahweh such as

Elijah has left significant traces in this tradition. Abraham himself is called 'a prophet' (Genesis 20:7). The prophetic Moses wishes 'that all Yahweh's people were prophets' (Numbers 11:29). E presents the past as the prophets understood it; it is a vision quite as partisan as, say, the modern Marxist interpretation of history.

The first substantial contribution by E to *Genesis* begins as late as chapter 20, and the Elohist does not show either his feelings or his outstanding skill until he tells the story of Abraham and Isaac in chapter 22. It is a story about a stern and terrible God, who can apparently destroy the very hope he has held out to Israel; who can put Abraham to the test by pretending that he demands the sacrifice of his 'only son', Isaac. But the worship of Yahweh in fact brings about the abolition of primitive practices such as human sacrifice: 'do not raise your hand against the boy.' God-fearing Abraham is assured that his descendants will 'possess the cities of their enemies' whose religion remains primitive. This powerful, endlessly suggestive story is set on 'one of the hills' three days' journey into the desert of Moriah, but as told by E it belongs to a country where Elijah and his disciples have fought and conquered the prophets of Baal. It has ancient roots, but as told by E it belongs to an age when God is to be worshipped with the sacrifice of the heart.

Many of the stories collected by E have been joined by a later editor with the J narrative, and we cannot always be certain where the joins come in the Bible which we have; and much of E's material provides scarcely any opportunity for a personal touch – for example, the law-code in the *Book of the Covenant* (see pages 180-4). But E's attitude of deep reverence for Yahweh and for Yahweh's servant Moses comes out clearly in the brief passage inserted between the Ten Commandments and the law-code (Exodus 20:18–21): 'When all the people saw how it thundered and the lightning flashed, when they heard the trumpet sound and saw the mountain smoking, they trembled and stood at a distance. "Speak to us yourself," they said to Moses, "and we will listen; but if God speaks to us we shall die." Moses answered, "Do not be afraid. God has come only to test you, so that the fear of him may remain with you and keep you from sin." So the people stood at a distance, while Moses approached the dark cloud where God was.'

For this Elohist, the familiarity with God shown in some of the J stories – for example, the picture of Yahweh 'walking in the garden at the time of the evening breeze' – is impossible. God is in 'the dark cloud'. When he makes himself known, it is often in dreams. He is not a God to be chatted with; he is a God to be feared and obeyed, according to laws which he has decreed. When Moses prays 'Show me thy glory', this God proclaims: 'I will be gracious to whom I will be gracious, and I will have compassion on whom I will have compassion. But my face you cannot see, for no mortal man may see me and live' (Exodus 33:19,20). The revelation of this transcendent God takes place through the Exodus and the associated events, under the towering figure of Moses. This is how the God whom E worships sums up the revelation:

> You have seen with your own eyes what I did to Egypt, and how I have carried you on eagles' wings and brought you here to me. If only you will now listen to me and keep my covenant, then out of all peoples you shall become my special possession; for the whole earth is mine. You shall be my kingdom of priests, my holy nation (19:4–6).

The defence of the worship of this God against Canaanite idolatry is prominent in the E narrative long before Canaan is reached. Aaron the brother of Moses makes an image of a bull-calf for the Israelites to worship, saying: 'These are your gods, O Israel, that brought you up from Egypt' (32:8). It is an echo of Jeroboam I's erection of 'two calves of gold' at Bethel and Dan in the tenth century, when the invitation or command to the northern tribes ran: 'Here

are your gods, Israel, that brought you up from Egypt'
(1 Kings 12:28). In E Moses acts like Elijah, crying: 'Who
is on Yahweh's side? Come here to me' (Exodus 32:26).
And on the orders of Moses, the Levites act with the ruthlessness of Jehu when he butchers the prophets of Baal
(32:27,29). So on this mountain-top from which E views
Israel's history, Moses and Elijah stand together as stern
prophets demanding an absolute loyalty to Yahweh.

THE D TRADITION: A REFORMATION AND ITS BACKGROUND

The third of the historians is the Deuteronomist or D. His
work is found not only in *Deuteronomy* itself but also in the
books of Joshua, Judges, Samuel, and Kings. But he, too, is
the editor of a tradition. We can see this right at the beginning of *Deuteronomy*, where there are at least two separate
introductions, imperfectly combined (chapters 1–4 and
5–11).

Almost certainly the D tradition originated in the north
under the impact of the great prophets, and was taken
south before Samaria fell to the Assyrians in 722–21. Over a
century it was then treasured more or less in secret. Part of
the tradition became the *Code of Deuteronomy*, published in
622–21 (see page 184). Then devout and scholarly men who
accepted this code as the law of Yahweh wanted to show
how its promises and threats had been fulfilled. They
determined to write a *History of Israel* governed by the *Code
of Deuteronomy*. Probably they had before them the example
of Jerusalem scribes who had already joined the J and E
narratives to make a single history of the patriarchs,
Moses, and the occupation of the Promised Land. Those
earlier scribes may well have been encouraged by the
patriotic atmosphere about 700 BC, in the time of King
Hezekiah and the prophet Isaiah. We know that the reign
of Hezekiah was a time of interest in the nation's past, for
Proverbs 25:1 shows that 'the men of Hezekiah king of

Judah' recorded some of the sayings which had been traditional in Israel. The date of the joining of the J and E narratives is not known for certain. It is not even certain that the narratives *were* joined before the final edition (which alone has survived) of the first five books of the Old Testament, but much detailed evidence within that final edition makes it reasonable to believe that 'JE' existed as one story before the D scribes got to work.

When we ask about the date of the history we call D, the Old Testament supplies some clues. The second book of Kings in its present edition concludes in 561–60 BC. It ends with a pathetic little sign that, despite its exile, some vitality might still be left in the royal house of David. The king of Babylon, we read, 'showed favour to Jehoiachin king of Judah. He brought him out of prison, treated him kindly and gave him a seat at table above the kings with him in Babylon. So Jehoiachin discarded his prison clothes and lived as a pensioner of the king for the rest of his life.' (By good fortune, some records of the rations of Jehoiachin and his family have been recovered by archaeologists.) The historian who chose that moment to end his work cannot have known that less than twenty years later Cyrus was to overthrow the Babylonian empire altogether – a far more convincing sign of Yahweh's favour to the Jews. So we may date this concluding passage about 550 BC.

But probably the bulk of D's work was done long before that. There are indications in this history that the Jerusalem temple is still standing. It is said of the poles on which the Ark rested in the temple: 'they are there to this day' (1 Kings 8:8). The accounts of Solomon's dedication of the temple (1 Kings 8:22–66) and of Josiah's equally enthusiastic reforms (2 Kings 22:3–23:25) do not seem overshadowed by any great tragedy. On the contrary, Huldah's prophecy that Josiah will be 'gathered to [his] grave in peace' (2 Kings 22:20) is mentioned without comment. All this suggests a date before the destruction of the temple in 586, and even before Josiah's violent death in 609. It is also noticeable that all events after Josiah's reforms – including the king's death and the two sieges of Jerusalem – are treated with a brevity unlike the eloquence of many previous passages: the narrative reads like an epilogue. This suggests that most of D's work was done in Josiah's lifetime.

When he incorporates traditional stories in the books of Joshua and Judges, D is surprisingly restrained in his moralizing. But even here he is colouring history, for he makes the 'judges' out to be more or less kings of a united Israel, and every judge or king is compared with Josiah. Not one – not even David, who is often praised – is Josiah's equal, for 'no king before him had turned to Yahweh as he did, with all his heart and soul and strength . . . nor did any king like him appear again' (2 Kings 23:25). To a greater or less extent, almost all the rulers of the Israelites did evil in the sight of Yahweh, and as this historian sums up their reigns – long or short, prosperous or sad – that is really all that needs saying about them. But two evil kings are specially noted: Jeroboam I and Manasseh.

Jeroboam I is singled out for repeated condemnation because after Solomon's death he led the northern tribes away from their proper allegiance to the religious and political authority in Jerusalem. A story is told of how 'a man of God from Judah, moved by the word of Yahweh, appeared at Bethel' – and foretold the coming of King Josiah in vengeance (1 Kings 13). About the great King Omri, D simply says: 'He followed in the footsteps of Jeroboam son of Nebat, repeating the sins which he had led Israel to commit, so that they provoked the anger of Yahweh their God with their worthless idols' (1 Kings 16: 26). When Samaria falls to the Assyrians, D shows no pity. Instead, he preaches one last, bitter sermon. 'The Israelites persisted in all the sins that Jeroboam had committed and did not give them up, until finally Yahweh banished the Israelites from his presence, as he had threatened through his servants the prophets, and they were carried into exile from their own land to Assyria; and there they are to this day' (2 Kings 17:22–23).

Manasseh, who reigned over Judah from 697–96 to 642–41, is given no credit for keeping his little state afloat for half a century when the ocean of world history was being churned up by Sennacherib and his two successors in control of the Assyrian empire at the height of its power. Instead, he is condemned for adopting pagan worship (some of which, no doubt, he felt he had to adopt as an Assyrian vassal anxious to display his loyalty). It is said that even Josiah's righteousness could not compensate for his grandfather Manasseh's wickedness (2 Kings 23:26).

Jeremiah also reckoned the sins of Manasseh as unforgivable (15:1–4). But it is interesting to compare this portrait of a wicked king with an account in a fourth-century source, the second book of Chronicles (33:20), which may include some reliable material based on 'the chronicles of the seers' (whatever they were). On the one hand, the Chronicler adds to the tradition about Manasseh's wickedness the particularly horrifying report that he burned his sons in sacrifice. On the other hand, the Chronicler says that the Assyrians 'captured Manasseh with spiked weapons, and bound him with fetters, and brought him to Babylon. In his distress he prayed to Yahweh his God . . . and God accepted his petition.' After this, we are told, Manasseh strengthened the fortifications of Jerusalem and the other cities of Judah, and restored the worship of Yahweh. Assyrian evidence lists Manasseh among the vassal-kings, and shows that gangs of men from Judah were forced to labour on public buildings in Nineveh; but no explanation is available to show why the Assyrians relaxed their grip towards the end of his reign – if they did.

In the second or first century BC, a Jew whose identity we do not know evidently thought that the later white-washing of this king's reputation had not gone far enough, and he composed the edifying *Prayer of Manasseh* to be found in the Apocrypha (although not in the Roman Catholic version). We need not go as far as that. But if there

is anything in what the Chronicler reports, it looks as if
D's portrait of Manasseh has been blackened by his hatred
of the king under whom the Code of Deuteronomy, and all
that it represented, had to lie underground.

However, even as he recounted the sins of Jeroboam I and
Manasseh, D was still very sure that Yahweh was alive,
active, and in control. After all, had not Jeroboam's kingdom fallen? And had not Manasseh's heir Josiah swept
away the evil of that reign? And had not the publication
of the *Code of Deuteronomy* won the day religiously? D was
rather like a man who has kept explosives secretly – and
who has then watched them detonate. While the echoes of
that explosion were still strong, he surveyed history with
grim pleasure.

We owe to him this summary now included in the book
of Joshua (21:43–45): 'Thus Yahweh gave Israel all the
land which he had sworn to give to their forefathers . . . He
gave them security on every side . . . Of all their enemies
not a man could withstand them . . . Not a word of Yahweh's
promises to the house of Israel went unfulfilled; they all
came true.' Whatever the disappointments after that
beginning, in this historian's ears always rang the words:
'It was not because you were more numerous than any
other nation that Yahweh cared for you and chose you, for
you were the smallest of all nations; it was because Yahweh
loved you . . .' (Deuteronomy 7:7,8). 'It is not because of
any merit of yours that Yahweh your God is giving you this
rich land to occupy; indeed, you are a stubborn people'
(9:6).

The Deuteronomist saw the road of his people through
the wilderness on the map of history, but the only thing he
really saw on the road was Yahweh leading onwards –
sometimes followed, usually defied. In words which were to
be of the highest significance to Jesus of Nazareth, D wrote:
'You must remember all that road by which Yahweh your
God has led you these forty years in the wilderness to humble
you, to test you and to discover whether or no it was in

your heart to keep his commandments. He humbled you and made you hungry; then he fed you on manna which neither you nor your fathers had known before, to teach you that man cannot live on bread alone but lives by every word that comes from the mouth of Yahweh' (8:2,3).

P AND THE CHRONICLER: THE PRIESTS' HISTORY

The fourth of these 'historians' is the Priest or P. He acted as editor for the tradition behind him in the sixth or fifth century BC. Many modern scholars believe that he did his work in exile, like Ezekiel and the compiler of the *Law of Holiness* (whose outlook was similar); but it is possible that P had returned to Palestine, and certainly he must have had access to Israel's historical traditions, whether or not these were embodied in documents.

His material, or a selection of it, was added to J, E, and D (which almost certainly were already joined) to make the Pentateuch (the first five books of the Bible). It seems that this final edition took place in the late fifth or early fourth century, and we should think of the whole Pentateuch as having been completed by a disciple of P – or by P himself. When they rejected the religious authority of Jerusalem, the Samaritans kept the Pentateuch and the book of Joshua (and *only* those books) as holy scripture; so that this final editorial work on the Pentateuch must have been done sufficiently long before the split to become authoritative. Unfortunately, however, we do not know exactly when the split became final (see page 167). The Hebrew of the Samaritan Pentateuch differs in many details from the standard (Masoretic) text. It is usually thought to have been written early in the fourth century, but no ancient copy has survived and some scholars think that its date should be set two centuries later.

At first sight P lacks the interest of J, E, and D. This priest is obsessed by the equipment and vestments of the sanctuary under Aaron the holy priest – not by Jacob courting Rachel, Abraham with his knife over Isaac, or the sins of the rulers of Israel. He goes in for long lists of things, places, and people; he seems a clerk as well as a priest. But much that at first sight seems dead comes alive once we realize that P has gone through the bitter experience of the Babylonian exile. Seen in that light, his long and imaginary description in *Leviticus* of the worship offered by Israel in the wilderness is moving, and even his record of the establishment of the Israelite sanctuary at Shiloh, with the land at peace and allocated to the tribes family by family, all around, is no longer boring (Joshua 18–21).

Moreover, P's contributions to the Bible's first five books do have a strong message. It is the message that God's agreement with man has always depended on man obeying certain laws. There never was an unconditional covenant. This message is of the utmost importance to this priest, for it enables him to be even more systematic than the Deuteronomist in explaining why Yahweh has allowed so many disasters to overtake his disobedient people.

The covenant between God and the first man had a condition: 'I give you all plants that bear seed everywhere on earth, and every tree bearing fruit which yields seed: they shall be yours for food' (Genesis 1:29). No meat! God's covenant with Noah and his sons, who were no longer compelled to be vegetarians, also had a condition: 'Every creature that lives and moves shall be food for you; I give you them all, as once I gave you all green plants. But you must not eat the flesh with the life, which is the blood, still in it' (9:3). God's covenant with Abraham was similarly conditional: 'circumcise yourselves, every male among you' (17:9–14). Indeed, Jewish tradition based on P has described the seven laws of the sons of Noah as binding on all mankind: the laws ordaining the worship of one God, establishing equity between men, and prohibiting blasphemy, murder, theft, incest, and cruelty to animals. Above all, God's covenant with the people of Israel, represented by Moses on Mount Sinai, was conditional

upon their obedience to all the laws assembled by P in
Exodus (12:1-27; 13:1-16; chapters 25-31 and 35-40),
Leviticus (chapters 1-16 and 27), and *Numbers* (1:1-10:10;
15:1-31; 27:1-11; chapters 18, 19, 28, 29, 30, 35, and 36).

The emphasis that God's covenant depends on men's
obedience certainly speaks of a priest's sense of discipline
and holiness – and, yes, of a priest's legalism. It is significant that in P no mention is made of sacrifices before God's
covenant with Moses, which lays down exactly what form
the sacrifices are to take (Leviticus 8). Gone is the picture
of a sheep-breeder giving God a lamb as the most natural
thing in the world. But it is only fair to P to remember that
he sets God's promises and warnings in the widest possible
context.

The table of the descendants of Noah (Genesis 10) shows
an amazingly wide interest in the geography and history of
the ancient world. Most scholars believe that much of this
list was already present in the J tradition, but that P has
expanded it. The prominence of Nimrod as a 'mighty
hunter' and as the founder of cities including Nineveh
suggests an origin in Mesopotamia. But this list traces the
descent of the Medes, Greeks, and Etruscans (under the
names Madai, Javan, and Tiras), with others, from Noah's
son Japheth; of the Ethiopians (Cush), the Egyptians (Put),
the Philistines, the Canaanites, and many others from
Noah's son Ham; and of many nations (our 'Semites')
from Noah's son Shem. Israel is not mentioned. The
Sumerians and Persians are also not mentioned, which
allows the list to be dated at any time in the fourteen centuries separating their empires.

The use of such a list is an example of P's care in preserving ancient traditions. And we can see his scholarly
merits by comparing him with the last of the historians to
be considered in this chapter: the Chronicler.

Probably the Chronicler was the editor of a group at
work in the fourth century BC. A Jewish tradition has
identified him with Ezra, but it is far more likely that he

was a priest strongly influenced by the *Law of Holiness* and by the example of P's historical work – and keen to follow up Ezra's reforms as D had followed up the reforms of Josiah. In particular, he was keen to reassert the position of Jerusalem against the schismatic Samaritans. The two books of the Chronicles are a history from Adam to the decree of Cyrus about rebuilding the Jerusalem temple. Appended to this work are the books of Ezra and Nehemiah, incorporating their memoirs. The lists of David's descendants (1 Chronicles 3) and of the priests (Nehemiah 12) both come down to about 400 BC.

However, the 'chronicles' turn out to be mere lists interspersed after the death of Saul with stories copied from D and some fresh material. When copying these stories the Chronicler adds some touches which seem to modern historians to be real possibilities as additions to historical knowledge; they may well be based on fuller 'annals of the kings' (2 Chronicles 24:27) now lost. But often the Chronicler's contributions simply project his own prejudices. On the whole he seems such an unreliable historian that even his opinion on a question quite near his own day – namely, the question: who came first, Ezra or Nehemiah? – is not now generally accepted as decisive. Certainly he left the books of Ezra and Nehemiah in considerable disorder, so that they have become a happy hunting ground for literary detectives.

The Chronicler's point of view is so narrow that the Deuteronomist appears in comparison a large-hearted liberal. The attitude throughout is that of the staff of the Jerusalem temple. It is characteristic that the Chronicler views King David mainly as a patron of the priests and singers attached to the temple, and as one who spent his time brooding over ecclesiastical architecture and organization. The Chronicler makes extensive quotations from five of the psalms, which he heard in the temple day by day; but the grandeurs and miseries of the history of Israel are seen remotely and vaguely, as if through a cloud of incense.

P, on the contrary, could write the first chapter of the Bible. Here this priest allows us to share his vision of God – the Lord of the covenant, but first, last, and all the time the Lord of creation. Much of this vision is, it seems, expressed by adapting the Babylonian *Epic of Creation*, which was recited every year during the New Year festival and which has been known again to scholars since AD 1876. If so, that makes P's work in Genesis 1:1–2:4 all the more impressive. Here a worshipper of Yahweh, perhaps in exile, never allowed himself for one second to be converted by alien religion, although Yahweh's own temple was distant and probably still lay in ruins. He used the Babylonian myth – to voice his own vision.

Genesis 1:1–2:4 is indeed so different from the Babylonian *Epic of Creation* that some modern scholars have denied that there is any direct connection. It is impossible to settle the matter definitely, but the Old Testament does show us that the essential ideas of the Babylonian myth were known to the Jews. The poem about creation in Job (chapter 26) is full of mythology about the sea-monster, 'the Rahab', who was killed by the Creator, and there are other references to 'the Rahab' or 'Leviathan' being killed in Isaiah 27:1 and 51:9,10 and in Psalms 74:14 and 89:10. Here the source of the mythology is clearly Canaanite, but it is highly probable that the Canaanites were themselves influenced by the civilization of Old Babylon, for long the dominant power in the Middle East. It may be that P encountered the Babylonian mythology through Canaanite and Israelite tradition. On the other hand, P has lived through the Jewish experience of exile in the Neo-Babylonian empire. He belongs to the same circle as Ezekiel and Ezra, a circle whose central aim was the maintenance of absolute loyalty to Yahweh 'by the waters of Babylon'. Probably he was stimulated by his own direct encounter with the Babylonian *Epic of Creation* more than a thousand years after that epic's composition.

The contrasts between the Old Babylonian and the

Jewish visions of creation are, indeed, immense. In the Babylonian epic the main theme is the triumph of Marduk the god of Babylon over gods who represent other cities and peoples; it is a political document, propaganda for the newly-established Old Babylonian supremacy. In the Jewish vision, however, there is no need to mention Israel.

The long Babylonian myth is peopled with gods, and complicated by many conflicts between them. In Genesis 1, there is only one God – and he does precisely what he wants, in seven days. In the Babylonian myth, the universe is created by Marduk out of the dead body of his enemy, the goddess Tiamat. In Genesis 1 creation comes out of 'the abyss' – out of the inconceivable. In the Babylonian myth, the sun, moon, and stars are made by the gods to be treated as sacred by men – for Babylonian religion was full of sun-worship, moon-worship, and astrology. In Genesis 1 the sun, moon, and stars are mere lamps, created by Yahweh to 'serve as signs both for festivals and for seasons and years' and 'to give light on earth'. In the Babylonian myth, the gods who have rebelled against Marduk's authority end up building a city and a temple for him on the earth. In Genesis 1, there is no city, no temple; only the mighty wind sweeping over the surface of the waters, the light and the darkness, the sky and the good earth, and the living creatures including man. On the seventh day God rests. He alone has done all that needed doing, leaving man on an earth which is an adequate temple. 'God saw all that he had made, and it was very good.'

Every people has its own myth of creation. It must be a myth, because the mind of man stops working when asked to contemplate reality before life, or matter, or time began. The imagination must take over, extrapolating from human experience in space and time to the origins. The imaginative reconstructions of the origins of the universe made by modern scientists are, no doubt, the least inaccurate myths at present available. But no human imagination has ever made a nobler myth than Genesis 1:1–2:4.

The formation of our planet is now known to have taken place about 5000 million years before the date implied by P (which Archbishop Ussher in the seventeenth century worked out as 4004 BC). Even the age when P wrote seems millions of years away, for it was so clearly pre-scientific; P could imagine green plants being created before the sun. But the real challenge of these histories of Ancient Israel is not so easily evaded. For at the heart of the matter, no scientific knowledge of nature or of man makes any essential difference – not even the science of modern historical research. In our greater sophistication we still face the same challenges because we are human. Every people needs to gather its traditions with something of the pride of the Yahwist. Every people needs to subject its history to a moral, prophetic commentary – as the Elohist did. Every people needs to judge its rulers by standards worthy of man's spiritual dignity – as the Deuteronomist did. Every people needs to cherish its best institutions – as the Priest did. And every people needs to see behind its history and its institutions the more important wonders of a universe which is at the same time awesomely mysterious and a 'very good' home.

CHAPTER 9

Jews in an Alien World

DANIEL AND THE MACCABEAN REVOLT

Obviously the books which Christians call 'the Old Testament' and 'the Apocrypha' do not deal with all the questions which arise when we ask whether or how the Jewish faith can survive in the modern world. But the key questions were already being heard in the second century BC. Then the Jewish religious heritage was under sustained attack – sometimes violent, sometimes cultural – from a civilization which seemed to many at the time to be overwhelmingly superior. The Old Testament and the Apocrypha include a number of books illustrating this challenge and the different Jewish responses. As we read them, we sometimes feel that the modern world is not far away.

Among the heirs of Alexander the Great in the control of the Middle East were the Seleucid kings, who finally gained possession of Palestine after defeating the Egyptians in 198 BC; and among these was a particularly tyrannical ruler, Antiochus IV. In a rehearsal for Hitler, he was set on making a new order in Palestine. The new *Reich* would be one where the dominant philosophy would be pagan, and where his own dictatorship would be recognized as divine; he called himself *Theos Epiphanes* or 'God Manifest'. He aroused the Jews' hatred by a ruthless campaign to suppress all that was distinctive in their religion and way of life – circumcision, the Sabbath, the food laws, the worship of Yahweh in the Jerusalem temple. First a gymnasium where races were run in the nude after the custom of the Greeks was erected within sight of the temple; then in 167 a general named Apollonius was sent to punish the hostile people of Jerusalem. Many of the citizens were butchered or raped;

many of their homes were destroyed; the temple treasures were looted and the city walls demolished; and with the stones a new fortress was built to intimidate the survivors. Worst of all, in the temple an altar to the father of the Greek gods, the Olympian Zeus, was erected; and on it a pig was offered in sacrifice.

In a village named Modin between Jerusalem and the sea, an old man called Mattathias started the revolt by striking down first a fellow-Jew who was about to offer a pagan sacrifice and then the superintending official. He had five sons, among them three men who became outstanding revolutionary generals: Judas (who won the nickname of *Maccabeus* or 'the Hammerer'), Jonathan, and Simon. These brothers led their people to victory, purifying the temple for the worship of Yahweh on 14 December 164, an event still celebrated in the Jewish feast of Dedication (*Hanukah*). Jonathan, Simon, and Simon's son John Hyrcanus were high priests as well as political rulers in Jerusalem, and this Maccabean kingdom endured until the Romans conquered Palestine a century later.

The story of the rebellion is told enthusiastically in the two books of the Maccabees included in the Apocrypha. The first, taking events down to 135, comes to us in a Greek translation of the lost Hebrew original which was written, probably in Jerusalem, towards the end of the second century BC. The second book is an abridgement of a lost five-volume history written by Jason of Cyrene at about the same time. The author writes in Greek. In this second book as in the first the atmosphere is strongly heroic, and the comments are proudly, sometimes fanatically, Jewish.

It is an exciting story – and the state which the Maccabean revolt established was the last Jewish state until Israel was established in AD 1948 as a direct response to the persecution of the Jews under Hitler. But the most influential legacy of the revolt in literature is *Daniel*, a historical novel found in the Old Testament. It seems to have been put together shortly after the outbreak of the revolt,

about 165 BC, although some of its contents are almost
certainly older. It reads like the work of one man, yet in the
version which has survived the story is told partly in the
third person and partly as Daniel's autobiography, partly
in Aramaic (2:4–7:28) and partly in Hebrew. The story is
splendidly meandering, incorporating poems, dreams, and
royal decrees. In places it resembles the *Arabian Nights*. But
it has a unity.

The unknown author is cautious in his attitude towards
the religious sincerity, and also towards the immediate
prospects, of the rebels. We read: 'Wise leaders of the
nation will give guidance to the common people; yet for a
while they will fall victims to fire and sword, to captivity
and pillage. But these victims will not want for help, though
small, even if many who join them are insincere. Some of
these leaders will themselves fall victims for a time so that
they may be tested, refined, and made shining white. Yet
there will still be an end to the appointed time' (11:33–35).
However, despite this caution, *Daniel* in effect raises a
signal for revolt. In a time of acute danger, it is propaganda for the Jewish religious heritage.

The book does not face the challenge of Greek culture
head on. Instead, it treats the struggle against the blasphemous Antiochus IV – perpetrator of 'the abominable
thing that causes desolation' (11:31; 12:11) – as only the
latest stage in the age-old battle needed to preserve the
Jewish identity under tyrannical oppressors. The scene is
set some four hundred years before, in the empire of Babylon
– although it is clear that the author has only the vaguest
ideas about the history of that time, believing (for example)
that the Babylonians were overthrown by the Medes, not
by Cyrus the Persian.

The hero, young Daniel, is a faithful Jew. His name,
which means 'God is Judge', was a stock name in Jewish
and even Canaanite tradition. ('What? are you wiser than
Daniel?' asks Ezekiel 28:3.) At the court of Nebuchadnezzar he is able to flourish on vegetables in order to avoid

contamination by heathen meat, and he is unharmed in
the blazing furnace where he has been sent for refusing to
worship an idol. In contrast, Nebuchadnezzar himself is
reduced to the condition of a wild animal until he decides
to worship 'the Ever-living one . . . the King of heaven', and
his successor 'Belshazzar' loses his kingdom to 'Darius the
Mede' although he has richly rewarded Daniel for interpreting the doom-laden vision at the final feast. Eventually
Daniel becomes one of the three chief ministers under
Darius. The moral of these colourful tales is made plain:
'the Most High is sovereign in the kingdom of men' (4:17).

The same message emerges from the second part of the
book. In chapters 7–12, we are told by Daniel of his own
dreams. These are visions of the empires rising and falling,
and therefore they are visions of beasts – a lion (the
Babylonians), a bear (the Medes), a leopard (the Persians),
a beast with great iron teeth and bronze claws (the
Seleucids). All gorge themselves on their victims, but all are
condemned at the throne of God:

Flames of fire were his throne and its wheels blazing fire;
a flowing river of fire streamed out before him.
Thousands upon thousands served him
and myriads upon myriads attended his presence.
The court sat, and the books were opened (7:9,10).

Finally there appears not a beast but *a man*, representing
'the saints of the Most High' (the faithful Jews). We read:
'I was still watching in visions of the night and I saw one
like a man coming with the clouds of heaven; he approached
the Ancient in Years and was presented to him. Sovereignty
and glory and kingly power were given to him, so that all
people and nations of every language should serve him; his
sovereignty was to be an everlasting sovereignty which
should not pass away, and his kingly power such as should
never be impaired' (7:13,14).

Daniel is sure of the coming triumph of Jewish steadfast-
ness, but implies alternative ways of viewing it. On the one

hand, it is to be a victory given by God to the Jews as they represent all the little men whom the empires have crushed. It is striking that this Jewish author has no doubt that his people are those who are truly human – not the Greek empires of Alexander and his successors described cryptically in chapter 11. 'I saw one like a man!' That is a sublime vision of the coming glory of man. On the other hand, the victory of the Jews is to be down-to-earth; indeed, it is to be the start of yet another empire. 'All people and nations of every language should serve him!'

This second, nationalist, prospect had the more immediate appeal. The revolt of the Maccabees, helped by propaganda such as *Daniel*, resulted in the establishment by military means of a political independence, and for a time the new Jewish state covered most of the area occupied eight hundred years before by the short-lived Israelite empire under David and Solomon. Over it the descendants of the Maccabees made themselves kings: the Hasmonaean dynasty. They ruled in a style which was more humane than their predecessors' but not what the author of *Daniel* had had in mind as the elevated finale of history. Indignant against the worldliness of the official religion under the Hasmonaean priest-kings, two puritan movements arose – the Pharisees who spread all over Palestine, and the Essenes who were stricter still, and who built the monastery at Qumran where the 'Dead Sea scrolls' were written and stored.

NOVELS OF NATIONALISM

Two other second-century novels included in the sacred literature of the Jews illustrate their militant nationalism.

One is *Esther*. It seems to have been written in Persia; it shows a familiarity with Persian customs, borrows a number of words from the Persian language, and is connected with the carnival or 'Lots' or *Purim*, a festival which is obscure in origin but which the Jews seem to have taken over from the

Persians (3:7). This novel must have had much the same propaganda effect as *Daniel* if, as is likely, its appearance in Palestine more or less coincided with the revolt of the Maccabees, but its religious content is distinctly less ardent. The nearest *Esther* came to mentioning God in its first edition was a vague promise that if Queen Esther refuses to help, 'relief and deliverance for the Jews will appear from another quarter' (4:14) – although this omission so troubled pious readers that before long some suitable prayers were added with other embellishments. This longer, revised edition is included in the Apocrypha; the first edition, however, finds a place in the Old Testament itself, to the embarrassment of many Jews and Christians.

The names of the principal characters in *Esther* reflect its Oriental background. King Ahasuerus, 'who ruled from India to Ethiopia', seems to be the Persian Xerxes. Mordecai, the most prominent Jew at his court at Susa, may echo the name of Marduk the god of Babylon. The 'beautiful and charming' Jewess, Esther, who becomes his queen, may be an echo of the goddess Ishtar (although 'Esther' may also come from the Persian meaning 'Star', and her Jewish name is also given: Hadassah, or Myrtle). The scene is one of feasts where 'the king's wine flowed freely as befitted a king'; of nights for which concubines needed a year's preparation with oil, myrrh, perfumes, and cosmetics; of dizzy power and luxury, and of gallows seventy-five feet high. With this sensational background, the story itself is a blend of pageantry, trickery, sex, and violence. It ends with Esther so fascinating the king (over the wine after dinner) that he issues a decree. This 'granted permission to the Jews in every city to unite and defend themselves, and to destroy, slay, and exterminate the whole strength of any people or province which might attack them, women and children too, and to plunder their possessions' (8:11).

Another nationalist novel which seems to have been published at about the same time as *Daniel* and *Esther* is

Judith, now in the Apocrypha. With equal gusto it tells of another Jewish heroine, a rich and merry young widow. She enters the camp of the Assyrians and enchants the commander-in-chief, Holophernes. After a banquet the general ends up in his tent alone with her. He is 'sprawled on his bed, dead drunk'. Judith, however, is sober enough to make a suitable prayer and cut off his head, which she hands to her maid, who puts it 'in her food-bag'. The Jews then loot the camp 'for thirty days' before striking up a hymn of thanksgiving with tambourines and cymbals.

We need not take such novels too seriously, certainly not as history. *Judith* opens with the error that Nebuchadnezzar 'reigned over the Assyrians', and *Daniel,* which does feature 'Nebuchadnezzar king of Babylon', is not much more accurate. Their chief characteristic is a delight in story-telling. In the Apocrypha are preserved further examples of this skill, as supplements to *Daniel.*

Two of these novelettes have some claim to be among the first detective stories ever written. In *Daniel, Bel, and the Snake,* Daniel proves that the Babylonian idol Bel does not really eat the twelve bushels of fine flour, the forty sheep, and the fifty gallons of wine provided for him every day – his priests do. Daniel proves this by scattering ashes over the temple floor at night. In the morning he is able to say to the king: 'Just look at the floor, and judge whose foot-prints these are!'

In *Daniel and Susanna,* Daniel proves that the 'very beautiful and devout' Susanna, the wife of the 'very rich' Joakim, is innocent of the charge that she has stripped off in the garden not in order to bathe in the heat of the day but for adultery. This charge has been brought by 'two elders' who have both been infatuated with her beauty and have been panting to take advantage of it. They bring the false accusation because Susanna has rejected their ad-vances in the garden and has sent up a great shout for help. Daniel examines them separately. Under what tree did they see Susanna and her young lover? 'Under a clove-

tree'. 'Under a yew-tree'. The dirty old men are led off to
execution while everyone else gives praise for the innocent
Susanna. Although the words of that song of praise are not
given, the *Song of the Three* does give the song which Daniel
and his companions recite at length in the fiery furnace
while their faith is being tested. They have the composure
of mind to call on all nature and all Israel to 'bless the
Lord'.

But some of the emotions which caused the writing and
the popularity of such fiction were serious enough; for an
enraged nationalism is never a laughing matter. What the
Jews in *Esther* were allowed to do in retaliation on any
people or province which might attack them, and what
Judith was able to do to the Assyrian general, was what
countless Jews longed to do to their oppressors. The
Maccabees rode to victory on these emotions.

NOVELS OF PEACE

Now we can turn to three novels where the Jewish response
is more peaceful.

'I believe God's word against Nineveh spoken by Nahum,'
says the author of the historical novel, *Tobit* now in the
Apocrypha and probably written about 200 BC. The novel
is set in the Assyrian empire towards the end of the eighth
century BC. Its hero, Tobit, refers to the book of Nahum,
which gloats over the impending or actual capture of the
Assyrian capital Nineveh by the Neo-Babylonians in 612
BC:

> Where now is the lions' den,
> the cave where the lion cubs lurked,
> where the lion and lioness and young cubs
>   went unafraid,
> the lion which killed to satisfy its whelps
> and for its mate broke the neck of the kill,
> mauling its prey to fill its lair,
>   filling its den with the mauled prey? (2:11–12)

Ah! blood-stained city, steeped in deceit,
full of pillage, never empty of prey!
    Hark to the crack of the whip,
the rattle of wheels and stamping of horses,
bounding chariots, chargers rearing,
    swords gleaming, flash of spears!
    The dead are past counting, their bodies lie in heaps,
corpses innumerable, men stumbling over corpses . . .
                                       (3:1–3)

'I believe God's word against Nineveh . . .' says Tobit.
'For I see that the place is full of wickedness and shameless
dishonesty' (14:4,10). But in the story Tobit and his family
remained exiles far from the Galilee where he had been
born. Nineveh would fall, as Nahum had announced – but
nothing could bring back the days before the Assyrian
conquest of the kingdom of Israel. Even the small state
which was eventually restored around the temple in
Jerusalem – and even the revolutionary nationalism of the
Maccabees – never knew the prosperity of the old days.
Either in Palestine or in exile (and the exiles were probably
better off), the Jews had to build up a life without most of
the usual boasts of nationhood. The interest of *Tobit* is that
it shows the qualities of character that made this achievement possible.

The tone of the book is self-assured. 'I, Tobit, made truth
and righteousness my lifelong guide; I did many acts of
charity for my kinsmen, those of my nation who had gone
into captivity with me at Nineveh in Assyria' (1:3). But
this smugness went with real kindness to Tobit's fellow-
Jews – and with courtesy to their conquerors, so that
Tobit soon found himself 'buyer of supplies' at the court of
the Assyrian empire, while his nephew Ahikar managed to
get himself appointed 'to supervise all the finances of the
kingdom'. The name 'Ahikar' is borrowed from another
novel, surviving in an Aramaic version of the sixth or fifth
century BC but possibly based on an Assyrian original,

about the maligned honesty of a non-Jewish official at the Assyrian court. It is significant that these novelists could place Daniel, Queen Esther, and Ahikar so high in the government of empires; for the fact was that in exile many of the Jews settled down. Not a few of them became comfortable, no doubt reflecting with Tobit that 'an honest life leads to prosperity' (4:6).

The main plot of *Tobit* (which is richly ornamented with sub-plots and speeches) concerns a visit which Tobit's son Tobias made to a kinsman Gabael in order to collect a large sum of money which Tobit had left on deposit twenty years ago – one sign that the honesty of Jewish merchants was authentic. Tobias was accompanied by the good angel Raphael, and by his dog (6:1). On his journey he stayed with another kinsman, Raguel, and with the angel's help married Raguel's 'sensible, brave, and very beautiful' daughter, Sarah. In order to make Sarah his wife he had to dispose of a troublesome demon, but a more everyday religion is indicated in the simple prayer which the boy and the girl offer on their wedding night (8:4–9). 'I now take this my beloved to wife,' Tobias says before God, 'not out of lust but in true marriage.' The angel Raphael sums up the values taught by this domestic tale: 'Better prayer with sincerity, and alms-giving with righteousness, than wealth with wickedness' (12:8). And Tobit himself sums up the gentle impact which this quality of life during the Exile will have on the world:

> Give him thanks, men of Israel, in the presence of the
>   nations,
> for he has scattered you among them;
> there he has shown you his greatness . . .
> Your light shall shine brightly to all the ends of the earth
>   (13:3,4,11).

In exile 'he has shown you his greatness' – that was a destiny more modest than any which the Jews would have chosen for themselves. (The dying Tobit still dreams of returning to a golden Jerusalem at 13:16.) But the quiet influence through integrity among the nations has been very considerable. It persuaded many in the ancient world to honour the Jews' peculiar religion; the New Testament shows that many 'God-fearers' were attached to the Jewish synagogues in many parts of the Roman empire. The same influence is real in our own time. When we say that 'Jews are good business-men' we are saying something not only about their intelligence, skill, and industry but also about the honesty which enables them to have reliable dealings with each other and with customers. When we say that 'Jewish family life is strong', we are saying something about the religious foundations of monogamy and of a stable, joyful home; and we are paying a tribute to *Tobit* and its age – for in all the laws included in the Old Testament, monogamy is nowhere commanded.

In addition to *Tobit*, two other historical novels are included in the Old Testament which show how some Jews regarded a peaceful, obscure contact with non-Jews as religiously better than an empire.

There is the exquisite little book, *Jonah*. It was included in the scroll made up of 'the twelve prophets', and these twelve are mentioned in the book called *Ecclesiasticus* at the end of the second century (49:10). There is no other clue to its date. The author may have used the name of an eighth-century prophet, the Jonah mentioned in the second book of Kings (14:25), but the name means 'Dove' and the dove was an old symbol for Israel. Certainly the hero or anti-hero of *Jonah* represents the whole Jewish people.

He was called by Yahweh to 'go to the great city of Nineveh . . . and denounce it, for its wickedness stares me in the face' (1:1). Instead he went in exactly the opposite direction – by ship to Tarshish (in Sardinia or perhaps in Spain). Yahweh replied to Jonah's disobedience by sending a storm: it is the rage of history surrounding the little kingdoms of Israel and Judah. Jonah was thrown into the sea and swallowed by a great fish: it is the exile of the Jews, their apparent disappearance from history. But then Jonah prayed, 'Yahweh spoke to the fish and it spewed Jonah out on to the dry land': it is the survival of the Jews and the return of some of the exiles to their homeland. So Jonah obeyed and found himself after all in Nineveh: it is the continuing exile of some Jews. He denounced Nineveh, and it repented with a great fast (in which even the animals joined): it is the spiritual influence of the Jews on other people including those who have made them exiles.

'Jonah was greatly displeased and angry': it is the pride of the Jews, unwilling to acknowledge how 'gracious and compassionate, long-suffering and ever constant' (4:2) is the God who has made them his people to serve him in his world. Jonah was again angry when a plant which had been sheltering him from the glare and heat of the day was killed by a scorching wind. And the voice of God came: 'You are sorry for the gourd, though you did not have the trouble of growing it, a plant which came up in a night and withered in a night. And should not I be sorry for the great city of Nineveh, with its hundred and twenty thousand who cannot tell their right hand from their left, and cattle without number?' Thus *Jonah* teaches the pity of God for the children, for the animals, and for all mankind. The Jews' mission in the world is to make known God's love, even to their national enemies.

Another small historical novel, *Ruth*, is probably older than *Jonah*. But it has the same charm – and the same theme that the gracious purpose of God embraces foreigners.

This particular foreigner is Ruth, a young woman of Moab – the same Moab that was scorned as Yahweh's 'wash-bowl' in Psalm 60:8 and denounced bitterly by many of Israel's prophets and law-givers. (In Deuteronomy 23:3, 6, we read: 'No Ammonite or Moabite, even down to the tenth generation, shall become a member of the assembly of Yahweh . . . You shall never seek their welfare or their good all your life long.') But when widowed, Ruth displayed a moving loyalty to her Jewish mother-in-law,

Naomi; it is the highest possible tribute to the friendship of
Jew and Gentile. 'Where you go, I will go, and where you
stay, I will stay. Your people shall be my people, and your
God my God. Where you die, I will die, and there I will be
buried' (1:16,17). And when taken by Naomi to Bethlehem,
Ruth received kindness from a farmer, Boaz, who made her
his wife; the friendship between Jew and Gentile, the
author seems to be saying, should not stop short of intermarriage. Their child was called Obed, and he became the
father of Jesse, the father of David. So King David was the
great-grandson of a Moabitess. Israel's hero was descended
from Arabs!

Like any good novel, *Ruth* does not openly preach. It is
enough to tell the tale for the myth of Israel's racial purity
and splendid isolation to crash in ruins.

JEWISH FAITH AND GREEK THOUGHT

In the second century BC many Jews were scattered not
only in the areas of the former Assyrian and Babylonian
empires but also in Egypt. There they faced the challenge
of Greek civilization, but the battle was fought with
weapons very different from those used in the clash between Antiochus IV and the Maccabees. It was a battle of
ideas, and two books included in the Apocrypha are records
of it.

The book called *Ecclesiasticus* was written about 190 BC in
Jerusalem by a scholar, Joshua or Jesus the son of Sirach,
and translated into Greek by the author's grandson who
settled in Egypt in 132. So the preface informs us. It was the
aim of this book to gather all that really mattered in a
Greek-dominated civilization; and to subordinate all this
dazzling treasury of heart and mind to the traditional
religion of the Jews. The theme is announced at the start of
chapter 1:

All wisdom is from Yahweh;
wisdom is with him for ever.

And the theme is pursued as this long book touches on many matters small and great.

Here we have the learning of a teacher who 'investigates all the wisdom of the past' and 'preserves the sayings of famous men', who 'travels in foreign countries and learns at first hand the good or evil of man's lot' (39:1-4). Here we have the ripeness of a man who prayed for wisdom 'when I was still young, before I set out on my travels' – and who found wisdom:

> From the first blossom to the ripening of the grape
> she has been the delight of my heart (51:15).

Now he runs a school (this is the only reference to a school in the Old Testament or Apocrypha):

> Come to me, you who need instruction,
> and lodge in my house of learning (51:23).

And he receives fat fees:

> Your share of instruction may cost you a large sum of
>   silver,
> but it will bring you a large return in gold (51:28).

This self-portrait of 'the man who devotes himself to studying the law of the Most High' (chapter 39) exudes self-satisfaction; it reminds one of Polonius in *Hamlet*.

But when it has completed all its discourses on the wonders of nature and on man in society, this book reaches a truth which Joshua the son of Sirach could have learned without moving an inch from Jerusalem – and could have taught without being paid a single piece of silver. For the climax is a long poem about the heroes of Israel's past.

This begins with the exhortation:

> Let us now sing the praises of famous men,
> the heroes of our nation's history (44:1).

And it ends with a highly flattering portrait of Simon II, the Jerusalem high priest (50:1-21). Every line of this poem glows with pride in the Jewish heritage as Ezra had reorganized it on the basis of 'the Law' and as it prospered before the persecution under Antiochus IV. Even Abraham is said to have 'kept the law of the Most High' (44:20). The fame of 'our forefathers' is contrasted with the oblivion of those who 'are unremembered; they are dead, and it is as though they had never existed' (44:9). This is not the verdict of one oppressed by the fame of Greeks such as Plato and Aristotle.

Another book in the Apocrypha, the *Wisdom of Solomon*, probably also comes from the second century, although some modern scholars date it as late as 50 BC. Here greater difficulty is experienced in answering the basic intellectual challenge of the Greeks, because the author (whose name we do not know) has felt its appeal more profoundly than Joshua the son of Sirach ever did. He wrote in Greek and almost certainly in Alexandria, then the greatest centre of Greek culture in the whole world.

He argues that 'wisdom' is still found in the Jewish religious tradition more clearly than anywhere else, but it is sure that he has sensed what Greek philosophy offers – nothing less than an understanding of the world. He writes:

> In wisdom there is a spirit intelligent and holy, unique in its kind yet made up of many parts, subtle, free-moving, lucid, spotless, clear, invulnerable, loving what is good, eager, unhindered, beneficent, kindly towards men, steadfast, unerring, untouched by care, all-powerful, all-surveying, and permeating all intelligent, pure, and delicate spirits. For wisdom moves more easily than motion itself, she pervades and permeates all things because she is so pure. Like a fine mist she rises from the power of God, a pure effluence from the glory of the Almighty; so nothing defiled can enter into her by stealth. She is the brightness that streams from ever-

lasting light, the flawless mirror of the active power of God and the image of his goodness. She is but one, yet can do everything; herself unchanging, she makes all things new; age after age she enters into holy souls, and makes them God's friends and prophets, for nothing is acceptable to God but the man who makes his home with wisdom. She is more radiant than the sun, and surpasses every constellation; compared with the light of day, she is found to excel; for day gives place to night, but against wisdom no evil can prevail. She spans the world in power from end to end, and orders all things benignly (7:22–8:1).

It is also clear that the author has seen for himself the dark side of the Greek view of life, for he is as eloquent as *Ecclesiastes* about the futility of human existence. 'What good has our pride done us?' he makes 'the godless' ask – and then he shows how deeply he has entered the mood of nihilism:

What can we show for all our wealth and arrogance? All those things have passed by like a shadow, like a messenger galloping by; like a ship that runs through the surging sea, and when she has passed, not a trace is to be found, no track of her keel among the waves; or as when a bird flies through the air, there is no sign of her passing, but with the stroke of her pinions she lashes the insubstantial breeze and parts it with the whirr and the rush of her beating wings, and so she passes through it, and thereafter it bears no mark of her assault; or as when an arrow is shot at a target, the air is parted and instantly closes up again and no one can tell where it passed through. So we too ceased to be, as soon as we were born; we left no token of virtue behind, and in our wickedness we frittered our lives away (5:8–13).

In the end, this deeply sensitive man is able to defend the faith that Yahweh, the God of Israel, orders human life. He is able to defend it by developing an element in Israel's tradition which the Old Testament leaves undeveloped: the belief that God's loving care of mankind is not ended by death.

As is shown in many of the psalms and in *Job*, even at a late stage in the composition of the Old Testament, and even in the most religiously thoughtful circles, it seemed very difficult or impossible to believe in eternal life as any kind of consolation or compensation for this world's evils. The Israelites accepted the reality of *Sheol*, the place of the departed spirits under the earth, but that seemed to them a bloodless, shadowy, and altogether undesirable half-existence. The story of how the medium at En-dor raised up the ghost of Samuel vividly illustrates the popular attitude: the ghost could utter no more terrible warning to King Saul than that 'tomorrow you and your sons shall be with me' (1 Samuel 28). More concisely, a woman from Tekoa reminded King David: 'We shall all die; we shall be like water that is spilt on the ground and lost' (2 Samuel 14:14). And a psalm summed it up:

> For men are like oxen whose life cannot last,
> they are like cattle whose time is short (49:20).

In *Sheol* life was no life at all:

> It is not the dead who praise Yahweh,
> not those who go down into silence (115:17).

Slowly the logic of their faith – together perhaps with some influence from the Persian religion, Zoroastrianism – drove some of the Jews towards a belief that a righteous God could not allow righteous, heroic men and women to be banished to *Sheol* or lost for ever. In particular, the martyrs of the Maccabean revolt were venerated because they accepted torture and risked everything rather than abandon the worship of Yahweh. Their courage still moved Christians when the New Testament was written (Hebrews 11:33–40). They would not be forsaken. It is therefore in *Daniel* that the Old Testament moves nearest to a vision of a coming resurrection, meaning by that the raising of dead bodies into new and eternal life. That will be infinitely better than *Sheol*, for it will be an age when

> Many of those who sleep in the dust of the earth will wake,
>   some to everlasting life
>   and some to the reproach of eternal abhorrence.
> The wise leaders shall shine like the bright vault of heaven,
>   and those who have guided the people in the true path
>   shall be like the stars for ever and ever (12:2,3).

In the *Wisdom of Solomon*, however, this trust in God for eternity is expressed in a form where there is no need of the idea of the resurrection of the body from 'the dust of the earth'. The author has evidently learned much from the Greek belief in the immortality of the soul, whether or not he has studied Plato's *Dialogues of Socrates* for himself. With the Greeks he thinks that 'a perishable body weighs down the soul' (9:15). Where he differs from Plato is that he bases man's eternal hope not on the 'soul' (which is a natural part of man and which is temporarily imprisoned in the body) but on the inexhaustible mercy of Yahweh. His conviction is that God created man, body and soul; that God always cares for man; and that God is always in control.

So this Jew, responding to the challenge of Greek culture in Egypt, views all human life from the peak of a faith which surmounts death:

> The souls of the just are in God's hand, and torment shall not touch them. In the eyes of foolish men they seemed to be dead; their departure was reckoned as defeat, and their going from us as disaster. But they are at peace, for though in the sight of men they may be punished, they have a sure hope for immortality; and after a little chastisement they will receive great blessings,

because God has tested them and found them worthy to be his. Like gold in a crucible he put them to the proof, and found them acceptable like an offering burnt whole upon the altar. In the moment of God's coming to them they will kindle into flame, like sparks that sweep through stubble; they will be judges and rulers over the nations of the world, and the Lord shall be their king for ever and ever. Those who have put their trust in him shall understand that he is true, and the faithful shall attend upon him in love; they are his chosen, and grace and mercy shall be theirs (3:1–9).

JOSEPH IN EGYPT

It is a pity that no novel survives to show the encounter between Jewish faith and Greek thought in second-century Egypt. But we do possess a book which through fiction illuminates an earlier encounter.

The last section of *Genesis* (chapters 37–50) is presumably based in part on stories told by some of the tribes of Israel about their founder, Joseph; Manasseh and Ephraim are mentioned particularly as Joseph's sons (41:50–52). Like the rest of *Genesis*, this section has been divided into the sources J and E. J says that Judah rescued Joseph from death, while E says it was Reuben; J says that Joseph was sold to some Ishmaelites, while E says he was found by some Midianites; J speaks of his father as Israel, while E calls him Jacob. There is also some P material. But most of this part of *Genesis* reads as one brilliant narrative, which may be regarded as a novel: *Joseph in Egypt*.

Either J or a later editor achieved in this section a level of story-telling comparable with the narrative of the succession to King David (see pages 53-7). For example, Judah's speech (44:18–34) is a masterpiece of eloquence. The worldly-wise narrator is clearly fascinated by life at court and by the problems of politics. But *Joseph in Egypt* is not a secular book. The author of the 'succession narrative' uses

an oblique method of disclosing his own devout mind, for the
religious comments which he offers are few and restrained
but crucial. When David has brought Bathsheba into his
house: 'But what David had done was wrong in the eyes of
Yahweh' (2 Samuel 11:27). When Bathsheba's second son,
Solomon, has been born: 'Yahweh loved him' (12:24).
When Absalom has rebelled: 'It was Yahweh's purpose
to . . . bring disaster upon Absalom' (17:14). And *Joseph in
Egypt* adopts much the same style. When Joseph is reunited
with his brothers: 'It was God who sent me ahead of you to
save men's lives' (Genesis 45:5). When Joseph looks back
on all his adventures: 'You meant to do me harm; but God
meant to bring good out of it by preserving the lives of
many people, as we see today' (Genesis 50:20).

The story shows the interest taken by some Jews in the
sophisticated 'wisdom' of Ancient Egypt. This is not the
philosophical wisdom of an Egypt dominated by Greek
thought, such as we have seen influencing the *Wisdom of
Solomon*. It belongs to an earlier period – probably in the J
stratum of this story to the age of Solomon himself, when
the new prosperity and political unity of Israel were
accompanied by a wholesale adoption of Egyptian influences. There may be a reflection of Solomon's centraliz-
ing bureaucracy in the admiration of this story-teller for
Joseph's control of the entire corn supply in Egypt on
behalf of Pharaoh.

This wisdom is really the know-how of a 'shrewd and
intelligent' man (41:33). It covers the interpretation of
dreams, and fortune-telling with the use of a silver goblet;
'you might have known that a man like myself would
practise divination' (44:15). But it also covers the administration of a state. The story-teller can readily picture
a leading Egyptian civil servant dressed in fine linen, with
a signet ring on his finger and a gold chain round his neck,
seated in a chariot with policemen clearing the way before
him (41:42,43).

The story of Potiphar's wife and her attempt to seduce

Joseph in chapter 39 reads somewhat like the conduct of the would-be adulteress in the *Tale of the Two Brothers* recorded in an Egyptian manuscript written about 1210 BC. The parallels are not close enough to suggest that the one story has been copied from the other, but the atmosphere is much the same: a woman bored by luxury is looking for new sex. Here as elsewhere we have evidence of a meeting between the Jew and an alien but seductive civilization – a meeting which prompts the urgent question: what does it mean to be a Jew? *Joseph in Egypt* unobtrusively suggests some answers to that question. And they are the answers implied in *Tobit*, *Jonah*, and *Ruth*.

The story shows that Joseph never chose to be in Egypt any more than Tobit or Jonah chose to be in Nineveh (or any more than Ruth chose to be widowed). He was taken to Egypt by slave-dealers, having narrowly escaped murder at the hands of his brothers. The mission of the Jews in the world is a heroic mission – but it is not a mission chosen by almost superhuman heroes. Here *Joseph in Egypt* parts company with *Daniel*.

The story also shows that Joseph's immature dreams of greatness ('the sun and moon and eleven stars were bowing down to me,' he announces at 37:9) were fulfilled when he, like Ruth or Tobit or Jonah or Daniel after him, made himself useful to those among whom he was compelled to live. When Joseph serves Pharaoh and the lesser Egyptians as a manager of the economy, perhaps we may go so far as to say that the truth is glimpsed that the mission of the Jews is to serve. At any rate, the eventual understanding of greatness in *Joseph in Egypt* is more mature than in *Esther* or *Judith*, although this story was told centuries before the writing of those novels. Its theme agrees with the advice which Jeremiah (29:5–7) was to give to the exiles in his day: 'Build houses and live in them; plant gardens and eat their produce. Marry wives and beget sons and daughters; take wives for your sons and give your daughters to husbands, so that they may bear sons and daughters and you may increase there and not dwindle away. Seek the welfare of any city to which I have carried you off, and pray to the Lord for it; on its welfare your welfare will depend.'

Joseph in Egypt – the concise Old Testament version, no less than the novel of twelve hundred pages which Thomas Mann wrote (*Joseph and his Brothers*, 1933–43) – dramatizes the effect of many adventures and much suffering on its hero's character. Joseph becomes great in a worldly sense when he rescues the Egyptians from famine; he becomes great in a spiritual sense when he rescues himself from bitterness. He forgives his brothers, and the story ends with a display of reconciling affection reminiscent of *Ruth*. 'He kissed all his brothers and wept over them, and afterwards his brothers talked with him'; and all the Egyptian court was delighted (45:15,16). This section of *Genesis* was presumably compiled in the form we possess when the J and E traditions were being joined by the Jerusalem scribes in the days of Hezekiah and Isaiah, and when many of the Israelites of the northern kingdom were exiled in the Assyrian empire. In its own way, it came near the universal mercy which inspired the *Jonah* vision of Yahweh brooding over Nineveh and 'being sorry for the great city'.

Included in the book of Isaiah (19:18–25) is a vision of Egypt swearing allegiance to Yahweh, finding its own deliverer in Yahweh, and allying with Assyria in order to worship Yahweh. This audacious vision of peace takes one's breath away; it is so unlike *Daniel*, or *Esther*, or *Judith*. But one finds that it is not unlike *Jonah*, or *Ruth*, or *Joseph in Egypt*:

> When that day comes there shall be five cities in Egypt speaking the language of Canaan and swearing allegiance to Yahweh of Hosts, and one of them shall be called the City of the Sun.
> When that day comes there shall be an altar to Yahweh in the heart of Egypt, and a sacred pillar set up for Yahweh upon her frontier. It shall stand as a token and a

reminder to Yahweh of Hosts in Egypt, so that when they appeal to him against their oppressors, he may send a deliverer to champion their cause, and he shall rescue them. Yahweh will make himself known to the Egyptians; on that day they shall acknowledge Yahweh and do him service with sacrifice and grain-offering, make vows to him and pay them. Yahweh will strike down Egypt, healing as he strikes; then they will turn back to him and he will hear their prayers and heal them.

When that day comes there shall be a highway between Egypt and Assyria; Assyrians shall come to Egypt and Egyptians to Assyria; then Egyptians shall worship with Assyrians.

When that day comes Israel shall rank with Egypt and Assyria, those three, and shall be a blessing in the centre of the world. So Yahweh of Hosts will bless them: A blessing be upon Egypt my people, upon Assyria the work of my hands, and upon Israel my possession.

CHAPTER 10

Songs for Every People

DREAMS OF A NEW AGE

After all that, what is the outcome?

In two places in the Old Testament the same great song of hope has been added to a prophet's warnings (Micah 4:1–4 and Isaiah 2:4). In this song, many nations come to Jerusalem, to its hill and to its temple:

> In days to come
> the mountain of Yahweh's house
> shall be set over all other mountains,
> lifted high above the hills.
> Peoples shall come streaming to it,
> and many nations shall come and say,
> 'Come, let us climb up on to the mountain of Yahweh,
> to the house of the God of Jacob,
> that he may teach us his ways
> and we may walk in his paths.'
> For instruction issues from Zion,
> and out of Jerusalem comes the word of Yahweh;
> he will be judge between many peoples
> and arbiter among mighty nations afar.
> They shall beat their swords into mattocks
> and their spears into pruning-knives;
> nation shall not lift sword against nation
> nor ever again be trained for war,
> and each man shall dwell under his own vine,
> under his own fig-tree, undisturbed.
> For Yahweh of Hosts himself has spoken.

But that hope was never fulfilled in Old Testament times. Indeed, the hope was so often disappointed that in another song of hope (Isaiah 25) the vision of the nations coming to Mount Zion has become fused with the vision of a life freed from the tragedy of all history, and from death itself:

> On this mountain Yahweh of Hosts will prepare
> > a banquet of rich fare for all the peoples,
> > a banquet of wines well matured and richest fare,
> > well-matured wines strained clear.
> On this mountain Yahweh will swallow up
> > that veil that shrouds all the peoples,
> > the pall thrown over all the nations;
> > he will swallow up death for ever.
> Then the Lord Yahweh will wipe away the tears
> > from every face
> and remove the reproach of his people from the whole
> > earth.
> > Yahweh has spoken.
>
> On that day men will say,
> See, this is our God
> for whom we have waited to deliver us;
> this is Yahweh for whom we have waited;
> let us rejoice and exult in his deliverance.

Isaiah or one of his disciples (11:1–9) saw that to bring deliverance a man was needed – a royal, anointed, or 'Messianic' descendant of Jesse the father of David:

> Then a shoot shall grow from the stock of Jesse,
> and a branch shall spring from his roots.
> The spirit of Yahweh shall rest upon him,
> > a spirit of wisdom and understanding,
> > a spirit of counsel and power,
> > a spirit of knowledge and the fear of Yahweh.
> He shall not judge by what he sees
> nor decide by what he hears;
> he shall judge the poor with justice
> and defend the humble in the land with equity;
> his mouth shall be a rod to strike down the ruthless,

and with a word he shall slay the wicked.
Round his waist he shall wear the belt of justice,
    and good faith shall be the girdle round his body.

But no such deliverer appeared on the throne in Old
Testament times. Indeed, that hope of the perfect king was
so often disappointed that it became mixed with the hope
of the perfect world. So this Messianic hope was enlarged:

Then the wolf shall live with the sheep,
    and the leopard lie down with the kid;
the calf and the young lion shall grow up together,
and a little child shall lead them;
    the cow and the bear shall be friends,
    and their young shall lie down together,
The lion shall eat straw like cattle;
    the infant shall play over the hole of the cobra,
and the young child dance over the viper's nest.
They shall not hurt or destroy in all my holy mountain;
    for as the waters fill the sea,
so shall the land be filled with the knowledge of Yahweh.

By the first century AD a convenient way of describing the
age which the Messiah was to inaugurate was to say 'the
kingdom of God' or 'the kingdom of heaven'. The phrase
makes its first appearance in the Old Testament inconspicu-
ously, when the first book of Chronicles speaks about 'the
kingdom of Yahweh over Israel' (28:5). The simple idea of
Yahweh as King of Israel is much earlier; Isaiah could
express his vision with the words, 'with these eyes I have
seen the King' (6:5). But it is only in late prophecy attached
to Zechariah's that we read the explicit announcement that
'Yahweh shall become king over all the earth' (14:9). For
it was only gradually that deepening disappointments
deepened the Jews' conviction that Yahweh was not yet
fully king, and intensified their longing for his reign.
    Although the hope of a royal deliverer (his title 'the
Messiah' is not an Old Testament phrase) no doubt

remained mainly nationalist and military, in some circles the hope was of a victory so complete that after it the vision could soar into the rule of God himself, above every problem of politics, every weapon of war, and every division among men. Such a vision was attached to the book of Zechariah (9:9,10):

> Rejoice, rejoice, daughter of Zion,
> shout aloud, daughter of Jerusalem;
> for see, your king is coming to you,
> his cause won, his victory gained,
> humble and mounted on an ass,
> on a foal, the young of a she-ass.
> He shall banish chariots from Ephraim
>   and war-horses from Jerusalem;
> the warrior's bow shall be banished.
> He shall speak peaceably to every nation,
> and his rule shall extend from sea to sea,
> from the River to the ends of the earth.

The Jerusalem to be entered by such a deliverer was itself to be a pure, new city of God, where 'every pot . . . shall be holy to Yahweh of Hosts' (Zechariah 14:21). Here the Old Testament merges into the literature known as 'apocalyptic'. An 'apocalypse' – meaning a 'disclosure' of the future – is usually attributed to some great figure of the past such as Daniel or Elijah or Moses or Abraham or Enoch (about whom Genesis 5:22–24 simply says: 'Enoch walked with God for three hundred years, and . . . was seen no more, because God had taken him away'). In the apocalyptic vision, history grows darker and darker with blasphemy, vice, violence, tyranny, famines, plagues, earthquakes, and eclipses. But the day of deliverance is thrillingly close at hand. In that day time is stopped by the miraculous intervention of God to judge the old world, and a new world arises, a world of glory and righteousness described in loving and defiant detail. A considerable number of Jewish books of this kind have survived from the period

200 BC–AD 100; some of them came to light among the Dead Sea scrolls. But the same atmosphere is found in some famous sections of the New Testament – in the warnings collected in chapter 14 of Mark's gospel, for example, or in the warnings and promises of the *Revelation of John*. We have already seen that the second book of Esdras is an apocalyptic book partly Jewish and partly Christian (page 70).

In comparison with many parts of the Old Testament, this apocalyptic atmosphere suggests despair. No longer does Abraham or Moses or Joshua lead his people confidently into the unknown; no longer is there a simple delight in the land of Canaan and in the life which it makes possible; no longer is there confidence in the old Jerusalem or in the political leadership of the House of David; no longer are the temple's sacrifices offered to Yahweh in the cheerful expectation of his blessings; no longer do the prophets announce that Yahweh is firmly in control of what the armies of Egypt, Assyria, Babylon, and Persia are doing; no longer do Nehemiah and Ezra rebuild the walls and the laws. A devil-dominated history is now thrown into the lake of fire, and it is through tearful eyes that men see beyond history 'the holy city, new Jerusalem, coming down out of heaven from God, made ready like a bride adorned for her husband': a city of gold and jewels, with no need of a temple or of sunshine, with gates which are never shut but which never admit anything unclean (Revelation 20: 7–22:5).

Such despair of history was the inevitable consequence of the repeated frustration of historical hopes. The Israelite or Jew in the Old Testament is someone whose good dreams never come completely true; who compensates for his disappointments by still more extravagant dreams; but who in the end has to face the fact that, in the world as it is, his dreams are always doomed. He then comes up with the solution that the world must be changed.

History has seldom been kind to such dreams. On the whole it has been on the side of Joseph's brothers: 'Here comes that dreamer. Now is our chance; let us kill him and throw him into one of these pits and say that a wild beast has devoured him. Then we shall see what will come of his dreams' (Genesis 37:19,20). But as the dreams have collided with history, sometimes history itself has been changed. The contempt which many Christians have felt for Judaism at the end of the Old Testament period is based on ignorance. The actual situation was far from being 'narrow' or 'stagnant'. Judaism in the first century AD was bursting with vitality. It produced many movements which propounded their own theories vigorously and which (something more remarkable) shaped their lives according to their theories – the conservative, aristocratic, and worldly Sadducees of Jerusalem; the Samaritans with their temple on Mount Gerizim; the Pharisees resolved on a holiness greater than the world's, yet in the world; among the Pharisees who taught loyalty to the Law, the great Rabbi Shammai but also the more liberal Hillel; the Zealots determined on an armed revolution; the disciples of John the Baptist; the disciples of Jesus. Much of this vitality survived the Romans' suppression of the Jewish revolt and their destruction of Jerusalem. Through many calamities the Jewish vision of life has continued to have an impact on people and events, to this day; and so has the hope of one Jew that 'the kingdom of God' would come on earth as in heaven.

Why have such dreams endured? And why have they continued to appeal to people remote in space and in time from the world of the Old Testament? To answer such questions, we have to listen to the songs which give the essence of Ancient Israel's faith. According to the gospels, two of these psalms were on the lips of Jesus of Nazareth while he was being tortured to death. One is a song out of the depths to the God whose power is known in Israel's history:

My God, my God, why hast thou forsaken me

and art so far from saving me, from heeding my groans?
O my God, I cry in the day-time but thou dost not
    answer,
    in the night I cry but get no respite.
And yet thou art enthroned in holiness,
    thou art he whose praises Israel sings.
In thee our fathers put their trust;
    they trusted, and thou didst rescue them (22:1–4).

And the other is the song of a man who, without this shelter,
would despair like a hunted animal:

With thee, O Yahweh, I have sought shelter,
    let me never be put to shame.
    Deliver me in thy righteousness;
bow down and hear me,
    come quickly to my rescue;
be thou my rock of refuge;
    a stronghold to keep me safe.
Thou art to me both rock and stronghold;
    lead me and guide me for the honour of thy name.
Set me free from the net men have hidden for me;
    thou art my refuge,
    into thy keeping I commit my spirit.
Thou has redeemed me, O Yahweh thou God of truth
                      (31:1–5).

SONGS ABOUT GOD

The psalms collected in the Old Testament are hymns used
in the temple at Jerusalem. That is about all we know for
certain about their origins.

Most of the old Hebrew versions say that seventy-three
of the hundred and fifty psalms are 'of David', but modern
scholars agree that he is most unlikely to have written all of
these before the temple was built. Eleven psalms are headed
'of the sons of Korah' and twelve 'of the sons of Asaph'.
These were two guilds of singers in the temple, but why the

psalms were theirs we do not know. Thirty of the psalms have the heading 'A song', whereas fifty-seven are called psalms; we do not know what the difference was, or why fifty-five have a heading 'To the choirmaster'. Seventy-one times the word *Selah* comes within a psalm, but we do not know whether this meant an interlude by the instrumentalists or a shout of assent by the people. It would seem that a translation such as the New English Bible is wise to omit all these meaningless Hebrew notes. And these are not the only riddles in the psalms.

Many of the psalms curse 'enemies' or 'evildoers', but we are never told exactly who these are. Sometimes they seem to be national enemies, fit to be cursed by a king. Sometimes they may be Canaanite sorcerers, the enemies of Yahweh's priests. At other times the attack seems to be against rich and arrogant Jews – the 'impious fool' who says in his heart 'there is no God' (Psalm 14, repeated in Psalm 53), or the man who is simply fat and nasty:

> Pride is their collar of jewels
> and violence the robe that wraps them round.
> Their eyes gleam through folds of fat;
> while vain fancies pass through their minds.
> Their talk is all sneers and malice;
> scornfully they spread their calumnies.
> Their slanders reach up to heaven,
> while their tongues ply to and fro on earth (73:6–9).

More seriously, we do not know why some psalms are so obviously congregational hymns ('All people that on earth do dwell' is based on Psalm 100 and 'Praise, my soul, the king of heaven' on Psalm 103), while others are so obviously the outpourings of one soul. It has been suggested that the 'individual' psalms were first used by the king as the representative of the people, or were composed by the priests for use by worshippers who could not find their own words, but no explanation is certain.

What is certain is that many of the psalms are 'songs of

Zion' (137:3). They voice a great love for Jerusalem. They 'proclaim glorious things' (87:3) about this city which is 'perfect in beauty' (50:2) and 'the joy of the whole earth' (48:2) – and particularly about its temple:

> How dear is thy dwelling-place,
>   thou Yahweh of Hosts!
> I pine, I faint with longing
>   for the courts of Yahweh's temple;
> my whole being cries out with joy
>   to the living God.
> Even the sparrow finds a home,
>   and the swallow has her nest,
> where she rears her brood beside thy altars,
>   O Yahweh of Hosts, my King and my God.
> Happy are those who dwell in thy house;
>   they never cease from praising thee.
> Happy the men whose refuge is in thee,
>   whose hearts are set on the pilgrim ways! (84:1–5)

Psalms 120–134 are a collection of 'Songs of Ascents' to be sung by the pilgrims who rejoice when they hear, 'Let us go to the house of Yahweh.' Psalm 42 declares that the longing to enter the temple 'among exultant shouts of praise, the clamour of the pilgrims' is an emotion 'as a hind longs for the running streams'.

Music was a vital part of the worship. Psalm 4, for example, is 'for strings', Psalm 5 'for flutes', and Psalms 9–10 'for oboe and harp'. Other psalms give us glimpses of the processions and the concerts:

> Thy procession, O God, comes into view,
>   the procession of my God and King into the sanctuary:
> at its head the singers, next come minstrels,
>   girls among them playing on tambourines.
> In the great concourse they bless God,
>   all Israel assembled bless Yahweh (68:24–26).

Sing out in praise of God our refuge,
　　acclaim the God of Jacob.
Take pipe and tabor,
take tuneful harp and lute.
Blow the horn for the new month,
　　for the full moon on the day of our pilgrim-feast
　　　　　　　　　　　　　　　　　　　　(81:1–3).

O Yahweh, it is good to give thee thanks,
to sing psalms to thy name, O Most High,
to declare thy love in the morning
　　and thy constancy every night,
　　to the music of a ten-stringed lute,
　　to the sounding chords of the harp (92:1–3).

Bow down to Yahweh in the splendour of holiness,
and dance in his honour, all men on earth (96:9).

　　With trumpet and echoing horn
acclaim the presence of Yahweh our king (98:6).

Praise him with fanfares on the trumpet,
　　praise him upon lute and harp;
praise him with tambourines and dancing,
　　praise him with flute and strings;
praise him with the clash of cymbals,
　　praise him with triumphant cymbals;
let everything that has breath praise Yahweh! (150:3–6)

The first thirty psalms show the different occasions and
moods in which an individual, whether king or commoner,
would go to the temple and recite the appropriate hymn.
One psalm is for use with the morning sacrifice:

　　Listen to my words, O Yahweh,
　　　　consider my inmost thoughts;
　　heed my cry for help, my king and my God.
　　In the morning, when I say my prayers,
　　　　thou wilt hear me.
　　　　I set out my morning sacrifice

and watch for thee, O Yahweh.
For thou art not a God who welcomes wickedness;
    evil can be no guest of thine.
  There is no place for arrogance before thee;
    thou hatest evildoers,
    thou makest an end of all liars (5:1–6).

And another is a relaxed evening hymn of happiness:

In my heart thou hast put more happiness
than they enjoyed when there was corn and wine in
    plenty.
Now I will lie down in peace, and sleep.
for thou alone, O Yahweh, makest me live unafraid
    (4:7–8).

One psalm is a lament in adversity:

How long, O Yahweh, wilt thou quite forget me?
How long wilt thou hide thy face from me?
How long must I suffer anguish in my soul,
    grief in my heart, day and night? (13:1,2)

And another is a thank-offering on recovery from illness:

  I will exalt thee, O Yahweh;
    thou hast lifted me up
and hast not let my enemies make merry over me.
O Yahweh my God, I cried to thee and thou didst heal
    me.
O Yahweh, thou hast brought me up from Sheol
    and saved my life as I was sinking into the abyss
        (30:1–3).

Some passages in other psalms show the reality of the
distress:

I lay sweating and nothing would cool me;
I refused all comfort.
When I called God to mind, I groaned;

as I lay thinking, darkness came over my spirit.
My eyelids were tightly closed;
I was dazed and I could not speak.
My thoughts went back to times long past,
    I remembered forgotten years;
all night long I was in deep distress,
as I lay thinking, my spirit was sunk in despair (77:2–6).

And other psalms show the reality of the deliverance:

    I love thee, O Yahweh my strength,
Yahweh is my stronghold, my fortress and my champion,
my God, my rock where I find safety,
my shield, my mountain refuge, my strong tower
                                    (18:1–2).

O God, thou art my God, I seek thee early
    with a heart that thirsts for thee
    and a body wasted with longing for thee,
like a dry and thirsty land that has no water.
    So longing, I come before thee in the sanctuary
    to look upon thy power and glory (63:1–2).

Thou art my hope, O Yahweh,
my trust, O Yahweh, since boyhood.
From birth I have leaned upon thee,
my protector since I left my mother's womb (71:5–6).

To the psalmist a moral offence was not so much a breach
of a code, or an insult to society, as a direct affront to his
God, and the psalmist's consolation in his sense of personal
sinfulness was that Yahweh's righteousness was shown all
the more clearly:

Wash away all my guilt
    and cleanse me from my sin.
For well I know my misdeeds,
and my sins confront me all the day long.
Against thee, thee only, I have sinned
and done what displeases thee,

so that thou mayest be proved right in thy charge
and just in passing sentence (51:2–4).

But because the judge was Yahweh, the psalmist was
ultimately confident:

In thee is forgiveness,
and therefore thou art revered.
I wait for Yahweh with all my soul,
I hope for the fulfilment of his word.
My soul waits for Yahweh
more eagerly than watchmen for the morning
(130:4–6).

As the heaven stands high above the earth,
So his strong love stands high over all who fear him.
Far as east is from west,
So far has he put our offences away from us (103:11–12).

Thou wilt show me the path of life;
in thy presence is the fullness of joy,
in thy right hand pleasures for evermore (16:11).

Repeatedly in the psalms it is announced: 'Yahweh is
king.' The 'king of glory' dominates every individual,
whatever that individual's mood may be. The main
purpose of every worshipper should be simply to 'gaze upon
the beauty of Yahweh' (27:4), to 'taste . . . and see that
Yahweh is good' (34:8).

Lift up your heads, you gates,
lift yourselves up, you everlasting doors,
that the king of glory may come in.
Who is the king of glory?
Yahweh strong and mighty,
Yahweh mighty in battle.
Lift up your heads, you gates,
lift them up, you everlasting doors,
that the king of glory may come in.

Who then is the king of glory?
The king of glory is Yahweh of Hosts (24:7–10).

Another psalm pictures Yahweh enthroned above all
nations:

> God has gone up with shouts of acclamation,
>   Yahweh has gone up with a fanfare of trumpets.
> Praise God, praise him with psalms;
> praise our king, praise him with psalms.
> God is king of all the earth;
>   sing psalms with all your art (47:5–7).

Indeed, Yahweh is thought of as lording it over any other
gods there may be:

> God takes his stand in the court of heaven
>   to deliver judgement among the gods themselves
>   (82:1).

Psalm 107 depicts men in their varied lives, all coming to
worship Yahweh in thanksgiving – men who have been
hungry and thirsty in the desert, who have been prisoners,
who have been ill, who have almost perished in a storm at
sea. Yahweh's mercy is like a compassionate father's for his
children (103:13); he is the 'father of the fatherless' (68:5).
Psalm 115 calls on 'those who fear Yahweh' (a term for non-
Jews willing to worship in the Court of the Gentiles), as
well as on the priests and the laity, to bless Yahweh and to
receive a blessing from him.

This everlasting God is high above mortal men:

> Lord, thou hast been our refuge
>   from generation to generation.
> Before the mountains were brought forth,
>   or earth and world were born in travail,
> from age to age everlasting thou art God.
> Thou turnest man back into dust;
> 'Turn back,' thou sayest, 'you sons of men';
> for in thy sight a thousand years are as yesterday;

a night-watch passes, and thou hast cut them off;
they are like a dream at daybreak,
they fade like grass which springs up with the morning
but when evening comes is parched and withered
(90:1–6).

Yet God's presence is everywhere:

Where can I escape from thy spirit?
Where can I flee from thy presence?
If I climb up to heaven, thou art there;
if I make my bed in Sheol, again I find thee.
If I take my flight to the frontiers of the morning
or dwell at the limit of the western sea,
even there thy hand will meet me
and thy right hand will hold me fast.
If I say, 'Surely darkness will steal over me,
night will close around me',
darkness is no darkness for thee
and night is luminous as day;
to thee both dark and light are one (139:7–12).

Again and again the psalms extol the 'steadfast love' or
'mercy' (in Hebrew *chesed*) of Yahweh. This love is experienced in the deliverance of the worshipper, which is a
part of the history of Israel; and from this viewpoint, it is
seen in all nature. Psalm 19 is an example of how in a single
song the worshipper could remind himself both that 'the
heavens tell out the glory of God' and that 'the law of
Yahweh is perfect.' The one belief followed from the other.
Psalm 50 lays bare the psychology of the Israelite religion
when it begins with a vision of Yahweh as the judge who
will vindicate his servants, and ends with a vision of
Yahweh the Creator. Yahweh speaks:

I need take no young bull from your house,
no he-goat from your folds;
for all the beasts of the forest are mine
and the cattle in thousands on my hills.

I know every bird on those hills,
   the teeming life of the fields is my care (50:9–11).

This God does not need the worship of the temple, but the
worshipper needs to love him back:

Great is Yahweh and worthy of all praise;
   his greatness is unfathomable.
One generation shall commend thy works to another
   and set forth thy mighty deeds.
My theme shall be thy marvellous works,
   the glorious splendour of thy majesty.
Men shall declare thy mighty acts with awe
   and tell of thy great deeds.
They shall recite the story of thy abounding goodness
   and sing of thy righteousness with joy (145:3–7).

Life teems with evil as well as with goodness, but the
knowledge of the God disclosed in personal experience and
in history is all that matters:

Whom have I in heaven but thee?
And having thee, I desire nothing else on earth.
Though heart and body fail,
   yet God is my possession for ever (73:25,26).

Songs such as these show why Ancient Israel's dreams of
a new age to be built by God as his kingdom have not been
dismissed, although the disappointments have been so
many. They are songs which can communicate with a
modern inquirer, as they have spoken to the Jewish and
Christian communities across the centuries. Despite the
riddle of their origins, they are the songs which sum up
Ancient Israel at its best; and because they are songs about
the real God, they are songs for every people.

CHAPTER 11

The Peoples of the Books

Muslims call both Jews and Christians by a term usually translated into English as 'the People of the Book'. They mean by this that the Jews and Christians by possessing divinely inspired scriptures are elevated above mere pagans, although they are beneath those who have 'surrendered' (*muslim*) to God (*Allah*) and his Prophet. It is a nice compliment. It is, however, not realistic about the practical importance of 'the Book' in the life of 'the People'.

One trouble is that there is no one people. Another is that there is no one book. Even if the Arabic phrase is translated as 'people of a book' (as it can be), it still does not do justice to the great differences between book and book, and between passage and passage, in the Jewish and Christian scriptures. Today a need is shared by Jews, Christians, and Muslims alike: the need to decide precisely which book among the scriptures, and which passage in it, has the greater authority for modern man. In this last chapter a few suggestions may be outlined which may serve as reverent and tentative gropings, or even as first steps, towards a new appreciation of this heritage which is not properly treated if treated with a blind loyalty.

We may begin with the household of 'Submission' (*Islam*), because the handling of the Jewish scriptures in the Prophet's 'Recital' (*Koran*) neatly shows us both the importance and the difficulty of the task now challenging every Jew, Christian, and Muslim. The most basic fact about the origins of Islam is that Mohammed, who died in AD 632, was a prophet and poet fit to be compared with any in the Jewish scriptures. Many passages in the Koran testify that Mohammed enjoyed – or rather, was dominated and driven

·by – a direct communion with that ultimate reality which, or whom, the Israelites worshipped as Yahweh.

It comes as no surprise when we find in the Koran many proofs of Mohammed's veneration of the Jewish religious giants. Thus we read (in *sura* 6) the words of Allah: 'We made Abraham strong against his people. We exalt whom We choose; for your Lord is wise and all-knowing. We gave him Isaac and Jacob, and We guided them as We guided Noah before them. Among his descendants were David and Solomon, Job, Joseph, Moses, and Aaron (thus are the righteous rewarded); Zacharias, John, Jesus, and Elijah (all were upright men); and Ishmael, Elisha, Jonah, and Lot. All these we raised above Our other creatures, as We raised some of their fathers, their children, and their brothers. We chose them and guided them to a straight path . . . To Moses We gave the Scriptures, a perfect code for the righteous, teaching them about all matters, a guide and a blessing to them, so that his people might believe in the last meeting with their Lord.' For a time, Mohammed even ordered his followers to observe the Jewish Day of Atonement, and always to turn to Jerusalem when praying. It is also not surprising that Mohammed, who felt this sense of spiritual kinship with the apostles of God in the Jewish scriptures, was disappointed by the human nature of the Jews whom he met in Arabia – the more disappointed because they were commercial rivals to his own ambitious Muslims. He would naturally feel something of the impatience of Ancient Israel's own prophets. 'Those to whom the burden of the *Torah* was entrusted but who refused to bear it,' he pronounced, 'are like a donkey laden with books' (62:5). To him, 'Abraham, Ishmael, Isaac, Jacob, and the tribes' were not Jews; they were Muslims, believers who worshipped and obeyed the true God (2:135–140). This theory enabled him to plunder, indeed to massacre, contemporary Jews who provoked his anger, and at the same time to appropriate what he liked in the Jewish scriptures. Characteristic was his decision that his followers need not obey the Jewish food laws – but that the Jews should continue to accept them, since they had been imposed by Allah as a punishment.

What is more surprising, and perhaps even more tragic, is that the Prophet of Islam was not led by his respect for the Jewish scriptures to examine them (or to hear them read, if the tradition is true that he was illiterate) with the care he expected his followers to bestow on his Koran. His failure here left a gap in the religion which he founded.

The sketchy nature of Mohammed's acquaintance with these books comes out in the inaccuracy with which he retells some of their great stories (for example, the stories about Moses, whose sister Miriam is also honoured in the Koran as the mother of Jesus). But it is also evident in his failure to come to terms with the deepest insights. He makes his own in an appropriately Arab style, and he communicates so much which we have come to know as the strength of Ancient Israel's tradition – the horror of idolatry and of uncontrolled sensuality; the submission to the sole Creator and the cosmic mystery; the grateful eye for beauty, of nature or of woman; the trust in the hands of the One who alone is the reliable guide; the conviction that God grants political stability and economic prosperity to those who in a practical way keep his laws; the faith which interprets defeats as God's rebukes; the austere but purposeful vision of life which looks to the Judgement and the Resurrection. But Mohammed never appreciates God's fatherly love, or at least never speaks clearly about it. He never approaches the God of Hosea, who lifted his people like a little child to the cheek (see page 93); or the God of Second Isaiah, who in giving birth to a better world for his people whimpered, panted, and gasped like a woman in labour (see page 161); or the God of Third Isaiah, who by his love and pity carried his children through all the disappointing years (see page 173). The majesty of Allah is undeniable, recalling the awe felt by Moses and the Israelites in the desert almost two thousand years before the Prophet of Arabia; but the mercy of Allah is harsh in comparison with the Good Shepherd of Ezekiel 34 and Psalm 23. And because Mohammed never reckons with this God of inexhaustible love, he does not express the all-embracing charity of *Jonah* or *Joseph in Egypt*. In the Koran he retells those stories, but misses their point of universal compassion.

Because of the reverence in which the Prophet is held by all Muslims, no doubt it would be asking too much to expect the quick adoption of a critical approach to the Koran; and because of the notorious conflicts of interest between Arabs and Jews in the twentieth-century Middle East, it would be asking too much to expect Muslims to learn universal compassion from Jews. It would be said that only a Christian could make such insensitive suggestions. A far more likely source of renewal in Islam is the mystical tradition in which many Muslim saints have not been inhibited from speaking of their love for a lovable Allah, and of wondering tenderness towards all of Allah's creation. Nevertheless the Jewish scriptures remain relevant to Islam. They remain relevant just because of the status of the Prophet and the Koran – for no one can study the evidence about Mohammed and doubt his debt to the message in the Jewish scriptures about the one, holy God.

It would be likely to seem an added impertinence if a Christian were to urge the Jews themselves to adopt a new estimate of their scriptures. Just as Muslims cannot be expected to learn the ways of peace from Jews, so Jews cannot be told about the inner meaning of Judaism by Christians, whose conduct towards 'God's ancient people' has been barbarous for many centuries and has reached a climax of evil in this twentieth century. Yet a Christian may be allowed to rejoice in the strengthening of two trends within modern Judaism. One is the trend away from the identification of Judaism with the kind of Zionism which is insensitive to the position of the Arabs in Palestine. Another is the trend away from the rigorous identification of loyalty to Judaism with meticulous obedience to dietary and other laws. Amid the tensions of the Middle East since the 1940s one has to be thankful for small mercies, even for silences; and it is a matter for thanksgiving that so very few Israelis have applied the scriptural thunders against the old Canaanites to the modern Arabs, or have wanted to demolish the Dome of the Rock in order to rebuild the temple for sacrifices.

When examined in the light of scholarship (which these scriptures repeatedly praise as part of the light held out to men by God), both the promises about the holy land and the commandments about the holy life can be seen to be related to the circumstances of history. Scholarly knowledge of these circumstances by no means excludes a divine initiative in the history, but it does make us include a human element in the response – and that awareness of the human element does make us hesitate before oversimplifying the contemporary relevance of these biblical passages. The love of the Ancient Israelites for the land which they possessed when the traditions which we call J, E, and D took shape, or which they longed for in the days of P, is moving. But it does not follow that it is right to treat the scriptures as if they settled twentieth-century political disputes. The desire of orthodox Jews to maintain their ancient traditions in diet, dress, and other matters is not an attitude which Gentiles should criticize: it is their own affair. But it does not follow that twentieth-century rabbis can teach without fear of contradiction that God dictated these laws to Moses, binding all Jews to the end of time and making it impossible for Gentiles who do not keep these laws to enjoy the same nearness to God. And the rabbis with a message for the modern world do not so teach.

Much modern Jewish experience shows that a scholarly understanding of their scriptures is helpful in liberating their religion into a wider life where it is somewhat easier for Jews and Gentiles to reach an understanding based on mutual respect. Thus the acceptance of 'biblical criticism', which sounds a purely academic exercise, is relevant to such urgently practical objectives as peace between Israelis and Arabs and mutual understanding between orthodox Jews and the rest of humanity. However, to applaud a scholarly and realistic attitude which relaxes the controversies and conflicts produced by fanaticism is not at all to welcome a complete abandonment of the Jewish religious tradition in favour of secularism.

One who was as great as Mohammed, but who had a more exact knowledge of Judaism because he was to the end of his days a devout rabbi and Pharisee, may be permitted to speak about this inheritance. Paul wrote to the Romans:

> What advantage has the Jew? What is the value of circumcision? Great, in every way. In the first place, the Jews were entrusted with the oracles of God ... They are Israelites; they were made God's sons; theirs is the splendour of the divine presence, theirs the covenants, the law, the temple worship, and the promises. Theirs are the patriarchs, and from them, in natural descent, sprang the Messiah. May God, supreme above all, be blessed for ever! Amen (3:1-2,9:4-5).

These riches remain when a scholarly understanding of the scriptures has placed them in their historical order and in their historical settings. No modern knowledge of the development of Ancient Israel detracts at all from the essential realities: the awe and the adoration; the wrestling of these very human people with their God 'supreme over all' in many perplexities and disasters; the conclusions which they reached and which the prophet Mohammed and millions of others learned (at least in part) from them; the audacious insights which were theirs alone, insights into the wounded heart of God. 'God is my possession for ever' sang the psalmist. That possession is not taken away from Jews merely because modern scholars deny that King David wrote all the psalms. On the contrary, the religion in their

Bible can come alive for Jews in a new way, now that their scholars can reconstruct the history while their archaeologists can uncover the physical remains; just as the whole life in their Bible can seem very near now that the farmers, the tradesmen, the women, and the children of Israel once again enjoy the land claimed by the rights of love and work.

For mankind's sake it is important that in the period into which we are moving Jews should overcome their recent obsession with the problems of Jewish identity. The most terrible catastrophe in the whole history of the Jews (the holocaust under Hitler) was followed within a few years by their most spectacular triumph (the establishment of the state of Israel in 1948), but Jews have still been suspected or disliked in many quarters despite the shame and the admiration which these events have caused. So it is easily understandable that Jews should ask only to be left alone – and should have asked themselves so often: how can the unpopularity be ended or ignored, how can the Jew be established as a full citizen of the modern world, how can the continuing Dispersion be linked with the new fact of Israel? But the treasures which the Jews retain in trusteeship for mankind are more precious than the pots which have contained them. We may dare to hope that the time will come soon when the confident mission of the Jew to the world can be resumed, preaching the peoples' God. A few modern Jews – one thinks of Martin Buber in Germany and Israel, or of Abraham Heschel in America – have already indicated what could be done. 'Should not I be sorry for the great city of Nineveh?'; 'the souls of the just are in God's hand'; 'a blessing be upon Egypt my people'. This is a vision of God which still impels those grasped by it to share it.

Among the peoples always indebted to these ancient books, and therefore to the Jews, are the Christians. If it is desirable for Muslims to study the Jewish apostles of Allah for themselves, and if it is essential for Jews to break out of some past interpretations in order to feel the true vitality and world-stirring power of their scriptures, it is no less important for Christians to recall that these books make up the other three-quarters of the Christian Bible. Such an acknowledgement of their religion's prophetic foundations helps Christians to understand what millions of Muslims have seen, and still see, in the prophet Mohammed. It also helps them to remove finally the anti-Semitism which has been Christianity's most hideous disgrace. But in addition to equipping them for more sympathetic dialogues with Jews and Muslims, the study of the Jewish scriptures helps Christians to understand Christianity: its origins, and its perpetual character. For if it ever forgets its Jewish origins, Christianity always betrays its own character. Too much Christian history declares this.

When Christians discover 'the Old Testament' and 'the Apocrypha', they rediscover vital facts. The Jewish-Christian religion is for men and women, not for hermits or for stained-glass saints. It is about the fields, the mines, the ocean, the crocodile, cities, marriages, battles, growing old, and suffering, and about the God met there; it is not about an escape above the bright blue sky. It is about the shrines which unite people and the heroes who lead them together into freedom; it is not only about pious individuals. It is about building nations and preserving them from corruption; it is not only about churches. It is about raising peoples from death and rebuilding communities on law as well as on love, as is necessary. It is the interpretation of the whole history of a nation and of mankind. It is both courage and humility in facing the present. It is changing the world because God works always and everywhere to create the world's future.

It is a religion arising within the world which it struggles to transform. In the twentieth century many have become convinced that Christianity needs a radical renewal: it has grown old, and must be born again. Understandably, many bored Christians have turned to the Eastern religions and have found there many treasures of the spiritual life. But it will be a disaster if the new contact with Eastern ways of meditation and self-purification is purchased at the expense of involvement in life and struggle. There is a tempting tendency in Eastern religion to treat life only as 'suffering' and struggle only as 'illusion' – while it has been the glory of the Jewish-Christian religion to find joy in life and meaning in struggle, even if a nation dies or a man is crucified in the process. The greater spiritual depth which is rightly sought by Christians can be reached more safely by using the resources within the Jewish-Christian tradition itself, for example the profound spirituality of the psalms.

Because it is a religion of life and struggle, it is always free to change and to grow. In the twentieth century many Christians reject the heavy emphasis there has been on intellectual system-building in theology and on doctrinal uniformity in religious discipline. They question the styles of authority exercised in the past by Christian theologians, priests, and preachers. They turn instead to a freely flowing religion, which involves the whole personality and not the intellect alone; which develops as life changes; which springs out of the life of the community, not out of the power of officials. But twentieth-century Christians are dangerously mistaken when they think that in order to have such a religion they must invent one. The religion which they seek is found in the New Testament, before Christianity was organized by Greek philosophers and Roman lawyers. It is also found in the Old Testament.

The faith of Ancient Israel was seldom expressed in intellectual propositions: it was a religion sung and shouted and lived before it was a religion thought. It was never expressed in a creed binding on all: theologically, it was chaotic. And not even after Ezra's work was the Jewish religion dominated by officials to the extent that the Christian Church has been. The priests of the Jerusalem temple had a limited role in teaching and discipline; the earlier priests of the local shrines seem to have had virtually no role at all in such spheres. The rabbis such as Ezra certainly did teach when they emerged towards the close of the Old Testament period, but it is significant that even such a highly intellectual rabbi as Saul of Tarsus was taught the trade of a tent-maker. Almost all the rabbis seem to have earned their livings in everyday jobs. They were immersed in the existence of their fellow-laymen, and it was their special task to answer religious questions thrown up by that lay life. It is very clear that Ancient Israel, leading into rabbinic Judaism, has much to teach the Christian Church about the health and development of a religious community.

But it was no accident that the controversies between Jews and Christians from the start concerned the nature of the law *of God*, the people *of God*, the kingdom *of God*. Today, when all religions are under great secular pressures, it needs to be remembered that this Jewish-Christian religion has always had at its heart a faith in a 'testament' or covenant or agreement between God and man; it has never been a religion of man talking to himself. It is a religion about the world, a religion of life and struggle, a communal religion – because the world is God's, the struggle is God's, and the community is God's. The Jewish-Christian religion has often been involved in politics but is not primarily a political movement. It does not chiefly seek to defend, or to overthrow, the established authorities. It does not give the highest priority to moral respectability, or to psychological health, or to social welfare. When modern Jews or Christians reduce their religion to those secular expressions, and declare that there is nothing more mysterious in it, they are simply forsaking their tradition; and the question to be asked is whether that betrayal is necessary. Here is a religion which claims to contain the truth and which confesses that it is thirsty for the living God who has been man's refuge from generation to generation.

We are right to think of 'the Jewish-Christian religion', and we are right to feel that the division between Judaism and Christianity has split the word of God. But in history, because human nature was at work, the division was more or less inevitable. The supreme emphasis placed by Jesus on intimate, trusting prayer to God as 'Father' (*Abba*) was not incompatible with the Jewish scriptures but unless the gospels misrepresent the matter it scandalized the rabbis by its directness. The claim of Jesus to forgive sinners, and his delight in fellowship with them, were so unconventional as to be shocking; and the mission of the Church of Jesus to every nation, welcoming Gentiles who were not to be made into Jews first, seemed nothing less than a claim to be a new Israel. The claim of Jesus that he was inaugurating the joyful new age when God would reign, and the insistence of the Christians that the Christ or Messiah had appeared, separated those who believed such good news from those to whom history remained much the same as before, often dull and often grim. So the Church healthily broke the exclusiveness of the Judaism which Nehemiah and Ezra had fashioned; but in embracing the world it made 'the Jews' an alien group, tragically liable to hostility and persecution. After nineteen centuries which have only increased the alienation between Christians and Jews, it is indeed a problem to know how such divisions can be healed. But the complexity of this problem makes it all the more necessary for Christians to cling to the original, truly world-embracing, truly God-based vision of Jesus the Jew, resulting in the authority for Christians of two Testaments.

It was necessary for Jesus himself to be schooled in the Jewish tradition and the Jewish truth. During the hidden years in Nazareth he searched the scriptures of his people, written over a thousand years. Only then did the day come when in the Nazareth synagogue 'he rolled up the scroll, gave it back to the attendant, and sat down; and all eyes in the synagogue were fixed on him. Then he began to speak . . .' (Luke 4:20–21).

CHAPTER 12

The Old Testament Today

UNCERTAINTIES IN HISTORY

The title of a book, *The Quest of the Historical Israel*, by G. W. Ramsey (1981), was an echo of the classic where Albert Schweitzer displayed the difficulties of writing a biography of Jesus. But it was more than a clever title. Recently the quest for the historical truth behind the Old Testament has been pursued as energetically as in any period in its own history. For more than two hundred years the quest has been seriously and systematically 'critical' (meaning truth-seeking). After various poineers a great German scholar, J. E. Eichorn, began to publish the results of his investigations in 1780; for examples, he maintained that the creation stories were 'myth' and that the book of Isaiah embodied the work of at least two prophets. Another giant in this field, Julius Wellhausen, expounded the relevance of his 'documentary hypothesis' about the composition of the Hebrew Scriptures in the first (and only) volume of the *History of Israel* in German in 1878, and in his article on 'Israel' in the 1881 edition edition of the *Encyclopaedia Britannica*; for example, he maintained that much of the 'Law of Moses' dated from after the exile. S. R. Driver's *Introduction to the Literature of the Old Testament* (1891) made such conclusions of German scholarship widely known and broadly acceptable in the English-speaking world, in contrast with the uproar that had overwhelmed the earlier attempts to criticize the sacred text. But debate and revision have never ceased, and recently the quest has still been a struggle, somewhat like a detective's, to find out what really happened.

Looking back on my previous chapters, which were first printed in 1976, I notice some places where I did not fully reckon with the difficulties of this quest. I have preserved at the end of this new edition the list of authorities on whom I mainly relied, but have added a short list of later books which themselves refer to many specialized works of research and disputation. I now gratefully offer in this chapter a short list of reconsiderations, but I would make a preliminary point about biblical scholarship in general.

Because it is a subject which tries to be scientifically historical, the 'critical' (which is too negative a word) study of the Bible is always changing and sometimes progressing. In each decade a few new facts are discovered, and more numerous suggestions are made about the correct interpretation of familiar documents. New theories seem convincing or at least become fashionable. That is a healthy situation – or at any rate, it is one that is inevitable and inescapable. But it would be foolish for anyone to try to base his or her religious faith on the accuracy of some detail in the picture provided by biblical scholars, because unless one is a complete fundamentalist or gets out of touch with the work of the scholars the detail is always liable to be altered. Religious faith is certainly connected with events in history and with the interpretation of historical literature, for we depend on the past as well as on our own experience. But faith's answers to the great questions about God and the human condition cannot depend on what we happen to know about the latest results of scholarly research and discussion probing the uncertainties of history and adding to the debates of literary criticism. If we are believers we do not put our trust in the details of events which occurred (or did not occur) thousands of years ago, or in the details of theories about the origins of literature. In my friendly dialogue with the conservative Evangelical leader John Stott, published as *Essentials* (1988), we found common ground in saying that we accept what the Bible taken as a whole affirms, although there are of course serious differences of opinion about exactly what in a particular passage of the Bible is permanently authoritative because it is the true (or 'infallible' or 'inerrant') word of God, and what may not be 'affirmed' in that way because it is the contribution of a mistaken individual or a vanished society (it is 'culture-bound'). The Second Vatican Council's Dogmatic Decree on the Divine Revelation (1965) taught that 'everything asserted by the inspired authors or sacred writers must be held to be asserted by the Holy Spirit' – which is a true statement, I believe, if 'asserted' is defined very carefully. But the Council did not go back on the blessing of critical scholarship given cautiously by Pius XII in 1943. It added, I think wisely: 'it follows that the books of Scripture must be acknowledged as teaching firmly, faithfully and without error that truth which God wanted put into the sacred writings *for the sake of our salvation.*' (The italics are mine.) We are not saved by details, so we should not put our trust in them.

In some places I probably was too cautious in 1976. On page 162, for example, I said that the authenticity of the Persian royal decree in Ezra 6:3–5 'although far from certain seems possible'. Most scholars now accept it as probably genuine. A handsome tomb in the valley outside the Old City of Jerusalem is possibly the one referred to in Isaiah 22:15–17:

> Go to this steward,
> to Shebna, comptroller of the household, and say:
> What right, what business, have you here,
> that you have dug yourself a grave here,
> cutting out your grave on a height
> and carving yourself a resting-place in the rock?
> Yahweh will shake you out,
> shake you as a garment is shaken out
> to rid it of lice. . . .

Some doubt must remain because the first half of the name of the owner has been obliterated and all that is left is '. . . yahu who is over the house', but recently other examples have been found of the full name Shebanyahu. The ninth-century sanctuary recently excavated at Kuntillet Ajrud, a remote place in the south, provides a fresh example of the mixture of the worship of Yahweh with Canaanite religion (syncretism) which is frequently denounced in the Bible: there, Yahweh was thought to have a consort, Ashera. Increasing numbers of little nude female figures in pottery have shown how widespread was the mixture of religion and sex in Canaan as the Israelites settled. On the other hand, many Yahwistic names have been found in seventh-century inscriptions, together with hundreds of jars marked 'of' or 'for' the king, illustrating both the reform of religion and the extension of royal power in the reign of Josiah, one of the Bible's heroes. And tablets which were the records of the banking firm of Murashu in fifth-century Nippur have been analysed as evidence that many Jews exiled to Mesopotamia preserved Yahwistic names. Those are only three examples of the support sometimes given to the Bible by archaelogy.

But of course if one is interested in sound scholarship one is chiefly worried about statements which may have been misleading because not quite cautious enough. The basic problem is that there is so little evidence about the history of Israel outside the Bible. Palestine's wet winters have rotted away almost all ancient documents, and its invaders or later generations have demolished almost all ancient buildings along with their inscriptions; thus for the history of the Philistines there seem to be no written documents or carved inscriptions at all. And there are not many references to Israel in non-biblical sources. Egyptian records say nothing about the captivity or Exodus of Israel. Although they do provide evidence about some forceful interventions in Palestinian affairs they leave the extent of Egyptian control or influence unclear in almost all periods.

We may be surprised to be told by 1 Samuel 1:4 that the two delinquent sons of Eli, a devoutly Yahwist priest, had Egyptian names, Hophni and Phinehas, and we may be even more surprised to be told of close connections between Egyptian civilization and the later 'wisdom' of educated men in and around Jerusalem. The so-called 'empire' of David and Solomon has left no trace on non-biblical documents and inscriptions that have been discovered. Its extent seems to have exaggerated in folklore, along with the quantity of Solomon's wealth, which I did call 'legendary' (page 107). Sober historians probably have to forget the Queen of Sheba – and when told that an Egyptian princess was sent to join Solomon's harem they probably have to remember that the known history of Ancient Egypt contains no similar marriage-alliance. In all the years after the exile there is not a single reference to the history of the Jews in a non-biblical source until the time of Alexander the Great, the 330s. Virtually all that archaeology contributes is a collection of silver coins marked *yhd*. For this period the biblical evidence is also scanty, and it is instructive to reflect on how much of the earlier material for a history of Israel is biblical.

The Old Testament is clearly a collection of documents which have been edited before reaching us – by men with strong convictions and little interest in the questions which scientific historians ask. In books such as *Joshua* and *Judges* the editor of the traditions was far more concerned to illustrate a religious message than to research into the actual process of the settlement of Palestine. The theology of *Deuteronomy* was vindicated by the successes of faithful Yahwists and by the disasters of backsliders: that was the plot of this semi-historical drama. Many mysteries seem to have been left permananetly mysterious – such as the origins of Moses (how Egyptian was he?), or the origins of the Levites (were they a tribe or were they landless?), or the origins of the psalms (were they composed after specific individuals' experiences, or for specific services in the

temple, and if so when?), or Jeremiah's attitude to Josiah
(how enthusiastic was he?), or the death of Josiah (reported
enigmatically), or the end of Ezra (whose story breaks off),
or the time of the split with the Samaritans, or the process
by which polygamy disappeared. Periods of time are often
referred to vaguely as 'forty years', and the '480 years' said
to have passed between the Exodus and the building of
Solomon's temple (1 Kings 6:1) cannot be fitted into the
Bible's own longer timetable. Jacob is said to have been in
his seventies when he sought a wife; Hiram of Tyre is said
to have been the ally both of David and of Solomon;
Hezekiah is said to have been born when his father was
aged eleven; and so forth. The first definite date in the
whole story is the fall of Jerusalem to the Babylonians. We
read in J. Alberto Soggin's *History of Israel* (1984) that King
Jehoiachin surrendered on 15–16 March 597 (the day was
calculated from sunset to sunset). This is recorded in the
Babylonian Chronicle, which, while not mentioning the
name of the king, basically confirms the facts given in 2
Kings 24. But the date when the city was once more
captured after the rebellion of Zedekiah is again uncertain.
As Professor Soggin says, 'scholars vacillate between 587
and 586 and it is impossible to make a decision'. Like other
historians, he also advises us that it is impossible to
disentangle the evidence about the relationship between
Nehemiah and Ezra – although the outline solution which
I accepted (pages 166–8) is still favoured.

On page 27 I quoted the lament over Saul and Jonathan
as David's, as 2 Samuel 1 does, but perhaps I ought to have
pointed out there (as I did on page 125) that David had
offered to fight for the Philistines in the battle which
brought about the deaths of Saul and Jonathan. I missed the
opportunity to raise the question whether this lament was
a proof of a noble generosity to the memory of Saul, or was
a piece of cynical propaganda by the guerrilla who
supplanted Saul's son as king, or was not really by David
– a question which cannot be answered conclusively. On

page 53 I called the narrative of David's own last years 'historical', but perhaps I ought to have stressed there that much of ancient history-writing would be classified as story-telling. It is legitimate to ask: since the bedroom scene in 2 Samuel 13 must be novelistic, what about the previous tale – the famous one about David's adultery and Nathan's rebuke? I have, I hope, always recognized that Israel's history-writing was not motivated by a search for accuracy: it shared a preference for vividness with all other ancient history-writing, just as it shared with many other peoples the motive of celebrating the favour of the local divinity. On page 124, for example, I was reserved about the accuracy of 'charming stories', and I left unanswered the historical question about who killed Goliath.

I would not deny that the later stories about David have been coloured, first by one story-teller anxious to defend him against Saul and then by another inclined to justify his son Solomon against the older Adonijah, when the truth seems to be that both David and Solomon began their reigns, which were on the whole successful, with treachery and murder. And increasingly I doubt whether the priest Abiathar, who had decided to back Adonijah, could have brought himself in retirement to tell the story of Solomon's triumph (page 54). However, I reflect that the glamour added to the David and Solomon of history was not entirely a bad thing. The absence of such a royal ideology or mythology in the northern kingdom was no asset to it. I also reflect that neither David nor Solomon was completely idealized. Despite some passages in the royal psalms there are remarkably few traces in Israel of the general tendency of the Middle East to claim that the local ruler was totally at one with the local divinity.

Exploring the history before the monarchy, I wrote on page 70 that 'tradition said' that Joshua started the ceremony at Shechem when the twelve tribes of Israel found unity by reciting blessings and curses. I was influenced by the eminent scholar Martin Noth, who from

1930 onwards made the idea of an early covenant between a tribal league ('amphictyony') and Yahweh an important key to understanding the Old Testament. His history of Israel included a section on 'the Institutions of the Confederation'. However, most recent scholars have viewed this key with suspicion, or have thrown it away, insisting that the tribal unity (never complete) and the emphasis on a covenant with Yahweh (never fully kept) probably developed much later in Israel's history. After alliances to meet emergencies under 'judges' who were local military chiefs, the tribes may have come together only under the monarchy – in a united kingdom which lasted for only two reigns. No less a scholar than Gerhard von Rad (accepted by Noth) maintained that the traditions of the Exodus and the revelation on Mount Sinai were recited by different groups at different festivals (at Gilgal and Shechem) until joined together under the monarchy; and von Rad's successors in the historical quest have tended to be even more sceptical about reports of a formalized early unity, reminding us that the Israelites had no fixed capital or central shrine until David's men captured Jerusalem. A clear and emphatic insistence on Israel's covenant with Yahweh became the controlling idea of *Deuteronomy*, inspiring the history which stretches to the end of *2 Kings*, but it may have owed much to the treaties imposed by the kings of Assyria in the seventh century when the kings of Judah were their vassals, expected to show a very practical expression of 'love' for their overlords. On page 144 I said that a shorter version of *Deuteronomy* was made public in the year 622–21. It is a convincing suggestion that this version consisted of chapters 12–26, where the term 'covenant' occurs only once (17:2), so that there may well be something in the further suggestion that this idea developed its full power only after that date. However, I am not persuaded by all the arguments of Noth's or von Rad's critics. Although Amos (for example) scarcely mentioned a 'covenant' and Hosea preferred to use the idea of a marriage, the prophets of both the two kingdoms, Israel and Judah, appealed to an accepted tradition about a relationship between all the Israelites and their God which was a covenant in all but name. It was a relationship between Yahweh's love understood as a steadfast loving kindness and mercy and a human love understood as grateful and loyal obedience. And if we seek to explore the background we have to remember that the Assyrian treaties with vassals were not the first treaties or covenants made in the history of the Middle East. It is not necessary to make the Old Covenant a late arrival on the Old Testament scene.

I do not now think that my agnosticism about the Patriarchs was large enough. To call Abraham an 'Amorite' (page 76) was to go beyond the sure evidence; in known history the Amorites were more shadowy than their (now diminished) fashionableness among some scholars has suggested. I am attracted, however, by a possible link with the tribe Raham, mentioned in an Egyptian inscription of about 1300 BC. I recognize that the ancient customs reflected in the stories of the Patriarchs (page 76) continued long after the dates traditionally attributed to Abraham, Isaac and Jacob – who may have been con-temporaries or, for that matter, may not have existed at all, since all we have to go on is an edited collection of folk tales which I did call 'legends' (page 73). Perhaps the best name for them is 'sagas' – a name familiar to scholars since Hermann Gunkel's commentary in 1901. Sagas are simple, dramatic stories about the heroic days of old, popular because full of human, family-centred interest. Although we cannot prove that the hero of a saga is as insubstantial as the smoke of the fire around which such stories were told, it is not necessary to treat him as a solid figure of history. The ancient farmer's creed which I quoted on page 69 did not mention Abraham, Isaac or Jacob (who may well have been different originally from Israel). It is possible that some or all of the Mesopotamian names in these stories

were learned as late as the Jews' exile under Babylon, an
example being 'Ur of the Chaldees' (Genesis 11:28). But it
is unlikely that this whole tradition, about the 'God of the
Fathers' being the God worshipped by Abraham, Isaac,
Jacob and Israel before he was named as Yahweh, is a late
invention.

Probably all the tribes whose shrines were associated
with the Patriarchs by legend or saga were formed within
Canaan. Professor Soggin has called this one of 'the facts
that we can take to have been established', and before him
Martin Noth began his *History of Israel* with the observation
that Israel 'cannot really be grasped as a historical entity
until it becomes a reality living on the soil of Palestine'. I
was not cautious enough about the biblical narrative on
page 81. It seems likely that the tribes of Judah, Ephraim
and Naphtali were called after their parts of Canaan, not
the other way round. The varying lists of the tribes, and the
complexities of their geography, seem to reflect a quite
prolonged fluidity.

I also now see that I was a shade too definite in some of
my references to the Exodus across the limited fluidity of
the Reed Sea. It is disquieting that the first Pharaoh to be
named in the Bible is Sheshonk, mentioned as Shishak in
1 Kings 14:25–27, where his victorious campaign against
Israel is dated to about 925 BC. (An inscription about it on
an Egyptian temple, mentioned on page 134, can be
interpreted to say that the campaign took place earlier and
humiliated King Solomon himself.) This was some 350
years later than the date tentatively suggested for the
Exodus (on page 83). But I am unconvinced by those
scholars who maintain that very few, if any, of the ancestors
of Israel were involved in any exodus from Egypt. I ask:
how and why were stories about the manifestation of
Yahweh's favour in the Exodus – stories which are referred
to in all kinds of places in the Old Testament – given such
religious prominence and emotional power if the memories
of the folk had preserved nothing at all of an escape from

Egypt? It could have been maintained that the Israelites were entitled to the land by right of long habitation blessed by the 'God of the Fathers', and that the decisive miracle was divine intervention in battles within Canaan, such as the thunderstorm which rescued Deborah's motley army from defeat (page 104). If it had no deep roots in folk memories, the story of the Egyptian connection was not necessary in order to claim that Yahweh's favour had been demonstrated. And although arguments from silence are notoriously precarious, it is interesting that we have no hint of claims by one or more of the tribes that its residence in Canaan had been continuous since the days of Abraham, Isaac and Jacob.

On page 102 I ought to have made clear that the only 'cities' or little towns in Canaan which are both shown by archaeology to have been destroyed, and claimed in the book of Joshua to have been conquered by him, are Lachish and Hazor. On page 113 I ought to have made clear that the Canaanites mourned the death of Baal each spring when the vegetation died (see Zechariah 12:11), before his resurrection marked by the autumn rains and the accompanying orgies. But the first point supports the view that the total extermination of the Canaanites desired by *Deuteronomy* was far from being a fact of history – and the second point supports the belief that the Canaanite religion was far from being superior to Yahwism. The fact that the origins of Yahwism are lost in obscurity (at Genesis 4:26 the source J maintains that it began in Adam's time) ought not to be allowed to outweigh the capacity of that religion to develop into something as unique as it has been precious. To say this is not to say that Yahwism was always as unique as some scholars have claimed. Its imagery, rites and laws all had much in common with the culture of surrounding peoples. In contrast with the bloodthirstiness of *Deuteronomy*, the stories about the Patriarchs seldom include conflict with the native Canaanites, and in this respect at any rate they appear to reflect real history. The uniqueness took time to develop, and Professor Giovanni Garbini can point to some facts when he argues that 'the religious message placed in the mouth of Moses was not something new that came from outside Palestine to change the religious face of the country of Canaan, but a reaction which originated in Palestine itself against a type of religion observed by the whole population'. Certainly the 'Law of Moses' as we have it assumes an agricultural, not a nomadic, population and has been influenced by prophets and priests (as I stressed in chapter 7). I recall that Martin Noth, for example, was sceptical about the historical basis of many of the Moses stories. However, I see no reason why we should go as far as Garbini in totally denying that Moses and those influenced by him influenced the Israelites. (The sceptical professor also denies that Ezra existed.) We ought to be cautious about denials too, specially when they reduce to vanishing point a Founder of the stature of Moses. The usual process in history exaggerates the work of the Founder but does not invent him.

Although the history of Judah during the last century and a half of its existence as a kingdom is comparatively well documented, the traditions incorporated into the Old Testament include stories which look like patriotic legends. For example, there is a discrepancy between the story in 2 Kings 18–20 that after an initial payment of a large sum in tribute a miracle saved Hezekiah and Jerusalem from Sennacherib's army, and the Assyrian inscription which records that Hezekiah simply became Sennacherib's vassal, paying tribute. The two accounts have sometimes been reconciled by saying that there was a second Assyrian campaign which ended in a retreat, but there is no evidence for a second campaign. It is possible that the story of a hasty retreat which occurs in the history of Herodotus is more reliable than the Assyrian royal inscription which has been preserved in its characteristically bombastic style of propaganda. (Perhaps biblical scholars ought to reckon more than they do with the chance that Assyrian inscriptions recording victories may not be infallible.) But it seems more likely that Hezekiah did buy the Assyrians off during the one campaign, and that Isaiah's assurances about Jerusalem's safety were given in that unromantic setting. Even more doubt must surround the story in *Chronicles* that Hezekiah's son Manasseh became a devout Yahwist. An earlier tradition merely says that he enjoyed a reign of fifty-five years while he 'did what was wrong in the sight of Yahweh' (2 Kings 21:2). Some observance of the Assyrian state religion would have been required of him in order to show his loyalty as a vassal, but the Chronicler may well have thought that the length of such a reign was due to Yahweh's favour in return for worship. I was cautious about these stories (on pages 141 and 212) – but probably not cautious enough.

More misleading perhaps was my overconfidence in assigning passages of the Old Testament in J, E, D and P, and in reconstructing the theologies which shaped those sources (in chapter 8). I still accept the division of the Scriptures into those traditions and I am still indebted to the interpretation of them by scholars of the stature of Martin Noth and Gerhard von Rad, but I now see more clearly than I did why the labelling, dating and attribution of motive should be accompanied by a decent sense of hesitation as one cuts up the Bible's history books. Scholarly commentaries on the books of the prophets also often leave you in uncertainty if you do not rely exclusively on any one scholar, for there is much disagreement about which oracles are original, which are the work of disciples and which are due to the final, post-exilic editing (redaction). One does not wish to disparage the enormous, and sometimes successful, efforts of the critical scholars if one observes that there is an element of speculation in the bulky literature which confronts the advanced student. It is not easy to separate the traditions combined in the biblical text or to excavate the layers beneath this surface so as to show when, how and why these traditions were formed and transmitted by speech or writing. The wonder is that the work is sometimes done conclusively. Yet I have also come to see more and more clearly that the uncertainties and the general air of remote antiquity which must surround the history and literature of Israel matter little in comparison with the power and the glory of the Scriptures as we have them.

The events which are studied and disputed by scholars are often petty incidents in the sordid and distant history of the Middle East – or can be sized up as such in the perspective of the secular historian. The origins of the traditions now combined in the Bible are often impenetrably obscure – or can seem so if one is more accustomed to modern certainties about the authorship and date of a book. Many of the beliefs about God or the world expressed in these ancient books are not beliefs which modern people can share. It is easy to see why the Protestant theologian Adolf von Harnack complained in 1921 that keeping the Old Testament as an authoritative document has been 'the consequence of religious and ecclesiastical paralysis'. But something more must be said. Like the prehistoric geological rift which begins in the Syrian mountains and continues down into Africa, to Lake Malawi, so the religion of Israel, immortalized in the Bible, constitutes a rift in the very widespread pattern of religion seen as the worship of rain or sex or monarchy. From Dan to Beersheba, the historic limits of Ancient Israel, the distance is about 150 miles; from the sea to the Jordan, only thirty-six. Yet this tiny area was the scene of an earthquake more momentous than the physical one recalled in Amos 1:1 and Zechariah 13:5. That changed the shape of the Mount of Olives. This spiritual earthquake changed the world.

DIVERSITY IN THE BIBLE

What, then, does the Bible affirm? Since writing the previous chapters, I have found no reason to abandon the answer which I then gave about the Old Testament: here are books which show that in the joys and sorrows of real life real people can meet the real God. But I have had cause to ponder a challenge very different from the complaint that I was not cautious enough about the history. So I now want to respond to the conservative challenge that a 'liberal' or 'critical' approach to Scripture does not reckon adequately with the authority of the sacred text.

In particular I now see that chapter 11 may seem too 'liberal' or 'critical' in a shallow way. In it I suggested that an acknowledgement of the real character of the Hebrew Scriptures could help Muslims to see that their Prophet failed to come to terms either with the books as actually written (the references to them in the Koran often being inaccurate) or with their emerging message about God's love (the Koran being often sublime literature that in the main proclaims God's transcendent and stern majesty). I also suggested to Jews that modern scholarship shows that God did not really promise the Holy Land to Abraham and his descendants exclusively and for ever, and did not really dictate every word of the Law of Moses. And I urged my fellow Christians to learn from the earthy as well as the heavenly elements in the Old Testament, renouncing past obsessions with church life and dogmatism (including fundamentalism and antisemitism). These suggestions were, I now realize, made in a tactless style which has inevitably aroused some response to the effect that I was being both superficial and arrogant by attempting to impose 'liberalism' on traditionally minded believers. I can see that I owe my readers a more careful – although necessarily brief – account of such understanding of biblical authority as I have attained, for only if Muslims, Jews or Christians are persuaded that the Scriptures are being treated rightly will they be persuaded that no form of fundamentalism is right.

The title of this book may create a false impression. I am not pretending that I can offer one new idea which will explain the whole meaning of the whole of the Old Testament. On the contrary, I hold – as do the vast majority of thoughtful readers nowadays – that mistakes were made when such claims were made in the past and should not be repeated. The Old Testament contains materials for the history of Ancient Israel, but with these materials a detailed history cannot be written if it is to confine itself to evidence of the kind usually accepted by good historians. In much the same way we have materials for a *Theology of the Old Testament*, but the theology cannot be thoroughly systematic if it is to be truly biblical. One of the merits of the *Theology of the Old Testament* by Walther Eichrodt, written in the 1930s, is that it meticulously acknowledged the nature of its materials while it used one idea as 'the central concept, by which to illuminate the structural unity and the unchanging basic tendency' at least in its first volume. The equally impressive *Theology* by von Rad (in two volumes from the 1950s, with his book on *Wisdom* in effect forming a third volume) returned to the older tradition of German scholars by approaching the subject historically. Von Rad brilliantly expounded a proclamation about Yahweh trumpeted by historians, renewed in relation to current problems by prophets, and further related to current knowledge by the scribes of 'wisdom'. And one of the advantages of being able to compare those two theologies is that it makes one realize how different can be the approaches which seem best to scholars equally great in learning and insight.

The concentration of orthodox Judaism on 'the Law of Moses', particularly after the Roman destruction of the temple but also during and after the Babylonian exile, did not do justice to most parts of the Scriptures. But the concentration of the Christian Fathers and the Middle Ages on passages which could be held to 'prefigure' the coming of Christ, or to foreshadow Christian belief in the Holy Trinity, often read meanings into the text which were not there originally, by the fanciful process called 'typology'. The concentration on the ethical splendour introduced by the prophets, accompanied by the denigration of 'legalism' and 'priestcraft', did not take the prophets' setting into account: they prophesied in sanctuaries and inspired lawmakers. Nor did it reckon with the much more worldly and prudential ethics of the proverbs. And the enrolment of these prophets among the pioneers of Socialism did not always take their religious passion into account: unlike most modern politicians, they advocated social justice because they were aflame with the conviction that this was the will of God. But the concentration on simple, timeless and relatively uncontroversial precepts of morality, characteristic of the Enlightenment (in the eighteenth century and from Spinoza to Kant), was in danger of dressing the Ancient Israelites in the clothes of middle class respectability.

The emphasis on the 'People of God' in biblical theology and the liturgical movement might fail to take into account the individualism of Ezekiel or *Job* and the profound and all-pervading sense, older than those books, of personal moral responsibility. But the emphasis on 'heroes' in many popular presentations of the Bible failed to expound the strong sense of corporate solidarity in Ancient Israel. The emphasis on 'God who acts', leading to a claim that Israel was unique in basing its whole religion on its beliefs about God's activity in history, could not account for the traditional division of the Hebrew Scriptures into the Law, the Prophets and the Writings, with no 'History'. But the existentialist emphasis on faith as a leap in the dark towards a Wholly Other could not account for the celebration of Yahweh's sovereignty over the universe, mankind and the congregation. The emphasis on atonement for sin through sacrifice has rightly taught that Yahweh delighted in 'the appointed sacrifices' because they enabled his people to receive his forgiveness (Psalm 51:19). But it could not account for the many passages of the Old Testament where sacrifices were treated as celebrations, denounced as escapism or ignored as irrelevant, such as Psalm 51:16–17:

> Thou hast no delight in sacrifice;
> if I brought thee an offering, thou wouldst not accept it.
> My sacrifice, O God, is a broken spirit;
> a wounded heart, O God, thou wilt not despise.

In recent years all those one-sided fashions in Old Testament interpretation have been more or less discredited. It has been acknowledged that no one idea entirely dominated this religion – that these people could let go of ideas as they could let go of physical objects as sacred as the ark or the temple. But a fresh effort has been made to stress the unity in this material by emphasizing that we have to deal with the final form of the biblical texts as authorized in the official 'canon' (whose obscure history I somewhat oversimplified on page 16) – so that the most important kind of 'criticism' is the humble attempt to see how a passage fits into the book as we have it. This is called 'canonical criticism'. However, as we try to make sense of the apparently bewildering diversity in the Old Testament it seems silly to make an idol of either the 'original author' or the 'final editor'. Neither the earliest nor the latest stage in the transmission of a biblical tradition is generally regarded as automatically authoritative. One reason is that it is often difficult to get at the identity and credentials of the author or the editor. Another reason is that it is often hard to tell what is canonical. What text is regarded as authentic? What books are regarded as canonical? In what order of importance are they placed? Is the New Testament regarded as the most important part of the canon, making it right to subordinate the Hebrew Scriptures (first called 'the Old Testament' by Clement of Alexandria in about AD 200)? And when these canonical books give different accounts or explanations or teachings, which is more canonical?

Yet another reason to be on our guard against attributing too much importance to the final editor is that no student of the Bible consistently prefers either the first or the last stages in the processes which have created the Old Testament. We do not think that the early source J is always more important for our moral and spiritual instruction than the much later source called P; the cosmic magnificence of the creation myth which begins the Bible comes from P. But it is equally true and right that we do not always prefer what is newer, for the attempt to read the Old Testament as a story of evolutionary progress goes against the evidence. P could become obsessed by ecclesiastical legalism and could reflect the prejudices of racism and tribalism. We do not regard the Chronicler, who was inspired by a P-type theology, as the most reliable of Ancient Israel's historians simply because he was the most recent. And we do not consider that the original teaching of Jesus was inferior to the editorial theology which organized the gospels. We give the highest place to what the Bible taken as a whole affirms. And what is that? Our own consciences have to tell us – instructed, we hope, by the Holy Spirit, by the common sense of the Christian (or other religious) tradition and community, by biblical scholarship and by our own knowledge and experience.

Sometimes the oldest does seem to be the best. But sometimes the final editing of these books added touches which were less truthful or less profound than the contents which were being edited. For example, the conventionally pious prologues and epilogues added to *Job* and *Ecclesiastes* do not match the power of those stupendous declarations of open-eyed and anguished faith. Sometimes the editorial work which added later material made a book richer and helped it to speak to later generations. For example, the final version of the books of all the great prophets included oracles or narratives contributed by their disciples and this enlargement has sometimes helped readers to see the relevance of the man whose name is used for the whole book. It is illuminating and moving to think that the work of Amos and Hosea inthe northern kingdom inspired other men to add prophecies directed at Judah – and that anonymous prophets during the exile and the return regarded themselves as standing in the tradition of Isaiah and Jeremiah, whose disciples they were proud to be. The book called *Daniel* (pages 221–5) is also illuminating in this connection, for in it many centuries come together. It portrays a Jew in exile in the sixth century who loyally mediates on the already sacred heritage of his people. But this portrait speaks not to that age but to a crisis four hundred years later, encouraging endurance and heroism during the Maccabean revolt. Here we are given glimpses of the spiritual power of an often renewed tradition. But it is also true that sometimes the editing of the Old Testament has reduced the impact of an historical figure. Later oracles of consolation blunt the force of pronouncements of doom by Amos (as when, in the words of Wellhausen, a disciple has added 'roses and lavender instead of blood and iron'). The mixture of his own ecstatic joy with an earlier prophet's despair can produce a highly confusing muddle (as when a single Isaiah was thought to have written the whole of the book which bears his name). The figure of David the warrior-king was made much larger than life – and therefore made unintelligible when studied carefully – by editors who attributed all the literary splendours of the psalms to his authorship, and who claimed that his chief interest was planning the worship in the temple. It is as if Elizabeth I had written the plays of Shakespeare and also the Book of Common Prayer. The Bible's dating of Ezra before Nehemiah made the reforming work of those two men hard to understand. And the attribution of all the written religious law to Moses made it agonizingly difficult to sort out the claims of the various parts of the law on the devout conscience, as is shown in (to give an ancient example) the letters of St Paul, reflecting on his experience as an anxious Pharisee.

There is also some danger that 'canonical criticism' may be used to divert attention from the straightforward question: what evidence is there that this event really took place? The best exponents of canonical criticism (Professor Brevard Childs, for example) are well aware of the labours of the historians and of the scholars who have investigated the origins of the biblical texts and have asked what was the original 'situation in life'. And those of us who still seek truth by using the older methods of criticism should be aware that texts may be late or legendary and still be valuable in moral and spiritual instruction, which conveys a kind of truth. A story-teller can witness to his (or his people's) experience of God precisely by telling a fictitious story, as when a priest summed up his people's experience in exile by telling the story of God's creative sovereignty that begins the Bible. But if religion is a search for truth, it cannot be irrelevant to ask whether a text agrees with older texts or tells us about a real event. The attempt to separate 'Scriptural truth' from the truth that is reached by the ordinary processes of investigation and reflection is liable to end up in the attitude that Scripture is not true in any worthwhile sense – and the attempt to separate 'salvation history' from the material which ordinary historians study (an attempt best made by von Rad) is liable to end up in the attitude that the Bible consists of nothing more than a tissue of myths not anchored in the real world. A crucial difference between the faith of Israel and the religion of surrounding peoples (for example, Egypt or Babylon) was that it contained very few 'myths', if by that ambiguous word is meant stories told about the activities of gods in a never-never land before or above history. The Israelites told stories about the activity of God in history. That is why it is morally necessary and spiritually fruitful to accept the results of the historical and literary investigation of the Bible – at least, if we have access to such knowledge. The duty of the quest of the historical Israel remains. So does the profit, even when the results are full of uncertainties.

I am therefore not persuaded that 'canonical criticism' should always replace the older kinds of criticism which tried to discover what actual events and real people lie behind the final form of the biblical texts. Often these difficult researches can help us to understand the Bible (*Daniel*, for example) and to benefit from its message to people having to cope with the events of their own time. When these researches increase our awareness of the diversity of the Old Tetament, it is a small price to pay.'

But I have not yet mentioned the most profoundly serious reason why it is wrong to oversimplify the Old Testament and its authority.

These Scriptures appear, I admit, to provide a number of simple ideas around which all the material can be arranged. In addition to the ideas just mentioned, three themes which may be called political are prominent: the covenant, the land and the monarchy. The idea of the tribes' covenant with Yahweh was used by Noth to give unity to the history and by Eichrodt to give unity to the theology. The promise and gift of the land of Canaan to Israel as part of this covenant (and of earlier covenants with the Patriarchs) have always been remembered by Jews, so that towards the end of the twentieth century the idea is still crucially important in the politics of the Middle East. The covenated promise by God to the monarchy is central in the royal psalms as well as in the books of Kings, and has deeply influenced Christian understanding of Jesus, the Son of David, as *Messiah*. Yet all these ideas supporting a people's pride are given to us by the Old Testament along with the intensely moving records of bitter disillusionment (for example the book, probably written amid the ruins of Jerusalem, called *Lamentations*). The covenant between Yahweh and Israel was broken – by Israel when other Gods were worshipped, other moralities embraced and other powers trusted and obeyed; and by Yahweh when both the little kingdoms of the Israelites were left to their fates. The land was occupied and ruled by Gentiles from dates within the Old Testament to AD 1948. The monarchy was denounced for oppression and other wickedness, torn apart by civil wars and eventually blotted off the political map. The experience of the Jews became predominantly tragic, and their religion provided no complete explanation of the terrible facts. The leading explanation is given repeatedly in their history books: the people sinned against Yahweh and therefore Yahweh punished them. The more I think about this explanation, the more amazed I am by its courage. Archaeology and history can produce small parallels to this explanation of danger and defeat by the anger of the national or tribal god against sin. But the verdict of Martin Noth stands up to repeated examination: 'There is no real parallel to this manifestation of prophecy anywhere else in human history.' Nowhere can we find literature of a people's self-condemnation on this scale – and in the modern world the confession of guilt by Germany, for example, or Japan or post-imperial Britain, has certainly not reached this thoroughness. However, the confession of guilt is not the only sound heard in the Old Testament. Isaiah 40:2 says that Israel's punishment was 'double measure for all her sins', and in his courageous chapter 18 Ezekiel rejects the whole tradition that one generation is rightly punished for the sins of another. A 'Song of the Suffering Servant' (pages 159–61) asserts the innocence of this figure who seems to be the embodiment of Israel, and *Job* (pages 62–7) makes a similar assertion about a figure who seems to embody suffering humanity. *Ecclesiastes* (pages 59–61) explicitly and consistently denies that God punishes the guilty and protects the innocent. And it is there, in that contradiction of *Deuteronomy*, that the Old Testament reaches the heights of eloquence.

In our century political independence has been recovered for the minority of the world's Jews living in Israel, but the iniquity of the Holocaust inflicted the largest disaster since the first century AD, and has been followed by the evil (as the Old Testament prophets would surely have seen it) of the Israeli treatment of the Palestinians. In our time we have a terrible reason to know that the apparently simple and cheerful ideas of the Old Testament must be questioned by the tragic realism of the Servant Songs, *Job* and *Ecclesiastes*. In the reality which includes Auschwitz faith is often not vindicated, and goodness is often not upheld and rewarded. We have to ask the questions which are asked with such courage in the Old Testament. Of what value is God's covenant? Does history bring salvation?

THE FAITH OF THE OLD TESTAMENT

At the end of my reconsiderations I repeat that here are books which show that in the joys and sorrows of real life real people can meet the real God. The chief merit of 'canonical criticism' of the Old Testament is that it has reminded students of a simple fact that may be obscured when scholars concentrate on the criticism which divides this material, stressing the differences between the books, and excavates beneath the surface in order to explore layers of authorship with different dates. The fact is that the Old Testament has been loved, from the time when it was assembled to our own day, chiefly because so many passages in it can communicate the sense of the presence of God. The ultimate reason why these Scriptures are canonical is that they have been held as sacred in the hearts of many millions because they have had this revelatory power. And one reason why the recent canonical criticism has interested many students is that it connects with a wider understanding of the power of great literature.

In the appreciation of non-religious literature (together with other forms of a culture) the insights of the intellectual movement called 'structuralism' can be helpful. This movement more or less disregards questions about how the text in our hands came to be in our hands – and in this attitude it expresses our own usual attitude when we settle down to learn from a great piece of literature. Structuralism asks instead how what the text says connects with what we are already thinking and feeling. In other words, it concentrates on the human concerns which change little from one generation to another. Among these concerns are the contrasts between good and evil, between health and sickness, between tranquillity and disorder, between male and female, and between old and young, which we use to make sense of our experience. And structuralism excavates beneath the surface, not in order to find dates (which, at a first glance, may be as uninteresting as the pottery which fascinates archaeologists) but in order to explore layers of meaning. Structuralism has its own techniques and jargon but essentially what such an approach to literature is trying to do is what we do whenever we seriously hear a portion of the Scriptures in church or synagogue and whenever we read it devotionally in private.

When we hear or read the Old Testament we often meet a faith which is very striking, although detailed problems about the history of Ancient Israel remain to vex the student and although a particular passage may seem untrue or unedifying or irrelevant to our own questions about what to believe or do. It runs through all the diversity and it emerges out of all the tragedy. It is faith in One God as Creator, Judge, Saviour, Shepherd and Sustainer. Here is the Father who accounts for what has been called the 'family likeness' of the books known as the Old Testament.

This faith arises out of the experience of the people and of individuals. It treats God as personal, with a name, because getting to know this God called Yahweh (or Elohim) is like getting to know a person. Like golden corn this faith springs up to nourish us out of the good days – out of the grandeur and beauty of nature, out of the flocks, the harvests and the victories, out of the joys of sex and family, out of the achievements of craftsmanship and wisdom, out of the unity which binds people together in justice, out of the *shalom* which combines righteousness, prosperity and peace. So this faith trusts God happily. But it survives in the bad days – in confusion and degradation under Canaanite influences, in defeat and exile, in the face of death and in almost total cynicism or despair. It does not give up its faith that God 'keeps faith' even when it cannot see into the future, as Moses could not; or even when it seems to be called to sacrifice everything as Abraham heard (or misheard) a command to sacrifice Isaac; or even when it seems to be wrestling in pain with an adversary not yet known to be God, as Jacob wrestled; or even when God is believed to be so angry or so indifferent that he is the enemy, as Jeremiah or Job at times believed; or even when the overwhelming mystery which it experiences provides no answers to intellectual questions, as the stunning disclosure to Job did not. This faith trembles – but it prays and it still trusts. It feels that God is 'holy, holy, holy' because different from anyone and anything, more powerful than any king, more righteous than any saint. But it also feels that God is undeniably there. His full nature cannot be known; he cannot be 'seen' and should not be named lightly. But his angel, glory, spirit, wisdom, word or deed can be known, and his will can be understood clearly enough to be obeyed.

So those who were ultimately received as the best teachers of Ancient Israel – the men whose teachings and editorial work constitute the Hebrew Scriptures – believed that something could be known of the character of his Holy One, mysterious and elusive as the divine presence and purpose must often be. I have sometimes asked myself whether it was wise to obtain permission for the use of Ancient Israel's chief name for God, 'Yahweh', in the questions from the New English Bible which formed the backbone of this book – but I have concluded that calling God 'the Lord', although it may be more devout (and I hope I am sensitive to Jewish feelings on that point), does not bring out the miraculous distinctiveness of Israel's perceptions. Often they compare Yahweh with a man of war, campaigning at first against Israel's enemies and then against Israel itself when the people's sins had at length got beyond even the divine patience. And often they compared Yahweh with a king, making his creation spring into being and life by his mere word, ruling without rival over history. And no interpretation of the Old Testament which wishes to be honest can make light of this adoration of transcendent power. But the abasement is the homage of people who are not exactly silenced by their humility. It is expressed in some of mankind's most majestic poetry. It has inexhaustible power – which leads a modern scholar, John Barton, to conclude that the Old Testament provides not information about history, theology or morality that is always authoritative, but 'materials which, when pondered and absorbed into the mind, will suggest the pattern or shape of a way of life lived in the presence of God'.

Since my previous chapters were written international discussion, well aware of the misuses of the ideas of the holy war and of monarchical masculinity, has tended to pick on those passages of Scripture speaking about God which are compatible with humane ideals and even with the ideas of pacifism, ecology and feminism. There certainly are such passages in the Old Testament, even if they are more marginal than many of the Old Testament's modernizers like to admit. The vision of peace in the books of Micah and Isaiah (page 244) is carved on the headquarters of the United Nations in New York, and the prophetic vision of nature in a harmonious order freed from human violence (page 146) might well be carved on the hearts of all ecologists and of the whole Green movement of our time. The story of *Jonah* with its revelation of God's love for the innocent people and the cattle in Nineveh (pages 231–2) becomes all the more remarkable when compared with the inscriptions surviving from the palaces of the Assyrian kings, with their boasts of utter ruthlessness. Because the

Hebrew words for 'wisdom' and 'spirit' are feminine, and because abstract ideas are personified where possible, other passages speak of the Wisdom or Spirit of God as if speaking of a subtle but all-knowing and powerful woman, 'kindly towards men, steadfast, unerring' (page 235). Alongside the song about Deborah the general, who is as bloodthirsty as any of the legendary lady-butchers of the Amazon army (pages 103–4), is the picture of her under a palm tree, peacefully dispensing justice (Judges 4:5); and the picture of Yahweh carrying the children like a tender mother is preserved together with the song about his fight against them as their enemy (Isaiah 63:9,10). The famous comparison between Yahweh and 'a woman in labour, whimpering, panting and gasping' as a new world is born (Isaiah 42:14) has recently been used by many as an acceptable key to the Old Testament's doctrine of God. The power of this daring image lies not only in the comparison of God with a woman. It lies also in the suggestion that before her purposes can be fulfilled God herself must suffer – a suggestion which not even *Job* was bold enough to make.

In the book of Jeremiah the agony of the prophet as he foresees the doom of the people is so close to the distress of Yahweh over his rejection by the people that it is sometimes not clear whether 'man or God is lamenting over 'my people'. But whatever the right interpretation of particular passages may be, the 'grief' of Yahweh is an Old Testament theme. It is, for example, clear from the book of Hosea that it was believed that Yahweh has strong feelings about Israel and that these may be described in terms of one of the most painful experiences known to humanity – the agony of the breakdown of a marriage over continuing and unrepented adultery. It is also clear that it was believed that Yahweh, who has no desire for any individual's death (Ezekiel 18:32), has a heart which throbs 'like a harp' in anguish for everyone in Moab as that people, traditionally hostile to Israel, is conquered and ruined (Isaiah 16:11;

Jeremiah 48:31). Here we are compensated for the crude *naïveté* in some of the pictures of God as a man ('anthropomorphism'). The best teachers of Ancient Israel believed that God is not remote from the best human feelings as love overcomes hurt, patience overcomes weariness and pity overcomes anger. Some of them even glimpsed what the New Testament, with its message of the cross, asserts – that these divine reactions are part of a love which includes an entry into suffering. God is affected by the responses of his children, as any human parent is. In that sense he is not as changeless as the Greek philosophers supposed. But what cannot change is his character, celebrated in the refrain in Psalm 136: 'his love endures for ever.' So Psalm 103:13–14 offers the deepest insight:

> As a father has compassion on his children,
> so has Yahweh compassion on all who fear him.
> For he knows how we were made,
> he remembers full well that we are dust.

In the last analysis that is why the Old Testament message about God is good news for all who will hear it. Ezekiel (2:9–3:3) had a vision of a scroll 'written all over on both sides with dirges and laments and words of woe'. His vision corresponds with many people's first impression of the Old Testament. But from behind the hand that held the scroll a voice seemed to come from eternity: 'Man, eat what is in front of you, eat this scroll . . . Swallow this scroll I give you, and fill yourself full.' The prophet did eat it, 'and it tasted as sweet as honey'.

Outline of Events

1250? Exodus from Egypt
1200–1020? Settlement in Canaan
1020–1000? Saul's reign
1000–960? David's reign
960–930? Solomon's reign
950? *Succession Narrative* and J
930? Division into kingdoms of Israel and Judah
886–853 Omri and Ahab over Israel
842–41 Jehu's revolution
830? *Book of Covenant* and E
750? Amos prophesies in Israel, then Hosea
741–40 Death of Uzziah and call of Isaiah
733 Most of Israel conquered by Assyrians
722–21 Samaria falls to Assyrians
701 Sennacherib besieges Jerusalem
700? Hezekiah's scribes join J and E?
697 Manasseh begins reign of 55 years
622–21 *Code of Deuteronomy;* Josiah's reform
612 Nineveh falls to Babylonians
609 Death of Josiah
597 Jerusalem falls to Babylonians; Jeremiah
586 Jerusalem destroyed; Ezekiel
561-60 Jehoiachin released; D completed
539 Babylon falls to Persians; Second Isaiah
538 Cyrus permits restoration of Jerusalem temple
515 Second temple consecrated
445 Nehemiah's first mission
398? Ezra's mission; *Law of Holiness* and P
350? *Chronicles*
333 Alexander defeats Persians at Issus
250? *Ecclesiastes* and *Job*
166 Maccabean revolt; *Daniel* and *Esther*
130 *Ecclesiasticus* translated into Greek
100? *Wisdom of Solomon*
63 Jerusalem falls to Romans

For Further Reading

*more advanced

*Ackroyd, P. R., *Exile and Restoration*, 1968

*Albright, W. F., *Yahweh and the Gods of Canaan*, 1968

Anderson, B. W., *The Living World of the Old Testament*, revised 1971

*Anderson, B. W. (ed.), *The Old Testament and Christian Faith*, 1964

*Baly, D., *The Geography of the Bible*, revised 1974

Bright, J., *The Authority of the Old Testament*, 1967

Bright, J., *A History of Israel*, revised 1972

Buber, M., *Moses*, 1951

Clements, R. E., *A Century of Old Testament Study*, 1976

*Eichrodt, W., *Theology of the Old Testament*, 2 vols., 1961, 1967

*Eissfeldt, O., *The Old Testament: An Introduction*, 1965

Ellis, P. F., *The Yahwist: The Bible's First Theologian*, 1968

Frank, H. T., *Discovering the Biblical World*, 1975

Gray, J., *The Canaanites*, 1964

Heaton, E. W., *Everyday Life in Old Testament Times*, 1956

Heaton, E. W., *Solomon's New Men*, 1974

*Hengel, M., *Judaism and Hellenism*, 1974

*Herrmann, S., *A History of Israel in Old Testament Times*, 1975

Kenyon, K. M., *Archaeology in the Holy Land*, revised 1969

*Knight, G. A. F., *A Christian Theology of the Old Testament*, revised 1964

Lindblom, J., *Prophecy in Ancient Israel*, 1962

McKenzie, J. L., *A Theology of the Old Testament*, 1975

May, H. G. (ed.), *Oxford Bible Atlas*, revised 1974

*Nicholson, E. W., *Deuteronomy and Tradition*, 1967

*Noth, M., *The History of Israel*, revised 1960

Ringgren, H., *The Faith of the Psalmists*, 1963

Ringgren, H., *The Religions of the Ancient Near East*, 1973

Rodinson, M., *Mohammed*, 1971

*Russell, D. S., *The Method and Message of Jewish Apocalyptic*, 1964

Sandmel, S., *The Enjoyment of Scripture*, 1974

*Spriggs, J. G., *Two Old Testament Theologies*, 1975 (Eichrodt and von Rad)

Stoltz, F., *Interpreting the Old Testament*, 1975

Thomas, D. W. (ed.), *Documents from Old Testament Times*, 1958

*Vaux, R. de, *Ancient Israel: Its Life and Institutions*, revised 1965

*Von Rad, G., *Old Testament Theology*, 2 vols., 1962, 1965

Von Rad, G., *Wisdom in Israel*, 1972

*Wiseman, D. J. (ed.), *The Peoples of the Old Testament*, 1973

Wouk, H., *This is My God: The Jewish Way of Life*, revised 1973

Yadin, Y., *Hazor: The Rediscovery of a Great Citadel of the Bible*, 1975

The best large one-volume commentaries are *Peake's Commentary on the Bible*, ed. M. Black and H. H. Rowley, 1962, and *The Interpreter's One-volume Commentary on the Bible*, ed. C. M. Laymon, 1971.

Too many good commentaries on the separate books are available to be listed here. The most up-to-date series are *The Cambridge Bible Commentary* based on the New English Bible and being published by Cambridge University Press, and the more advanced *Old Testament Library*, based largely on the Revised Standard Version and being published by SCM Press, London, and Westminster Press, Philadelphia. The most recent series by Jewish scholars is *Soncino Books of the Bible*, ed. A. Cohen (1945–52).

Recent Books 1989

HISTORY

John Bright's conservative but not fundamentalist *History of Israel* was last revised in 1981. Recent trends in scholarship were summed up by J. Alberto Soggin's *History* (1984). J. Maxwell Miller and John H. Hayes collected essays of high quality on *Israelite and Judean History* (1977) and provided a straightforward account of the facts in *A History of Ancient Israel and Judah* (1986). German histories of Israel in Old Testament times, translated into English, include those by S. Herrmann (revised in 1981) and H. Jagersma (1982). Stimulating scepticism was expressed in J. van Seters, *In Search of History* (1983), and Giovanni Garbini, *History and Ideology in Ancient Israel*, translated in 1988, although the sceptics are sceptical about each other. Norman K. Gottwald interpreted the Old Testament sociologically as a plea for brotherhood, including justice to the poor in memory of Israel's fraternal but lowly origins in *The Tribes of Yahweh* (1979), set in a wider context in *The Hebrew Bible: A Socioliterary Introduction* (1985). John Rogerson surveyed *Anthropology and the Old Testament* (1978). All these scholarly books have bibliographies. For the physical background see specially Jerome Murphy-O'Connor, *The Holy Land* (revised in 1986), and the two panoramic studies by Y. Aharoni, *The Land of the Bible* (1979) and *The Archaeology of the Land of Israel* (1982).

LITERATURE

For students alarmed by 'critical' methods *Beginning Old*

Testament Study edited by John Rogerson (1983) is a good introduction. J. Alberto Soggin's critical *Introduction to the Old Testament* was revised in 1988. Another comprehensive *Introduction*, by Otto Kaiser, was revised and translated in 1980. The New Oxford Bible Series includes the smaller *The Old Testament: A Literary and Historical Introduction* by R. J. Coggins, and presentations of *Narrative* by D. M. Gunn, *Poets and Psalms* by P. R. Ackroyd and *Wisdom and Law* by Joseph Blenkinsopp. More advanced discussion about how a Christian may legitimately extract a meaning, ancient or modern, from the final text of Scripture was stimulated afresh by Brevard S. Childs, *Introduction to the Old Testament as Scripture* (1979), and his *Old Testament Theology in a Canonical Context* (1985). James Barr, *Holy Scripture: Canon, Authority, Criticism* (1983), John Barton, *Reading the Old Testament* (1984), and J. A. Sanders, *From Sacred Story to Sacred Text* (1987), were among the contributions to the debate. For the intellectual background see D. H. Kelsey, *The Use of Scripture in Recent Theology* (1975), J. D. Smart, *The Past, Present and Future of Biblical Theology* (1979), and R. E. Clements, *A Century of Old Testament Study* (revised in 1983). The debate in German was summed up by A. H. J. Gunneweg, *Understanding the Old Testament* (translated in 1978 in the Old Testament Library series which has maintained a very high standard in its commentaries). Taking account of up-to-date studies, W. H. Schmidt, *The Faith of the Old Testament* (1983), still argued for the uniqueness of Yahweh, and E. W. Nicholson, *God and His People* (1986), for the covenant. These were among the useful attempts to find a unity, but John Goldingay surveyed recent scholarly discussion of *Theological Diversity and the Authority of the Old Testament* (1987). John Barton, *The People of the Book?* (1988), tackled the question of the biblical basis of Christianity at a new depth.

However, 'the use of books is endless and much study is wearisome' (Ecclesiastes 12:12).

Index

Index

Also available in Fount Paperbacks

BOOKS BY C. S. LEWIS

Reflections on the Psalms

'Absolutely packed with wisdom. It is clearly the fruit of very much reflection . . . upon one's own darkness of spirit, one's own fumbling and grasping in the shadows of prayer or of penitence.'

Trevor Huddleston

Miracles

'This is a brilliant book, abounding in lucid exposition and illuminating metaphor.'

Charles Davey, The Observer

The Problem of Pain

'Written with clarity and force, and out of much knowledge and experience.'

Times Literary Supplement

Surprised by Joy

'His outstanding gift is clarity. You can take it at two levels, as straight autobiography, or as a kind of spiritual thriller, a detective's probing of clue and motive . . .'

Isabel Quigley, Sunday Times

Also available in Fount Paperbacks

BOOKS BY C. S. LEWIS

Fern-Seed and Elephants

'The magic of his writings shows no abatement . . . the final essay
alone makes the paperback worth its weight in gold . . . a substantial
and most helpful analysis of the doctrines of the end of the world
and the final judgement.'

R. L. Roberts, Church Times

The Screwtape Letters

'Excellent, hard-hitting, challenging, provoking.'

The Observer

Screwtape Proposes a Toast

Screwtape appears again but this time to propose a toast at a
diabolical banquet. These essays are witty, original, outspoken,
offering abundant and delightful nourishment to the half-starved
Christian imagination of our time.

Till We Have Faces

'An imaginative retelling of the myth of Cupid and Psyche, with
Christian overtones, to which the author brings his customary
clarity of thought and superlative story-telling powers.'

British Weekly

Also available in Fount Paperbacks

BOOKS BY DAVID KOSSOFF

Bible Stories

'To my mind there is no doubt that these stories make the Bible come alive. Mr Kossoff is a born storyteller. He has the gift of making the old stories new.'

William Barclay

The Book of Witnesses

'The little stories are fascinating in the warm humanity they reveal. Right from the first one the reader is enthralled . . . bringing the drama of the New Testament into our daily lives with truly shattering impact.'

Religious Book News

The Voices of Masada

'This is imaginative historical writing of the highest standard.'

Church Times

The Little Book of Sylvanus

Sylvanus, the quiet, observant man, tells his version of the events surrounding the 'carpenter preacher' of Nazareth, from the Crucifixion to Pentecost. A moving and unforgettable view of the gospel story, and a sequel to *The Book of Witnesses*.

Also available in Fount Paperbacks

Fount Children's Bible
ANDREW KNOWLES

Bible stories retold in a simple and dramatic way, delightfully illustrated in full colour.

'It is not only the children who will enjoy and profit from this publication. I have enjoyed it myself and have learnt a lot from it.'

Stuart Blanch, Archbishop of York

Mr God, This is Anna
FYNN

'No review can do justice to this outstanding account of a short life lived to the full, but I commend it to all who are willing to learn from a child the way of wholeness of life.'

Dorothy Entwistle, Way of Life

Children's Letters to God
ERIC MARSHALL and STUART HAMPLE

'A hilarious and sometimes touching book . . . allowing the children to express their wishes, doubts and beliefs . . . half the charm of the book is that . . . the letters . . . are printed as the children wrote them with spelling mistakes and scrawling writing.'

James Laing, Scottish Sunday Mail

Bedtime Stories and Prayers
RITA SNOWDEN

A collection of charming stories and prayers which help a child to learn to pray. Beautifully illustrated, this book will be a joy to parents and children alike.

Fount Paperbacks

Fount is one of the leading paperback publishers of religious books and below are some of its recent titles.

- [ ] FRIENDSHIP WITH GOD David Hope   £2.95
- [ ] THE DARK FACE OF REALITY Martin Israel   £2.95
- [ ] LIVING WITH CONTRADICTION Esther de Waal   £2.95
- [ ] FROM EAST TO WEST Brigid Marlin   £3.95
- [ ] GUIDE TO THE HERE AND HEREAFTER
                              Lionel Blue/Jonathan Magonet   £4.50
- [ ] CHRISTIAN ENGLAND (1 Vol) David Edwards   £10.95
- [ ] MASTERING SADHANA Carlos Valles   £3.95
- [ ] THE GREAT GOD ROBBERY George Carey   £2.95
- [ ] CALLED TO ACTION Fran Beckett   £2.95
- [ ] TENSIONS Harry Williams   £2.50
- [ ] CONVERSION Malcolm Muggeridge   £2.95
- [ ] INVISIBLE NETWORK Frank Wright   £2.95
- [ ] THE DANCE OF LOVE Stephen Verney   £3.95
- [ ] THANK YOU, PADRE Joan Clifford   £2.50
- [ ] LIGHT AND LIFE Grazyna Sikorska   £2.95
- [ ] CELEBRATION Margaret Spufford   £2.95
- [ ] GOODNIGHT LORD Georgette Butcher   £2.95
- [ ] GROWING OLDER Una Kroll   £2.95

All Fount Paperbacks are available at your bookshop or newsagent, or they can be ordered by post from Fount Paperbacks, Cash Sales Department, G.P.O. Box 29, Douglas, Isle of Man. Please send purchase price plus 22p per book, maximum postage £3. Customers outside the UK send purchase price, plus 22p per book. Cheque, postal order or money order. No currency.

NAME (Block letters) _____

ADDRESS_____

_____

_____

While every effort is made to keep prices low, it is sometimes necessary to increase them at short notice. Fount Paperbacks reserve the right to show new retail prices on covers which may differ from those previously advertised in the text or elsewhere.